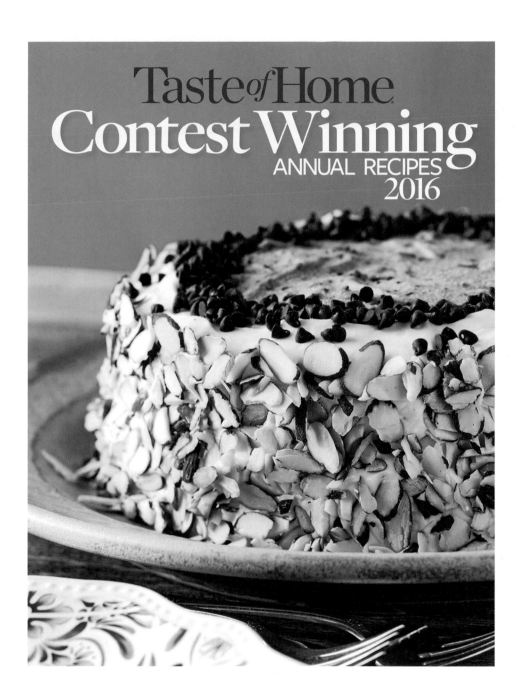

Taste of Home

Contest Winning
ANNUAL RECIPES
2016

Taste of Home
Contest Winning
ANNUAL RECIPES

PICTURED ON THE FRONT COVER: Marvelous Cannoli Cake, page 211.
PICTURED ON THE BACK COVER: Homemade Chicken Alfredo Pizzas, page 125; Ozark Mountain Berry Pie, page 204; Cappuccino Brownies, page 186; Cranberry Orange Pancakes, page 81.

TABLE OF CONTENTS

MORE THAN 350
PRIZEWINNING RECIPES & TIPS
FOR TODAY'S FAMILY COOKS!

For years *Taste of Home* has shared favorite recipes from family cooks in its books, magazines and online forums. It's no surprise, then, that *Taste of Home* contests continue to feature the best-of-the-best dishes...and now you can own them in one collection—*Contest Winning Annual Recipes!*

Take a look inside and you'll discover more than 300 prize-worthy specialties *from* today's home cooks made specifically *for* today's home cooks. From appetizers and snacks to weeknight dinners and holiday entrees, these sensational dishes are sure to impress—after all, they're contest winners!

Whether you need an eye-opening brunch bake, crowd-pleasing dessert or bake sale contribution, you'll steal the show with the classics here. Need a hearty appetizer? Look no further. Want to bake bread guaranteed to turn out every time? The perfect recipe is in your hands.

Inside this colorful cookbook, you'll find satisfying comfort foods as well as tasty new ways to lighten up your dinner routine. In fact, the lighter dishes in *Contest Winning Annual Recipes* include nutrition facts and even Diabetic Exchanges when applicable. What better way to offer healthy alternatives at mealtime than with dishes that won prizes in a recipe competition?

Serve up all the flavor, goodness and convenience you'd expect from *Taste of Home* today. Let *Contest Winning Annual Recipes* show you how!

Fresh Tomato & Cucumber Salad, page 31

A YEAR'S WORTH OF TASTY CONTEST WINNERS

The award-winning recipes found here come from an assortment of cooking contests, covering everything from brunch staples and grilled greats to make-ahead specialties and five-ingredient delights.

All the recipes in this cookbook are organized by major ingredient or course. See the contents on page 3 for a better understanding of where you'll find particular recipes or check out the indexes that begin on page 230. The General Index is a great tool to help find the ideal dish for any occasion.

Below is a complete list of contests from which the dishes in *Contest Winning Annual Recipes* were featured, as well as the first-place recipient of each competition. In addition, the icon **GRAND PRIZE** is scattered throughout the chapters so you can quickly find the recipes that received top honors in their respective contests. These cream-of-the-crop entries will certainly be winners with your family!

LET'S DO BRUNCH
Rise and shine! Let these prizewinning dishes jump-start your day. From pancakes and egg bakes to scones and coffee cakes, these eye-opening delights will steal the show. Consider Grand Prize winner Southwest Breakfast Tart (p. 76) for a change-of-pace contribution to your next brunch.

CHICKEN CHAMPS
When it comes to quick and easy entrees, versatile chicken is a winner in its own right. This contest offered all sorts of juicy options for mealtime success and demonstrated how family cooks are jazzing up the delicious staple. The tasty winning dish, Grilled Tomatillo Chicken (p. 124), is a perfect example!

FANTASTIC IN FIVE
The winners of this contest prove you don't need a lot of ingredients to whip up a new family favorite. With the exception of water, salt, pepper and oil, these fast dishes call for no more than five ingredients. The trophy went to Crispy Buffalo Chicken Roll-ups (p. 138).

DUDE FOOD
From hearty appetizers to savory entrees, there's nothing better than food meant for the man cave. Piled high with flavor, Meat-atarain Sub (p. 57) claimed the top spot in this manly-man contest loaded with all the stick-to-your-ribs comfort foods a guy could ask for.

HOT POTATOES

Feeding a meat-and-potatoes crew? The top picks in this contest promise to become mealtime lifesavers. From hearty side dishes like contest winner Durango Potato Casserole (p. 174) to satisfying main courses, these simply "spud-tacular" recipes are tops!

FRESH IS BEST

Whether you're trying to eat healthier, finish a bumper crop of homegrown produce or simply enjoy the best Mother Nature has to offer, you'll find plenty of ideas in *Contest Winning Annual Recipes*. Fresh Tomato & Cucumber Salad (p. 31) is a delicious example.

GRILLING

Enjoy the thrill of the grill with classic flame-broiled fare. From burgers and dogs to chicken and ribs, these are recipes you'll make again and again. Try them with a side of top-rated Marvelous Mediterranean Vegetables (p. 168).

SWEET ON CORN

Few things usher in summer like golden ears of sweet corn. Learn how family cooks are serving it with the winners of this contest. Smoky Grilled Corn Salsa (p. 16) is a fun new way to enjoy summer's best, and it received the blue ribbon!

GO GREEN

For some, meatless entrees are a way of life; others rely on them for an occasional change of pace. Regardless of your preference, you'll find plenty of refreshing recipes in this collection. Pesto Veggie Pizza (p. 155) is so delicious, no one will mind that it's meatless!

MAKE IT SIZZLE

When it comes to cooking over an open flame, home cooks are coming up with all sorts of enticing new ideas. Take Shrimp Salad with Peaches (p. 39), for example—which calls for cooking the shrimp *and* the peaches on the grill. The entree salad took home top honors in this fiery competition.

BERRIED TREASURES

What's your pick—blueberries, strawberries or raspberries? Maybe blackberries or gooseberries? The main ingredient in this colorful contest is obvious. The recipe for Chipotle Salmon with Strawberry Mango Salsa (p. 145) rose to the top, but plenty of other delightful submissions made the cut, too. The popular berry dishes are scattered among various chapters.

THE NEW SOUTHWEST

When it comes to full-flavored comforts, it's hard to top burritos loaded with cheese, nachos stacked with savory favorites, and other spicy sensations. Liven up weeknight dinner routines with twists on Southwestern standbys. Terrific Turkey Enchiladas (p. 136) have all the taste you'd expect from a Grand Prize winner!

LIGHTENED-UP ITALIAN

Featuring full-flavored herbs and spices, fresh vegetables and all the appeal family cooks crave, Italian foods are easier to trim down than you might think. Big on taste and small on calories and fat, Turkey Meatballs and Sauce (p. 130) is a great example of an Italian dish that keeps healthy-eating goals on track.

FROM SCRATCH

Nothing tops a homemade meal, and cooking from scratch is a trend that's sweeping the nation—again! Take a sip of winner Butternut Squash & Pear Soup (p. 51) and see how yummy from-scratch cooking can be. Best of all, these prizewinners come together quicker than you'd expect!

MAKE-AHEAD MARVELS

Everyone seems to keep busy schedules these days, making it tough to set a homemade meal on the table. You'll beat the clock with a little planning and these award winners. From make-ahead entrees to icebox desserts, these foolproof recipes will always get you out of the kitchen in a hurry. Hosting a party? Try Grand Prize winner Blue Cheese Walnut Tart (p. 11).

HEALTHY SEAFOOD

If you're looking to cut calories, trim fat or skim back on sodium, you'll enjoy the fresh favorites from this contest. Pineapple Pico Tuna Steaks (p. 158) offer a healthy way to mix up dinnertime routines and surprise your family with a colorful meal.

OUT-OF-THE-BOX DESSERTS

Don't have time to bake dessert? Think again! Cinnamon & Sugar Cake (p. 202) promises to brighten up the kitchen in moments because it starts with a boxed mix. In fact, all of the recipes from this competition call for a mix to speed up preparation. What could be easier?

NUTS ABOUT NUTS

It's time to think outside the shell! Nuts are wonderful in desserts—consider blue-ribbon winner Butter Pecan Cheesecake (p. 229)—but they add crunchy texture and earthy flavor to all sorts of courses, including salads, entrees and side dishes.

THANKSGIVING: THE SEQUEL

The only thing better than Thanksgiving dinner is all those leftovers! Use yours creatively with the stick-to-your-ribs specialties from this contest. Stuffing Dumpling Soup (p. 65), for instance, makes the most of the extra turkey, stuffing and green beans you might have on hand after the big feast.

SENSATIONAL CITRUS

As the days grow darker and colder, citrus fruits grow brighter and juicier! Learn the best ways to use lemons, oranges, limes and grapefruit with the top entries from this colorful contest. Consider Roasted Chicken with Lemon Sauce (p. 117) for dinner tonight.

HOLIDAY DESSERTS

Ring in the holidays with Best Maple-Cranberry Cheesecake (p. 219) or any of the winners from this lineup of yuletide sweets. Easy yet impressive, they'll steal the show on any buffet table, Christmas menu or winter get-together, making your event one to remember.

Whether you're cooking for a holiday, bake sale, potluck, backyard barbecue or simple weeknight dinner, you'll win thumbs up from everyone with the top-rated dishes found here! With *Taste of Home Contest Winning Annual Recipes*, serving up a winning dish has never been easier!

Italian Meatball Buns, page 19

10

12

8

Snacks & Appetizers

Looking for a **satisifying starter** for your next get-together? With a collection of most-requested appetizers, **delicious dips** and sweet sips, your guests will have all they need to get the party started!

Salsa Roja

With the help of my food processor, I can have fresh homemade salsa ready in 15 minutes. The lime juice works wonders bringing out all the flavors, and you can really taste the cilantro.
—**AMBER MASSEY** ARGYLE, TX

START TO FINISH: 15 MIN.
MAKES: 7 CUPS

- 1   **can (28 ounces) whole tomatoes, drained**
- 1   **can (14½ ounces) diced tomatoes with garlic and onion, drained**
- 1   **can (14½ ounces) Mexican stewed tomatoes, drained**
- 1   **can (10 ounces) diced tomatoes and green chilies, drained**
- 1   **medium onion, quartered**
- 2   **banana peppers, seeded and coarsely chopped**
- 2   **jalapeno peppers, seeded and coarsely chopped**
- 3   **garlic cloves, minced**
- 2   **teaspoons salt**
- ¼   **teaspoon ground cumin**
- ½   **cup minced fresh cilantro**
- ¼   **cup lime juice**
- 2   **medium ripe avocados, peeled and cubed**
     Tortilla chips

1. Place the first 10 ingredients in a food processor; cover and process until chopped. Add cilantro and lime juice; cover and pulse until combined.
2. Transfer to a bowl; stir in avocados. Serve with the tortilla chips.
NOTE *Wear disposable gloves when cutting hot peppers; the oils can burn skin. Avoid touching your face.*

Cola Hot Wings

These are so easy to make, and they offer year-round versatility, from summer cookouts to autumn tailgates. My husband likes them so much he'll stand out in the snow to grill them!
—**LISA LINVILLE** RANDOLPH, NE

PREP: 15 MIN. • **GRILL:** 40 MIN.
MAKES: ABOUT 2½ DOZEN

- 3   **pounds chicken wings**
- 1   **cup Louisiana-style hot sauce**
- 1   **can (12 ounces) cola**
- 1   **tablespoon soy sauce**
- ¼   **teaspoon cayenne pepper**
- ¼   **teaspoon pepper**
     Blue cheese salad dressing

1. Cut chicken wings into three sections; discard wing tip sections. In a small bowl, combine hot sauce, cola, soy sauce, cayenne and pepper.
2. Prepare grill for indirect heat, using a drip pan. Moisten a paper towel with cooking oil; using long-handled tongs, rub on grill rack to coat lightly. Grill chicken wings, covered, over indirect medium heat 10 minutes. Grill 30-40 minutes longer, turning occasionally and basting frequently with the sauce until wings are nicely glazed. Serve wings with salad dressing.
NOTE *Uncooked chicken wing sections (wingettes) may be substituted for whole chicken wings.*

"Try these unique little tarts as an appetizer before a special meal, or save them for a surprisingly different dinner finale. They're sweet, creamy and crunchy—and very addictive!"

—ANGELA VITALE DELAWARE, OH

White Chocolate Brie Cups

START TO FINISH: 25 MIN.
MAKES: 15 APPETIZERS

- 1 package (1.9 ounces) frozen miniature phyllo tart shells
- 1½ ounces white baking chocolate, chopped
- 2 ounces Brie cheese, chopped
- ⅓ cup orange marmalade
    Kumquat slices, optional

1. Preheat oven to 350°. Fill each tart shell with chocolate, then cheese. Place on an ungreased baking sheet. Top with marmalade.
2. Bake 6-8 minutes or until golden brown. Serve warm. If desired, top with kumquat.

Watermelon Spritzer

Beverages don't get much easier than this bright spritzer. Watermelon blended with limeade is cool and refreshing. It's a wonderful thirst quencher on a hot summer day. Best of all, it only requires four ingredients!

—**GERALDINE SAUCIER** ALBUQUERQUE, NM

PREP: 5 MIN. + CHILLING
MAKES: 5 SERVINGS

- 4 cups cubed seedless watermelon
- ¾ cup frozen limeade concentrate, thawed
- 2½ cups carbonated water
    Lime slices

1. Place watermelon in a blender. Cover and process until blended. Strain and discard pulp; transfer the juice to a pitcher. Stir in limeade concentrate. Refrigerate for 6 hours or overnight.
2. Just before serving, stir in carbonated water. Garnish servings with lime slices.

Topsy-Turvy Sangria

I got this recipe from a friend a few years ago. It's perfect for relaxed get-togethers. It tastes best when you make it the night before and let the flavors steep.

—**TRACY FIELD** BREMERTON, WA

START TO FINISH: 10 MIN.
MAKES: 10 SERVINGS (¾ CUP EACH)

- 1 bottle (750 milliliters) merlot
- 1 cup sugar
- 1 cup orange liqueur
- ½ to 1 cup brandy
- 3 cups lemon-lime soda, chilled
- 1 cup sliced fresh strawberries
- 1 medium lemon, sliced
- 1 medium orange, sliced
- 1 medium peach, sliced
  Ice cubes

In a pitcher, stir the wine, sugar, orange liqueur and brandy until sugar is dissolved. Stir in soda and fruit. Serve over ice.

Wonton Pot Stickers with Soy Reduction

Bok choy is a type of Chinese cabbage with white stems and dark green leaves. In a pinch, regular cabbage will do. These appetizers—full of sausage, cilantro, ginger, and onion—freeze so well, I always make large batches. Then I have extras to pull out of the freezer at a moment's notice.

—**MICHAEL ANGELO** SPRING, TX

PREP: 45 MIN. + FREEZING • **COOK:** 15 MIN./BATCH
MAKES: ABOUT 3½ DOZEN (¾ CUP SAUCE)

- ½ cup mirin (sweet rice wine)
- ½ cup balsamic vinegar
- ¼ cup reduced-sodium soy sauce
- 2 fresh basil leaves

POT STICKERS
- 1½ cups finely chopped bok choy
- 2 tablespoons minced fresh cilantro
- 1 tablespoon minced fresh gingerroot
- 1 tablespoon chopped green onion
- 1 tablespoon oyster sauce
- ¾ teaspoon toasted sesame oil
- 1 pound ground pork
- 45 wonton wrappers

ADDITIONAL INGREDIENT
- 1 to 4 tablespoons toasted sesame oil

1. In a small saucepan, combine mirin, balsamic vinegar and soy sauce. Bring to a boil; cook until liquid is reduced by half, about 15 minutes. Add basil; cover and steep for 2 minutes. Remove basil and discard. Cool sauce; set aside.
2. For pot stickers, combine the first six ingredients in a large bowl. Crumble pork over mixture and mix well.
3. Place about 1 tablespoon pork mixture in center of each wonton wrapper. (Cover remaining wrappers with a damp paper towel until ready to use.) Moisten edges with water. Fold one corner diagonally over filling; press edges to seal.
4. In a large skillet, cook pot stickers in oil in batches over medium-high heat for 1-2 minutes on each side or until golden brown. Serve with sauce.

FREEZE OPTION *Place sauce in freezer container; freeze. Place filled and folded pot stickers on a waxed paper-lined 15x10x 1-in. baking sheet; freeze until firm. Transfer to resealable plastic freezer bags. May be frozen for up to 3 months. To use pot stickers, thaw sauce in the refrigerator overnight. Arrange a fourth of the frozen pot stickers 1 in. apart in a greased steamer; place in a large saucepan over 1 in. of water. Bring to a boil; cover and steam 12-14 minutes or until a thermometer inserted into filling reads 160°. Repeat with remaining pot stickers. In a large skillet, cook pot stickers in oil in batches over medium-high heat for 1-2 minutes on each side or until golden. Serve with sauce.*
NOTE *Look for mirin in the Asian condiments section.*

Triple Berry Salsa

Blueberries are nutritious, low in calories and packed with vitamin C, fiber and disease-fighting antioxidants. This chunky salsa is a fresh, flavorful blend of berries and veggies and would be great over grilled chicken, too.

—RAYMONDE BOURGEOIS SWASTIKA, ON

START TO FINISH: 20 MIN.
MAKES: 22 SERVINGS

- 1½ cups fresh blueberries
- ¾ cup chopped fresh strawberries
- ¾ cup fresh raspberries
- 1 medium tomato, seeded and chopped
- 1 small sweet yellow pepper, chopped
- ¼ cup finely chopped red onion
- ¼ cup minced fresh cilantro
- 1 jalapeno pepper, seeded and minced
- 2 green onions, chopped
- 1 tablespoon cider vinegar
- 1 tablespoon olive oil
- 2 teaspoons lime juice
- 2 teaspoons orange juice
- 1 teaspoon honey
- ¼ teaspoon salt
  Baked tortilla chip scoops

In a large bowl, combine the first nine ingredients. In a small bowl, whisk the remaining ingredients. Drizzle over salsa; toss to coat. Chill until serving. Serve with chips.
NOTE *Wear disposable gloves when cutting hot peppers; the oils can burn skin. Avoid touching your face.*
PER SERVING *¼ cup (calculated without chips) equals 20 cal., 1 g fat (trace sat. fat), 0 chol., 28 mg sodium, 3 g carb., 1 g fiber, trace pro.* **Diabetic Exchange:** *Free food.*

Blue Cheese Walnut Tart

This simple yet elegant tart gives any casual gathering a touch of class. It's wonderful as a lunch entree and also perfect as part of a springtime brunch buffet.

—ERIN CHILCOAT CENTRAL ISLIP, NY

PREP: 30 MIN. • **BAKE:** 15 MIN.
MAKES: 12 SERVINGS

- 1 sheet refrigerated pie pastry
- 1 package (8 ounces) cream cheese, softened
- ⅓ cup crumbled blue cheese
- 1 garlic clove, minced
- ¼ cup heavy whipping cream
- 1 egg
- ¼ teaspoon cayenne pepper
- ¼ teaspoon coarsely ground pepper
- ⅓ cup chopped roasted sweet red peppers
- 3 tablespoons chopped walnuts, toasted
- 2 tablespoons minced fresh parsley

1. Press pastry onto the bottom and up the sides of an ungreased 9-in. fluted tart pan with removable bottom; trim edges. Bake at 425° for 8-10 minutes or until lightly browned. Cool completely on a wire rack.
2. In a large bowl, beat the cream cheese, blue cheese and garlic until blended. Add the cream, egg, cayenne and pepper; beat well. Spread mixture into crust. Sprinkle with red peppers, walnuts and parsley. Cover and freeze for up to 3 months, or bake, uncovered, at 375° for 15-20 minutes or until center is set.
TO USE FROZEN TART *Remove from the freezer 30 minutes before baking (do not thaw). Uncover; place on a baking sheet. Bake at 375° for 30-35 minutes or until center is set.*

GRAND PRIZE WINNER ★★★★

Caramelized Fennel Tarts

Fennel is a favorite of mine no matter how it's cooked, but I think it is really amazing sauteed until rich and golden, then baked on delicious puff pastry. I've served these as an appetizer and a side dish.

—MARY LISA SPEER PALM BEACH, FL

PREP: 45 MIN. • **BAKE:** 15 MIN.
MAKES: 2 DOZEN

- 2 medium fennel bulbs, quartered and thinly sliced
- 2 tablespoons olive oil
- 1½ teaspoons minced fresh thyme or ½ teaspoon dried thyme
- 1 teaspoon balsamic vinegar
- ¼ teaspoon salt
- ⅛ teaspoon pepper
- 1 package (17.3 ounces) frozen puff pastry, thawed

1. In a large skillet, saute the fennel in oil until softened. Reduce heat to medium-low; cook, uncovered, for 40 minutes or until deep golden brown, stirring occasionally. Stir in the thyme, vinegar, salt and pepper.
2. Unfold each puff pastry sheet onto an ungreased baking sheet. Using a knife, score 1 in. from the edges of each pastry. Spread the fennel mixture to within ½ in. of edges.
3. Bake at 400° for 12-15 minutes or until golden brown. Cut each tart into 12 pieces.
FREEZE OPTION *Freeze the cooled pastries in a freezer container, separating layers with waxed paper. To use, reheat the pastries on an ungreased baking sheet in a preheated 400° oven until crisp and heated through.*

FENNEL FACTS

Fennel is an aromatic herb with a large pale green bulb, celery-like stems and feathery leaves. Uncooked fennel has a mild licorice flavor and crunchy texture. When cooked, the flavor becomes more delicate and the texture softens. Fennel can be sauteed, braised or baked.

Tropical Guacamole

Fresh pineapple stars in this fruity guacamole that really hits the spot! Kids and adults have enjoyed it as a poolside snack or as a satisfying appetizer at a summer barbecue.

—SARAH WHITE SALT LAKE CTY, UT

START TO FINISH: 20 MIN.
MAKES: 3½ CUPS

- 3 medium ripe avocados, peeled
- 2 cups finely chopped fresh pineapple
- 1 medium tomato, seeded and chopped
- 2 jalapeno peppers, seeded and chopped
- ⅓ cup minced fresh cilantro
- 2 tablespoons lime juice
- 3 garlic cloves, minced
- 1 teaspoon salt
- ½ teaspoon pepper
  Tortilla chips

In a small bowl, mash two avocados. Stir in the pineapple, tomato, jalapenos, cilantro, lime juice, garlic, salt and pepper. Coarsely chop the remaining avocado; gently stir into guacamole. Serve with chips.
NOTE *Wear disposable gloves when cutting hot peppers; the oils can burn skin. Avoid touching your face.*
PER SERVING *¼ cup (calculated without chips) equals 77 cal., 6 g fat (1 g sat. fat), 0 chol., 173 mg sodium, 7 g carb., 3 g fiber, 1 g pro.* **Diabetic Exchanges:** *½ starch, ½ fat.*

I created this for a Cinco de Mayo party, and it was a hit! It's so easy, yet has a serious wow factor. The creamy dipping sauce mellows out the shrimp's heat perfectly.

—MANDY RIVERS LEXINGTON, SC

Grilled Chipotle Shrimp

PREP: 25 MIN. + MARINATING
GRILL: 10 MIN.
MAKES: ABOUT 5 DOZEN (1¼ CUPS SAUCE)

- ¼ cup packed brown sugar
- 2 chipotle peppers in adobo sauce, chopped plus ¼ cup adobo sauce
- 6 garlic cloves, minced
- 2 tablespoons water
- 2 tablespoons lime juice
- 1 tablespoon olive oil
- ¼ teaspoon salt
- 2 pounds uncooked large shrimp, peeled and deveined

CILANTRO CREAM SAUCE

- 1 cup sour cream
- ⅓ cup minced fresh cilantro
- 2 garlic cloves, minced
- 1½ teaspoons grated lime peel
- ¼ teaspoon salt
- ¼ teaspoon minced fresh mint

1. In a small saucepan, bring the brown sugar, chipotles, adobo sauce, garlic, water, lime juice, oil and salt to a boil. Reduce heat; cook and stir for 2 minutes longer. Remove from the heat; cool completely.

2. Transfer pepper mixture to a large resealable plastic bag. Add the shrimp; seal bag and turn to coat. Refrigerate for up to 2 hours.

3. Meanwhile, combine the sauce ingredients; chill until serving.

4. Drain and discard the marinade. Thread shrimp onto metal or soaked wooden skewers. Using long-handled tongs, moisten a paper towel with cooking oil and lightly coat grill rack.

5. Grill shrimp, covered, over medium heat or broil 4 in. from the heat for 6-8 minutes or until shrimp turn pink, turning once. Serve with sauce.

Roasted Grape Tomatoes

Everyone loves this mouthwatering starter, which needs just a few ingredients. We appreciate that it's a fast, simple way to use extra tomatoes from our garden.

—**LINDA GREEN** ARDMORE, OK

START TO FINISH: 25 MIN.
MAKES: 4 CUPS

- ½ cup cider vinegar
- ¼ cup packed brown sugar
- 2 tablespoons canola oil
- 4 garlic cloves, minced
- ½ teaspoon salt
- ½ teaspoon pepper
- 1 pound grape tomatoes
- 1 tablespoon minced fresh parsley
  Assorted crackers and Gouda cheese slices

1. In a large bowl, whisk the first six ingredients. Add tomatoes; toss to coat. Transfer to a greased 15x10x1-in. baking pan. Sprinkle with parsley.
2. Bake, uncovered, at 375° for 12-14 minutes or until softened, stirring occasionally. Serve with crackers and cheese slices.

TIME-SAVER

Typically, ½ teaspoon minced garlic from a jar equals one fresh garlic clove, minced. The *Taste of Home* Test Kitchen staff finds the jarred garlic to be slightly milder and prefers to use fresh. However, you may find the convenience of using jarred minced garlic is well worth it. Try it and see.

Prosciutto-Wrapped Asparagus with Raspberry Sauce

Grilling the prosciutto with the asparagus gives this appetizer a salty crunch that makes it perfect for dipping into a sweet glaze. When a delicious appetizer is this easy to prepare, you owe it to yourself to try it!

—**NOELLE MYERS** GRAND FORKS, ND

START TO FINISH: 30 MIN.
MAKES: 16 APPETIZERS

- ⅓ pound thinly sliced prosciutto or deli ham
- 16 fresh asparagus spears, trimmed
- ½ cup seedless raspberry jam
- 2 tablespoons balsamic vinegar

1. Cut prosciutto slices in half. Wrap a prosciutto piece around each asparagus spear; secure ends with toothpicks. Moisten a paper towel with cooking oil; using long-handled tongs, lightly coat the grill rack.
2. Grill asparagus, covered, over medium heat 6-8 minutes or until the prosciutto is crisp, turning once. Discard the toothpicks.
3. In a small microwave-safe bowl, microwave jam and vinegar on high for 15-20 seconds or until jam is melted. Serve with asparagus.
PER SERVING *1 asparagus spear with 1½ teaspoons sauce equals 50 cal., 1 g fat (trace sat. fat), 8 mg chol., 184 mg sodium, 7 g carb., trace fiber, 3 g pro.* **Diabetic Exchange:** *½ starch.*

Chili-Cheese Egg Rolls

More than an inventive way to use leftover or store-bought chili, this is the No. 1 request in the Bender household. Give these change-of-pace egg rolls a try and you'll understand why.

—JENNIFER BENDER BALDWIN, GA

PREP: 15 MIN. • **COOK:** 5 MIN./BATCH
MAKES: 8 EGG ROLLS

 1 **can (15 ounces) chili without beans**
 1 **cup (4 ounces) shredded cheddar cheese**
 2 **tablespoons finely chopped onion**
 2 **tablespoons finely chopped seeded jalapeno pepper**
 8 **egg roll wrappers**
    Oil for deep-fat frying
    Sour cream and guacamole, optional

1. In a small bowl, combine the chili, cheese, onion and jalapeno. Place ¼ cup chili mixture in the center of one egg roll wrapper. (Keep remaining wrappers covered with a damp paper towel until ready to use.) Fold bottom corner over filling. Fold sides toward center over filling. Moisten remaining corner with water; roll up tightly to seal. Repeat.
2. In an electric skillet, heat 1 in. of oil to 375°. Fry egg rolls for 1-2 minutes on each side or until golden brown. Drain the egg rolls on paper towels. Serve with sour cream and guacamole if desired.
NOTE *Wear disposable gloves when cutting hot peppers; the oils can burn skin. Avoid touching your face.*

Creole Scallop Cakes

Experimenting in the kitchen is a passion of mine. One day I had some scallops and decided to create scallop cakes, which turned out to be a great decision. Both the cakes and aioli can be made the day before, so all you have to do is cook the scallop cakes just before serving.

—IISHA LEFTRIDGE-BROOKS SACRAMENTO, CA

PREP: 25 MIN. + CHILLING • **COOK:** 5 MIN./BATCH
MAKES: 20 SCALLOP CAKES (1½ CUPS AIOLI).

  1   **egg, beaten**
  ½   **cup seasoned bread crumbs**
  2   **tablespoons finely chopped sweet red pepper**
  2   **tablespoons finely chopped leek (white portion only)**
  4   **garlic cloves, minced**
  2   **tablespoons honey mustard**
  1   **tablespoon minced fresh thyme**
  1   **tablespoon chopped fennel fronds**
  2   **teaspoons salt-free lemon-pepper seasoning**
 1½   **teaspoons Creole seasoning**
  1   **pound sea scallops**
COATING
  1   **cup panko (Japanese) bread crumbs**
  4   **teaspoons dried parsley flakes**
  2   **teaspoons coarsely ground pepper**
SPICY HONEY AIOLI
  1   **cup mayonnaise**
  ⅓   **cup honey mustard**
  1   **tablespoon lemon juice**
  1   **tablespoon unsweetened apple juice**
  1   **teaspoon paprika**
  1   **teaspoon Creole seasoning**
  ½   **teaspoon Cajun seasoning**
  ⅓   **cup canola oil**

1. In a large bowl, combine the first 10 ingredients. Place scallops in a food processor; cover and pulse until just pureed. Fold into egg mixture.
2. In a shallow bowl, combine the bread crumbs, parsley and pepper. Drop 2 tablespoons scallop mixture into crumb mixture. Gently coat and shape into a ½-in.-thick patty. Repeat with remaining mixture. Cover and refrigerate for at least 30 minutes.
3. Meanwhile, in a small bowl, whisk the mayonnaise, mustard, lemon juice, apple juice and seasonings. Cover and refrigerate until serving.
4. In a large skillet over medium heat, cook patties in oil in batches for 2-3 minutes on each side or until golden brown. Drain on paper towel. Serve with aioli.
NOTE *The following spices may be substituted for 1 teaspoon Creole seasoning: ¼ teaspoon each salt, garlic powder and paprika; and a pinch each of dried thyme, ground cumin and cayenne pepper.*

Smoky Grilled Corn Salsa

Our backyard grill is the perfect place to cook up the ingredients for a homemade corn salsa. It's yummy with tortilla chips or as a topping for meat, poultry and fish.
—**ALICIA DEWOLFE** GLOUCESTER, MA

START TO FINISH: 30 MIN.
MAKES: 6 CUPS

- 6 plum tomatoes, halved
- 4 medium ears sweet corn, husks removed
- 2 medium sweet yellow peppers, halved
- 2 medium green peppers, halved
- 3 jalapeno peppers, halved and seeded
- 1 medium red onion, cut into ½-inch slices
- ¼ cup minced fresh cilantro
- 3 tablespoons olive oil
- 3 tablespoons red wine vinegar
- 5 garlic cloves, minced
- 1 teaspoon salt
- ½ teaspoon sugar
- ½ teaspoon pepper

1. Grill the tomatoes, corn, peppers and onion, covered, over medium heat for 10-12 minutes or until tender, turning occasionally. Allow vegetables to cool slightly. Remove corn from cobs; transfer to a large bowl. Chop the remaining vegetables and add to corn.
2. In a small bowl, whisk the cilantro, oil, vinegar, garlic, salt, sugar and pepper. Pour over vegetables; toss to coat. Serve warm or cold.
NOTE *Wear disposable gloves when cutting hot peppers; the oils can burn skin. Avoid touching your face.*
PER SERVING *¼ cup equals 40 cal., 2 g fat (trace sat. fat), 0 chol., 102 mg sodium, 6 g carb., 1 g fiber, 1 g pro.* **Diabetic Exchange:** *½ starch.*

GRAND PRIZE
WINNER
★★★★★

“Sweet, smoky, tangy, fresh—the flavors in this distinctive appetizer are sure to perk up taste buds for dinner. I sprinkle the warm squares with basil and add a dollop or two of a mascarpone cheese topping.”
—**MERRY GRAHAM** NEWHALL, CA

Cranberry Bacon Galette

PREP: 25 MIN. • **BAKE:** 20 MIN. + COOLING
MAKES: 12 SERVINGS

- 1 carton (8 ounces) mascarpone cheese
- 1 tablespoon orange marmalade
- 1 tablespoon jellied cranberry sauce
- 2 tablespoons sugar
- 1 cup chopped red onion
- 1 cup dried cranberries
- ¾ cup chopped fresh mushrooms
- 1 tablespoon olive oil
- ½ teaspoon lemon-pepper seasoning
- ¼ teaspoon salt
- ¼ teaspoon smoked paprika
- 3 tablespoons cranberry-tangerine juice
- 1 sheet frozen puff pastry, thawed
- 5 cooked bacon strips, crumbled
- ¼ cup minced fresh basil

1. Preheat oven to 400°. For topping, in a small bowl, combine cheese, marmalade and cranberry sauce. Refrigerate until serving.
2. In a large skillet, cook sugar over medium-high heat 1-2 minutes or until it just begins to melt. Add onion; cook and stir 2 minutes longer.
3. Stir in cranberries, mushrooms, oil, lemon pepper, salt and paprika; cook and stir 2 minutes. Reduce heat. Stir in juice; cook and stir until the mushrooms are tender, about 4 minutes.
4. Unfold puff pastry onto a greased baking sheet. Spread cranberry mixture to within 1½ in. of edges; sprinkle with bacon. Bake 18-22 minutes or until pastry is golden brown. Cool 10 minutes. Sprinkle with basil. Serve galette warm with topping.

Three-Pepper Bean Dip

My husband's great-grandmother and I spent time together creating this recipe after trying a similar version from his aunt. So it not only tastes delicious, but also has a lot of sentimental value.
—**AMBER MASSEY** ARGYLE, TX

PREP: 15 MIN. • **BAKE:** 30 MIN.
MAKES: 5 CUPS

- 1 **can (16 ounces) refried beans**
- 1½ **cups (12 ounces) reduced-fat sour cream**
- 1 **cup salsa**
- 4 **green onions, chopped**
- 1 **can (4 ounces) chopped green chilies**
- 3 **ounces reduced-fat cream cheese**
- 1 **jalapeno pepper, seeded and chopped**
- 2 **tablespoons chopped chipotle peppers in adobo sauce**
- 1½ **teaspoons ground cumin**
- ½ **teaspoon chili powder**
- 1 **cup (4 ounces) shredded Colby-Monterey Jack cheese**
  Tortilla chips or assorted fresh vegetables

1. In a large bowl, combine the first 10 ingredients. Transfer to a greased 1½-qt. baking dish. Cover and bake at 325° for 25 minutes.
2. Sprinkle with cheese. Bake, uncovered, 5-10 minutes longer or until bubbly. Serve warm with chips.
NOTE *Wear disposable gloves when cutting hot peppers; the oils can burn skin. Avoid touching your face.*
PER SERVING *¼ cup (calculated without chips or vegetables) equals 84 cal., 4 g fat (3 g sat. fat), 16 mg chol., 211 mg sodium, 7 g carb., 2 g fiber, 4 g pro.* **Diabetic Exchanges:** *1 fat, ½ starch.*

Chipotle Pea Hummus

I've always loved to cook. I also love hummus, so I made a version with peas and smoky bacon. It took a few tries to come up with a recipe that everyone loved. I hope you enjoy it, too!
—**FRANCES "KAY" BOUMA** TRAIL, BC

START TO FINISH: 20 MIN.
MAKES: 1½ CUPS

- 2 **cups frozen peas**
- ⅓ **cup grated Parmesan cheese**
- 3 **cooked bacon strips, chopped**
- ¼ **cup reduced-fat sour cream**
- 2 **tablespoons olive oil**
- 1 **tablespoon lime juice**
- 2 **garlic cloves**
- 1 **to 2 teaspoons minced chipotle pepper in adobo sauce**
- ¼ **teaspoon pepper**
  Assorted fresh vegetables or crackers

1. In a small saucepan, bring 4 cups water to a boil. Add peas; cover and cook for 1 minute. Drain and immediately place peas in ice water. Drain and pat dry.
2. Place peas in a food processor; add the cheese, bacon, sour cream, oil, lime juice, garlic, chipotle pepper and pepper. Cover and process until smooth. Serve with vegetables or crackers.
PER SERVING *¼ cup (calculated without vegetables) equals 129 cal., 8 g fat (2 g sat. fat), 11 mg chol., 207 mg sodium, 8 g carb., 2 g fiber, 6 g pro.* **Diabetic Exchanges:** *1½ fat, ½ starch.*

Melon-Mango Salsa

After tasting a similar salsa atop fresh fish at a fishing tournament, I went home and tried to duplicate it. This is my surprising result. It's terrific with cinnamon pita chips.
—**SYLVIA FINCHAM** NEW BERN, NC

START TO FINISH: 20 MIN.
MAKES: 4 CUPS

- 1 **cup finely chopped cantaloupe**
- 1 **cup finely chopped honeydew**
- 1 **cup finely chopped peeled mango**
- ½ **cup chopped cucumber**
- ½ **cup finely chopped sweet red pepper**
- 1 **green onion, thinly sliced**
- 3 **tablespoons lemon juice**
- ¼ **teaspoon ground cinnamon**
- ¼ **teaspoon cayenne pepper**
  Cinnamon sugar baked pita chips

In a large bowl, combine the first six ingredients. Combine the lemon juice, cinnamon and cayenne. Pour over fruit mixture; toss to coat. Chill until serving. Serve with the pita chips.
PER SERVING *¼ cup (calculated without pita chips) equals 17 cal., trace fat (trace sat. fat), 0 chol., 3 mg sodium, 4 g carb., 1 g fiber, trace pro.* **Diabetic Exchange:** *Free food.*

Italian Meatball Buns

These soft little rolls come with a surprise inside—savory Italian meatballs. They're wonderful dipped in marinara sauce, making them fun for everyone. I love how easy they are to put together.
—**TRINA LINDER-MOBLEY** CLOVER, SC

PREP: 30 MIN. + RISING • **BAKE:** 15 MIN.
MAKES: 2 DOZEN

- 12 **frozen bread dough dinner rolls**
- 1 **package (12 ounces) frozen fully cooked Italian meatballs, thawed**
- 2 **tablespoons olive oil**
- ¼ **cup grated Parmesan cheese**
- ¼ **cup minced fresh basil**
- 1½ **cups marinara sauce, warmed**

1. Let dough stand at room temperature 25-30 minutes or until softened.
2. Cut each roll in half. Wrap each portion around a meatball, enclosing meatball completely; pinch dough firmly to seal. Place on greased baking sheets, seam side down. Cover with kitchen towels; let rise in a warm place until almost doubled, about 1½-2 hours.
3. Preheat oven to 350°. Bake buns 12-15 minutes or until golden brown. Brush tops with oil; sprinkle with cheese and basil. Serve with marinara sauce.

Touchdown Brat Sliders

It's game time when these minis make an appearance. Two things my husband loves—beer and brats—get stepped up a notch with crunchy flavored chips.

—**KIRSTEN SHABAZ** LAKEVILLE, MN

START TO FINISH: 30 MIN.
MAKES: 16 SLIDERS

- 5 thick-sliced bacon strips, chopped
- 1 pound uncooked bratwurst links, casings removed
- 1 large onion, finely chopped
- 2 garlic cloves, minced
- 1 package (8 ounces) cream cheese, cubed
- 1 cup dark beer or nonalcoholic beer
- 1 tablespoon Dijon mustard
- ¼ teaspoon pepper
- 16 dinner rolls, split and toasted
- 2 cups cheddar and sour cream potato chips, crushed

1. In a large skillet, cook bacon over medium heat until crisp. Remove to paper towels with a slotted spoon; drain, reserving drippings. Cook bratwurst and onion in drippings over medium heat until meat is no longer pink. Add garlic; cook for 1 minute longer. Drain.

2. Stir in the cream cheese, beer, mustard and pepper. Bring to a boil. Reduce heat; simmer, uncovered, for 8-10 minutes or until thickened, stirring occasionally. Stir in bacon. Spoon ¼ cup onto each roll; sprinkle with chips. Replace tops.

BACON BITS

Always check the date stamp on packages of vacuum-sealed bacon to make sure the meat is fresh. The date reflects the last date of sale. Once the package is opened, bacon should be used within a week. For longer storage, you can freeze bacon for up to a month.

Crispy Lime Chips with Crab

Creamy crab dip tops the lime-flavored chips perfectly. These are popular at parties, so it's good the recipe makes a lot.
—**TRACEY STONE** GETTYSBURG, PA

PREP: 45 MIN. • **BROIL:** 5 MIN.
MAKES: 80 APPETIZERS

- 1 tablespoon kosher salt
- 2 teaspoons grated lime peel
- 10 flour tortillas (10 inches)
- ¼ cup olive oil

TOPPING

- 1 package (8 ounces) cream cheese, softened
- 2 tablespoons lime juice
- 2 teaspoons seafood seasoning, divided
- 2 cans (6 ounces each) lump crabmeat, drained
- 6 green onions, finely chopped
- ½ cup shredded sharp white cheddar cheese

1. In a small bowl, combine salt and lime peel; set aside.

2. Using a 3-inch star-shaped cookie cutter, cut eight star shapes from each tortilla. In a large skillet over medium-high heat, heat half of the oil. Fry tortilla stars, a few at a time, until golden brown on both sides. Add more of the oil as needed. Drain stars on paper towels; immediately sprinkle with salt mixture.

3. In a small bowl, beat the cream cheese, lime juice and 1 teaspoon seafood seasoning until blended. Fold in crab and onions. Arrange chips on ungreased baking sheets. Top with crab mixture; sprinkle with cheddar cheese.

4. Broil 3-4 in. from the heat for 1-2 minutes or until cheese is melted. Sprinkle with remaining seafood seasoning. Serve immediately.

Curried Tropical Nut Mix

This nutty concoction is an easy make-at-home food gift guaranteed to spice up the snack table at any party. Good luck keeping the bowl filled!
—**MARY ANN DELL** PHOENIXVILLE, PA

PREP: 20 MIN. + COOLING
MAKES: 7½ CUPS

- 2 tablespoons curry powder
- 1 tablespoon butter
- 1 tablespoon olive oil
- 1 teaspoon ground cumin
- ½ teaspoon cayenne pepper
- 2 cups salted roasted almonds
- 2 cups salted cashew halves
- 2 cups salted peanuts
- 1 cup flaked coconut
- ½ cup dried mangoes, chopped

1. In a large microwave-safe bowl, combine the first five ingredients. Microwave, uncovered, on high for 30 seconds. Add almonds, cashews, peanuts and coconut; toss to coat.

2. Cook, uncovered, 5-6 minutes longer or until lightly browned, stirring after each minute. Add mangoes. Spread onto waxed paper to cool. Store in an airtight container.

NOTE *This recipe was tested in a 1,100-watt microwave.*

Olive Caprese Salad, page 42

26

28

34

Special Salads

Enjoy **garden-fresh flavor** at every meal with this colorful collection. Turn here when you need a green, fruit, potato or main dish salad. You'll even find **easy-as-can-be** tuna and chicken salads, as well as great ways to use up tomatoes, cucumbers, apples and other **farmers market favorites.**

Turkey Spinach Salad with Cranberry-Raspberry Dressing

A colorful way to keep celebrating, this dish works as an entree or a side salad. If you don't want to use macadamia nuts, try fried wonton strips.

—BETSY KING DULUTH, MN

START TO FINISH: 30 MIN.
MAKES: 6 SERVINGS (⅔ CUP DRESSING)

- ½ cup whole-berry cranberry sauce
- 2 tablespoons raspberry vinegar
- 2 tablespoons seedless raspberry jam
- ¼ teaspoon salt
- ⅓ cup olive oil

SALAD

- 8 cups fresh spinach, torn
- 3 medium kiwifruit, peeled and sliced, divided
- 1 cup fresh raspberries, divided
- ½ cup whole-berry cranberry sauce
- 2 cups diced cooked turkey breast
- ¾ cup coarsely chopped macadamia nuts, toasted

1. In a blender, combine the cranberry sauce, vinegar, jam and salt. Cover and process until smooth. While processing, gradually add the oil in a steady stream. Refrigerate until chilled.

2. To serve, combine the spinach, half of the kiwi, ½ cup raspberries and cranberry sauce in a large bowl. Add ½ cup dressing; toss to coat. Transfer to a serving platter. Arrange the turkey, macadamia nuts and remaining fruit over top; drizzle with remaining dressing. Serve immediately.

"This salad offers the best that summer produce has to offer, and it looks so beautiful layered in a glass bowl. It's almost too pretty to dig in to...almost! And it's perfect for potlucks."

—JODI ANDERSON OVERBROOK, KS

Favorite Layered Salad

START TO FINISH: 20 MIN.
MAKES: 8 SERVINGS

- 2 cups torn romaine
- 2 cups fresh baby spinach
- 1 cup sliced fresh mushrooms
- 1 cup grape tomatoes
- ½ cup shredded carrot
- 1 medium red onion, halved and sliced
- 1 medium sweet red pepper, chopped
- 1 medium cucumber, sliced
- 1 cup frozen peas, thawed
- ½ cup Miracle Whip Light
- 3 tablespoons sugar
- ½ cup shredded cheddar cheese
- 3 tablespoons crumbled cooked bacon

In a 3-qt. trifle bowl or glass bowl, combine romaine and spinach. Layer with mushrooms, tomatoes, carrot, onion, pepper, cucumber and peas. Combine Miracle Whip and sugar; spread over peas. Sprinkle with cheese and bacon. Chill until serving.

PER SERVING *1½ cups equals 131 cal., 6 g fat (2 g sat. fat), 14 mg chol., 293 mg sodium, 16 g carb., 3 g fiber, 5 g pro.* ***Diabetic Exchanges:** 1 vegetable, 1 fat, ½ starch.*

Chicken Poppy Seed Salad

Juicy berries, crisp sugar snap peas and crunchy pecans complement the lime-marinated chicken in this pretty salad. The homemade sweet-sour dressing is simply delicious.

—REBEKAH RADEWAHN WAUWATOSA, WI

PREP: 30 MIN. + MARINATING • **COOK:** 15 MIN.
MAKES: 4 SERVINGS PLUS 1 CUP LEFTOVER DRESSING

- 3 **tablespoons thawed limeade concentrate**
- ¼ **teaspoon pepper**
- ¾ **pound boneless skinless chicken breasts, cut into thin strips**
- 1 **tablespoon canola oil**

DRESSING
- ½ **cup white vinegar**
- ⅓ **cup sugar**
- 1 **teaspoon dried minced onion**
- 1 **teaspoon ground mustard**
- ½ **teaspoon salt**
- 1 **cup canola oil**
- 1 **tablespoon poppy seeds**

SALAD
- 1 **package (6 ounces) fresh baby spinach**
- 2 **cups sliced fresh strawberries**
- 1 **cup fresh sugar snap peas, trimmed**
- 1 **small red onion, chopped**
- ½ **cup pecan halves, toasted**

1. In a large resealable plastic bag, combine limeade concentrate and pepper; add the chicken. Seal bag and turn to coat. Refrigerate for 2 hours.

2. Drain and discard marinade. In a large skillet, saute chicken in oil until no longer pink.

3. Meanwhile, in a blender, combine the vinegar, sugar, onion, mustard and salt. While processing, gradually add oil in a steady stream. Stir in poppy seeds.

4. Divide the spinach among four salad plates; top with strawberries, peas, onion and chicken. Drizzle each serving with 2 tablespoons dressing; sprinkle with pecans. Refrigerate leftover dressing.

Hot Beef and Hazelnut Salad

In my kitchen, leftover roast frequently ends up in this filling salad.

—**RUTH GOODING** LOS ANGELES, CA

PREP: 20 MIN. + STANDING
MAKES: 4 SERVINGS

- 1 **pound boneless beef sirloin steak, sliced across grain into thin strips**

MARINADE
- ¼ **cup sliced green onions**
- 2 **garlic cloves, minced**
- 2 **tablespoons reduced-sodium or regular soy sauce**
- ¼ **tablespoon canola oil**
- 1 **tablespoon water**

DRESSING
- 2 **tablespoons cider vinegar**
- 2 **tablespoons reduced-sodium or regular soy sauce**
- 2 **tablespoons canola oil**
- 1 **garlic clove, minced**
- 1 **teaspoon sugar**
- ¼ **teaspoon curry powder**
- ¼ **teaspoon ground ginger**
- 8 **to 10 cups torn salad greens**
- ¼ **cup coarsely chopped hazelnuts, toasted**
  Sliced green onions
  Chopped sweet red or green peppers

1. Place beef in a glass bowl. Combine marinade ingredients; pour over beef. Allow to stand at room temperature 30 minutes.

2. Meanwhile, combine dressing ingredients; set aside. Place greens in a large salad bowl; refrigerate. In a skillet over high heat, brown half the beef and marinade. Remove and then brown remaining beef. Drain and add all beef to greens.

3. In the same skillet, heat dressing. Pour over salad and quickly toss. Top with hazelnuts, onions and peppers. Serve immediately.

PER SERVING *One serving (using reduced-sodium soy sauce) equals 329 cal., 22 g fat (0 sat. fat), 70 mg chol., 423 mg sodium, 6 g carb., 0 fiber, 28 g pro.* **Diabetic Exchanges:** *3½ meat, 1 vegetable, 1 fat.*

Turkey Pinto Bean Salad with Southern Molasses Dressing

This salad is a welcome alternative to the usual after-Thanksgiving fare. It's a tasty main dish loaded with protein. What a tasty fall dish!

—**LILY JULOW** LAWRENCEVILLE, GA

PREP: 35 MIN. + CHILLING
MAKES: 6 SERVINGS

- ½ **cup oil-packed sun-dried tomatoes**
- 1 **garlic clove, peeled and halved**
- ½ **cup molasses**
- 3 **tablespoons cider vinegar**
- 1 **teaspoon prepared mustard**
- ½ **teaspoon salt**
- ¼ **teaspoon coarsely ground pepper**
- 3 **cups cubed cooked turkey breast**
- 2 **cans (15 ounces each) pinto beans, rinsed and drained**
- 1 **medium green pepper, diced**
- 2 **celery ribs, diced**
- 1 **cup chopped sweet onion**
- ¼ **cup minced fresh parsley**

1. Drain the tomatoes, reserving 2 tablespoons oil. Place garlic and tomatoes in a food processor; cover and process until chopped. Add the molasses, vinegar, mustard, salt, pepper and reserved oil. Cover and process until smooth.

2. In a large bowl, combine the turkey, beans, green pepper, celery, onion and parsley. Add dressing and toss to coat. Cover and refrigerate for at least 2 hours.

PER SERVING *1⅓ cups equals 379 cal., 7 g fat (1 g sat. fat), 60 mg chol., 483 mg sodium, 49 g carb., 7 g fiber, 29 g pro.* **Diabetic Exchanges:** *4 lean meat, 2½ starch, 1 vegetable, 1 fat.*

Smoky Spanish Potato Salad

I created this recipe for red potatoes, but fingerlings and Yukon Golds work fine, too. With artichoke hearts added, it will liven up your next picnic.

—**HELEN CONWELL** PORTLAND, OR

PREP: 1 HOUR + COOLING
MAKES: 8 SERVINGS

- 1¾ pounds red potatoes (about 7 medium)
- 2 tablespoons olive oil
- 1 teaspoon smoked Spanish paprika
- ½ teaspoon salt
- 1 jar (6 ounces) marinated quartered artichoke hearts
- 1 cup (8 ounces) sour cream
- ¼ cup mayonnaise
- 1 celery rib, thinly sliced
- 2 tablespoons capers, drained
- 2 green onions, sliced
- 3 tablespoons minced fresh basil

1. Scrub potatoes; cut into 1-in. pieces. Place in a large bowl; drizzle with oil and sprinkle with paprika and salt. Toss to coat. Transfer to a greased 15x10x1-in. baking pan. Bake at 425° for 35-40 minutes or until tender, stirring occasionally. Cool.

2. Drain the artichokes, reserving 2 tablespoons marinade; place artichokes and potatoes in a large bowl. In another bowl, combine the sour cream, mayonnaise, celery, capers, onions, basil and reserved marinade. Pour over potato mixture and toss to coat. Chill until serving.

SMOKED PAPRIKA

Smoked Spanish paprika is made by drying chili peppers over wood fires. This type of paprika is best in dishes where an intense smoky, woodsy flavor is desired. If you'd like a strong paprika flavor without the smoked taste, simply purchase Spanish paprika or Hungarian paprika.

Caramelized Grapefruit Salad

Grapefruit segments are treated to a slight caramelization in a hot skillet just before topping this colorful salad. It's finished with a light honey mustard dressing, bacon and avocado.
—**MARIA DAVIS** FLOWER MOUND, TX

START TO FINISH: 25 MIN.
MAKES: 4 SERVINGS

⅓ cup pecan halves
2 tablespoons plus ¼ cup sugar, divided
1 medium grapefruit, peeled and cut into segments
4 cups spring mix salad greens
¾ cup chopped cucumber
2 green onions, sliced
½ medium ripe avocado, peeled and cubed
2 bacon strips, cooked and crumbled
3 tablespoons reduced-fat honey mustard salad dressing
¼ teaspoon coarsely ground pepper

1. In a small nonstick skillet over medium heat, cook and stir pecans and 2 tablespoons sugar for 2-4 minutes or until sugar is melted. Spread on foil to cool.
2. Coat grapefruit segments with remaining sugar. Coat the same skillet with cooking spray; cook grapefruit over medium heat for 2-3 minutes on each side or until browned.
3. In a large bowl, combine the salad greens, cucumber, onions, avocado and bacon. Drizzle with salad dressing and toss to coat.
4. Divide salad among four serving plates. Top with grapefruit and pecans; sprinkle with pepper.

Cathy's Tomato-Bean Salad

This is a variation on a salad that my mother and grandmother taught me to make. When I was trying to impress my husband, who is a chef, I added a can of chickpeas and olives. That was many years ago, and I'm still serving it the same way today!
—**CATHY MEIZEL** FLANDERS, NY

PREP: 15 MIN. + CHILLING
MAKES: 8 SERVINGS

1 can (15 ounces) garbanzo beans or chickpeas, rinsed and drained
4 large ripe tomatoes, thickly sliced
1 cup thinly sliced red onion
1 can (6 ounces) medium pitted ripe olives, drained and halved
½ cup olive oil
5 to 6 large fresh basil leaves, snipped, or 1 tablespoon dried basil
½ teaspoon dried oregano
¼ teaspoon pepper
  Salt to taste
⅛ teaspoon garlic powder

1. In a large salad bowl, layer beans, tomatoes, onion and olives. Combine all remaining ingredients; pour over the vegetables.
2. Cover and chill at least 3 hours or overnight. Serve chilled or at room temperature.

OLIVE OILS

Bottles simply labeled olive oil (previously called pure olive oil) contain oil with up to 3% acidity. It is usually a blend of refined olive oil and virgin or extra-virgin oil. It has a light color and mild flavor. You will likely find bottles labeled light olive oil on the market, too. The word "light" refers to the color and flavor of the oil, not its calorie content. Light olive oil also contains up to 3% acidity. It has gone through a fine filtration process, giving it a very mild flavor and light color. This oil is perfect for cooking and baking.

Roasted Sweet and Gold Potato Salad

I added Mexicorn and black beans to a potato salad for a festive look and taste. The zesty dressing is easy to throw together.

—JEANNIE TRUDELL DEL NORTE, CO

PREP: 1½ HOURS
MAKES: 16 SERVINGS (¾ CUP EACH)

- 2½ pounds Yukon Gold potatoes (about 8 medium)
- 1½ pounds sweet potatoes (about 2 large)
- 2 tablespoons olive oil
- 1 tablespoon ground cumin
- 2 teaspoons chili powder
- 2 teaspoons garlic powder
- 4 thick-sliced bacon strips, chopped
- 4 green onions, sliced
- 1 medium sweet red pepper, finely chopped
- ½ cup minced fresh cilantro
- 2 hard-cooked large eggs, chopped
- ¾ cup mayonnaise
- 1 tablespoon chopped chipotle pepper in adobo sauce
- 2 teaspoons sugar
- 1 large ripe avocado, peeled and finely chopped
- 2 tablespoons lime juice

1. Peel and cut potatoes and sweet potatoes into ¾-in. cubes. Place in a large bowl; drizzle with oil and sprinkle with seasonings. Toss to coat. Transfer to two greased 15x10x1-in. baking pans. Bake at 450° for 45-55 minutes or until tender, stirring occasionally. Cool slightly.
2. In a small skillet, cook bacon over medium heat until crisp. Remove to paper towels with a slotted spoon; drain.
3. In a large bowl, combine the potatoes, bacon, onions, red pepper, cilantro and eggs. Combine the mayonnaise, chipotle and sugar; pour over potato mixture and toss to coat. In a small bowl, toss avocado with lime juice; gently stir into salad. Serve warm or cold.
PER SERVING *¾ cup equals 236 cal., 14 g fat (2 g sat. fat), 33 mg chol., 145 mg sodium, 24 g carb., 3 g fiber, 4 g pro.*
Diabetic Exchanges: 2½ fat, 1½ starch.

Chopped Salad with Parmesan Dressing

Our two children and I have mixed up this attractive salad for brunch on Father's Day. It's always been enjoyed wherever I have served it.

—MARILYN NORRIE KING CITY, ON

START TO FINISH: 15 MIN.
MAKES: 6-8 SERVINGS

- ½ head iceberg lettuce, chopped into bite-size pieces
- 1 small head romaine lettuce, chopped into bite-size pieces
- ¼ pound Italian salami, finely diced
- ¼ pound part-skim mozzarella cheese, finely chopped
- 1 cup garbanzo beans or chickpeas, rinsed and drained

DRESSING
- 5 tablespoons canola oil
- 2 tablespoons white wine vinegar
- 1 teaspoon ground mustard
- 1 teaspoon salt, optional
- ½ teaspoon black pepper
- ½ cup grated Parmesan cheese

Combine salad ingredients in a glass bowl; chill while mixing dressing. Combine dressing ingredients in a jar with a tight-fitting lid; shake well. Pour dressing over salad just before serving and toss lightly. Serve immediately.

GRAND PRIZE
WINNER
★ ★ ★ ★

Fresh Tomato & Cucumber Salad

This bright, fresh recipe is so easy to prepare. It helps us to find a use for the many vegetables we accumulate from our garden and from friends who kindly share vegetables, too.

—JODIE GHARBI SHREVEPORT, LA

START TO FINISH: 20 MIN.
MAKES: 6 SERVINGS

- ¼ **cup lemon juice**
- ¼ **cup olive oil**
- 1 **tablespoon minced fresh basil or 1 teaspoon dried basil**
- 1 **tablespoon white wine vinegar**
- 1 **garlic clove, minced**
- 1 **teaspoon minced fresh mint or ¼ teaspoon dried mint**
- ⅛ **teaspoon kosher salt**
- ⅛ **teaspoon coarsely ground pepper**
- 4 **plum tomatoes, seeded and chopped**
- 2 **medium cucumbers, chopped**
- ½ **cup Greek olives, sliced**
- 2 **cups torn mixed salad greens**
- ¾ **cup crumbled feta cheese**
- ¼ **cup pine nuts, toasted**

1. In a small bowl, whisk the first eight ingredients; set aside.

2. In a large bowl, combine the tomatoes, cucumbers and olives. Drizzle with half of the dressing; toss to coat. Arrange salad greens on a large serving plate; spoon tomato mixture over top. Sprinkle with cheese and pine nuts and drizzle with remaining dressing.

Grilled Romaine Toss

PREP: 25 MIN. • **GRILL:** 10 MIN.
MAKES: 10 SERVINGS

- ¼ **cup olive oil**
- 3 **tablespoons sugar**
- 1 **teaspoon dried rosemary, crushed**
- 1 **teaspoon dried thyme**
- ¼ **teaspoon salt**
- ¼ **teaspoon pepper**
- 8 **plum tomatoes, quartered**
- 2 **large sweet onions, thinly sliced**

GRILLED ROMAINE

- 4 **romaine hearts**
- 2 **tablespoons olive oil**
- ¼ **teaspoon salt**
- ¼ **teaspoon pepper**

DRESSING

- ¼ **cup olive oil**
- ¼ **cup balsamic vinegar**
- 3 **garlic cloves, peeled and halved**
- 2 **tablespoons brown sugar**
- ¼ **cup grated Parmesan cheese**

1. In a large bowl, combine the first six ingredients. Add tomatoes and onions; toss to coat. Transfer to a grill wok or basket. Grill, covered, over medium heat for 8-12 minutes or until tender, stirring frequently. Set aside.

2. For grilled romaine, cut the romaine hearts in half lengthwise, leaving ends intact. Brush with oil; sprinkle with salt and pepper. Place romaine halves cut sides down on grill. Grill, covered, over medium heat for 3-4 minutes on each side or until slightly charred and wilted.

3. For dressing, place the oil, vinegar, garlic and brown sugar in a food processor; cover and process until smooth.

4. Coarsely chop romaine; divide among 10 salad plates. Top with tomato mixture; drizzle with dressing. Sprinkle with cheese.

NOTE *If you do not have a grill wok or basket, use a disposable foil pan. Poke holes in the bottom of the pan with a meat fork to allow liquid to drain.*

"I often double this fantastic salad, and it's always history by the end of the night. During inclement weather, simply prepare it under the broiler."

—TRISHA KRUSE EAGLE, ID

Mushroom Panzanella

My fresh take on classic Italian bread salad pairs great with grilled or roasted meats.

—JENNIFER BECKMAN FALLS CHURCH, VA

PREP: 35 MIN.
MAKES: 8 SERVINGS

- 4 **cups cubed sourdough bread**
- 6 **tablespoons olive oil, divided**
- 1 **teaspoon salt, divided**
- 1 **pound sliced fresh assorted mushrooms (such as shiitake, oyster and cremini)**
- 1 **garlic clove, minced**
- 2 **tablespoons balsamic vinegar**
- 1 **tablespoon stone-ground mustard**
- 1 **teaspoon honey**
- 4 **cups fresh arugula**
- 1 **cup grape tomatoes, halved**
- 2 **tablespoons pine nuts, toasted**
- 2 **tablespoons golden raisins**
- 2 **ounces fresh goat cheese, crumbled**

1. Preheat oven to 450°. In a large bowl, combine bread, 2 tablespoons oil and ¼ teaspoon salt; toss to coat. Transfer to an ungreased baking sheet. Bake 8-10 minutes or until golden brown. Cool to room temperature.

2. Combine mushrooms, 2 tablespoons oil, garlic and ¼ teaspoon salt; transfer to a greased baking sheet. Bake at 450° for 10-12 minutes or until tender.

3. In a large bowl, whisk vinegar, mustard, honey and remaining oil and salt. Add arugula, tomatoes, pine nuts, raisins, toasted bread and mushrooms; toss to coat. Sprinkle with goat cheese. Serve immediately.

PER SERVING *1 cup equals 210 cal., 13 g fat (2 g sat. fat), 5 mg chol., 506 mg sodium, 20 g carb., 2 g fiber, 6 g pro.*
Diabetic Exchanges: *2 fat, 1 starch, 1 vegetable.*

*"*You may never go back to 'plain' potato salad. I haven't! It goes great with lots of different foods as a side dish, but is also hearty enough to be a meal in itself.*"*

—KATHY SCOTT LINGLE, WY

Dublin Potato Salad

PREP: 25 MIN. • **COOK:** 20 MIN.
MAKES: 8 SERVINGS

- 3 **large white potatoes (about 1½ pounds)**
- 2 **tablespoons white vinegar**
- 2 **teaspoons sugar**
- 1 **teaspoon celery seed**
- 1 **teaspoon mustard seed**
- ¾ **teaspoon salt, divided**
- 2 **cups finely shredded cabbage**
- 12 **ounces cooked or canned corned beef, cubed**
- ¼ **cup chopped dill pickle**
- ¼ **cup sliced green onion**
- 1 **cup mayonnaise**
- ¼ **cup milk**

1. Cover potatoes in lightly salted water and boil until tender. Drain, peel and cube. Combine vinegar, sugar, celery seed, mustard seed and ½ teaspoon salt; drizzle over still-warm potatoes. Cover and chill.

2. Just before serving, gently fold in cabbage, corned beef, pickle and onion. Combine mayonnaise, milk and remaining ¼ teaspoon salt; pour over salad. Gently toss. Serve in cabbage-lined bowl.

3. In a small bowl, whisk the vinegar, lemon juice, mustard, sugar, garlic and remaining oil, salt and pepper. Add to potato mixture; toss to coat. Sprinkle with tarragon. Serve warm or at room temperature. Refrigerate leftovers.

NOTE *If you do not have a grilling grid, use a disposable foil pan. Poke holes in the bottom of the pan with a meat fork to allow any liquid to drain.*

PER SERVING *¾ cup equals 215 cal., 12 g fat (2 g sat. fat), 0 chol., 312 mg sodium, 24 g carb., 3 g fiber, 3 g pro.* **Diabetic Exchanges:** *2 fat, 1½ starch.*

Lemonade Fruit Salad

Here's a simple side that lets fresh fruit shine. I've taken it to several picnics, where it's always well received. Any combination of fruit will work equally well.

—**CLAIRE L. WATSON** CAPE GIRARDEAU, MO

START TO FINISH: 25 MIN.
MAKES: 16 SERVINGS (¾ CUP EACH)

- ½ **cup water**
- 3 **tablespoons sugar**
- 2 **teaspoons grated lemon peel**
- 1 **teaspoon grated orange peel**
- 1 **tablespoon lemon juice**
- 1 **fresh pineapple, peeled and cubed**
- 1½ **pounds seedless red grapes**
- 1 **pound fresh dark sweet cherries, pitted**

1. In a small saucepan, bring water and sugar to a boil; add lemon and orange peels. Remove from the heat; cool completely. Stir in lemon juice.
2. In a large bowl, combine the fruit. Drizzle with syrup and toss gently to coat.

Here's a potato salad that has no mayo. I think it is perfect for outdoor picnics, plus it looks just as good as it tastes.

—**HOLLY BAUER** WEST BEND, WI

Backyard Red Potato Salad

PREP: 25 MIN. • **GRILL:** 10 MIN.
MAKES: 9 SERVINGS

- 2½ **pounds small red potatoes**
- 1 **medium onion, cut into ½-inch slices**
- ½ **cup olive oil, divided**
- 1 **teaspoon salt, divided**
- ½ **teaspoon pepper, divided**
- 3 **tablespoons balsamic vinegar**
- 2 **tablespoons lemon juice**
- 1 **tablespoon Dijon mustard**
- 2 **teaspoons sugar**
- 2 **garlic cloves, minced**
- ¼ **cup minced fresh tarragon**

1. Place potatoes in a large saucepan and cover with water. Bring to a boil. Reduce heat; cover and cook for 10 minutes. Drain; cool slightly. Cut each in half.
2. In a large bowl, combine the potatoes, onion, ¼ cup oil, ½ teaspoon salt and ¼ teaspoon pepper; toss to coat. Arrange the vegetables, cut side down, on a grilling grid; place on a grill rack. Grill, covered, over medium heat for 8-10 minutes or until vegetables are tender and lightly browned, turning occasionally. Chop onion. Place onion and potatoes in bowl.

Strawberry Salad with Mojito Vinaigrette

Mojitos are a fun summery drink and the inspiration behind this refreshing side salad. No rum was used in my recipe, but it certainly could be added to the vinaigrette.

—DONNA MARIE RYAN TOPSFIELD, MA

START TO FINISH: 20 MIN.
MAKES: 5 SERVINGS

- ¼ **cup white wine vinegar**
- 4 **fresh strawberries, hulled**
- 2 **tablespoons water**
- 2 **tablespoons lime juice**
- 2 **tablespoons coarsely chopped fresh mint**
- 2 **tablespoons honey**
- ¼ **teaspoon salt**
  Dash pepper
- 2 **tablespoons olive oil**

SALAD

- 1 **package (5 ounces) spring mix salad greens**
- 2 **cups fresh strawberries, hulled and sliced**
- 1 **small red onion, thinly sliced**
- 3 **ounces fresh goat cheese, crumbled**
- ¼ **cup chopped walnuts**

1. In a blender, combine the first eight ingredients. While processing, gradually add oil in a steady stream. Set aside.

2. Divide salad greens among five plates; top with the strawberries, onion, cheese and walnuts. Drizzle with vinaigrette.

PER SERVING *1½ cups salad with 2 tablespoons vinaigrette equals 178 cal., 11 g fat (3 g sat. fat), 11 mg chol., 195 mg sodium, 17 g carb., 3 g fiber, 4 g pro.* ***Diabetic Exchanges:*** *2 fat, 1 vegetable, ½ starch, ½ fruit.*

Grilled Lebanese Salad

PREP: 30 MIN. • **GRILL:** 10 MIN.
MAKES: 13 SERVINGS (¾ CUP EACH)

- 8 **plum tomatoes**
- ½ **pound whole fresh mushrooms**
- 2 **medium red onions**
- 2 **medium green peppers**
- 6 **tablespoons olive oil, divided**
- ½ **teaspoon garlic salt**
- 4 **cups cubed French bread**
  (¾-in. cubes)
- 2 **teaspoons dried thyme**
- 1 **teaspoon dried oregano**
- ½ **teaspoon salt**
- ½ **teaspoon pepper**
- 1 **medium cucumber, peeled, seeded**
  and sliced
- ½ **cup fresh basil leaves, thinly sliced**
- 3 **tablespoons balsamic vinegar**

1. Cut tomatoes and mushrooms in half; place in a large bowl. Cut onions and peppers into ½-in.-thick slices; add to bowl. Drizzle vegetables with 4 tablespoons oil and sprinkle with garlic salt; toss to coat.

2. Place bread cubes in another large bowl. Drizzle with the remaining oil. Sprinkle with thyme, oregano, salt and pepper; toss to coat. Thread on metal or soaked wooden skewers.

3. Transfer vegetables to a grill wok or basket. Grill, uncovered, over medium heat for 8-12 minutes or until tender, stirring frequently. Grill the bread cubes, covered, over medium heat for 1-2 minutes or until toasted, turning occasionally.

4. Coarsely chop the tomatoes, onions and peppers; place in a large bowl. Add the mushrooms, bread cubes, cucumber and basil; drizzle with vinegar and gently toss to coat.

NOTE *If you do not have a grill wok or basket, use a disposable foil pan. Poke holes in the bottom of the pan with a meat fork to allow liquid to drain.*

PER SERVING *¾ cup equals 113 cal., 7 g fat (1 g sat. fat), 0 chol., 239 mg sodium, 12 g carb., 2 g fiber, 2 g pro.*
***Diabetic Exchanges:** 1 starch, 1 fat.*

Amazingly, even our kids eat their greens, herbs and garden veggies when prepared this way. Fresh and healthy never tasted more delicious!
—**TRISHA KRUSE** EAGLE, ID

Pecan-Crusted Chicken Salad with Fig Vinaigrette

Here's a delicious way to get greens into your diet. The salad is so flavorful, it's great for family dinners as well as casual summertime entertaining. Pecan-crusted chicken and homemade fig vinaigrette make it just as good as any restaurant salad. Give it a try!

—**KELLY BOE** WHITELAND, IN

PREP: 35 MIN. • **BAKE:** 20 MIN.
MAKES: 6 SERVINGS

- 1 **cup chopped pecans**
- ½ **cup panko (Japanese) bread crumbs**
- 1 **teaspoon dried rosemary, crushed**
- ½ **teaspoon salt**
- ½ **teaspoon dried sage leaves, crushed**
- ¼ **teaspoon dried basil**
- ⅛ **teaspoon cayenne pepper**

- 1½ **pounds boneless skinless chicken breasts, cut into 1-inch strips**

FIG VINAIGRETTE
- 6 **tablespoons fig preserves**
- 3 **tablespoons balsamic vinegar**
- 1 **small garlic clove, minced**
- 6 **tablespoons olive oil**

SALAD
- 9 **cups torn mixed salad greens**
- ¾ **cup crumbled goat cheese**
- 3 **tablespoons dried blueberries**

1. Place pecans in a food processor; cover and process until finely chopped. Add the bread crumbs, rosemary, salt, sage, basil and cayenne; process until combined. Transfer to a shallow bowl.

2. Coat chicken strips with pecan mixture. Place in a greased 15x10x1-in. baking pan. Bake, uncovered, at 375° for 20-25 minutes or until no longer pink, turning once.

3. For vinaigrette, in a small saucepan over low heat, melt the fig preserves. Transfer to a small bowl; add vinegar and garlic. Gradually whisk in oil.

4. Divide salad greens among six plates; sprinkle with the cheese and blueberries. Top with chicken. Drizzle with vinaigrette. Serve immediately.

Fresh Apple Salad

This salad is a perfect fall dish that always gets rave reviews. I clipped the recipe out of a newspaper years ago. Now I find myself preparing it whenever company is coming over.

—**BECKY DRUETZLER** INDIANAPOLIS, IN

PREP: 20 MIN. + CHILLING
MAKES: 16 SERVINGS

- 8 **cups chopped tart apples**
- 1 **can (20 ounces) pineapple chunks, drained, with juice reserved**
- 2 **cups seedless green grapes**
- 1 **to 2 teaspoons poppy seeds**
- 1½ **cups toasted pecans**

DRESSING
- **Reserved pineapple juice**
- ¼ **cup butter**
- ¼ **cup sugar**
- 1 **tablespoon lemon juice**
- 2 **tablespoons cornstarch**
- 2 **tablespoons water**
- 1 **cup mayonnaise or ½ cup reduced-calorie mayonnaise and ½ cup plain yogurt**

1. Combine apples, pineapple chunks, grapes and poppy seeds in large glass bowl, cover and refrigerate.

2. Meanwhile, for dressing, combine the reserved pineapple juice, butter, sugar and lemon juice in a small saucepan. Heat to boiling.

3. Combine the cornstarch and water to make a smooth paste; add to the hot mixture; cook until thick and smooth. Chill completely before stirring in mayonnaise/yogurt.

4. Toss fruit salad with chilled dressing; refrigerate until time to serve. Stir in pecans right before serving.

❝Over the years my husband and I have collected recipes from all over the United States. This flavorful salad recipe comes from New York. I serve it for luncheons, and it's one of my husband's very favorites.❞

—LINDA WHEATLEY GARLAND, TX

Spinach Salad with Goat Cheese and Beets

Here's a super easy salad that looks and tastes festive for the wonderful Christmas season. Vinaigrette dressing coats the greens nicely.

—NANCY LATULIPPE SIMCOE, ON

PREP: 45 MIN. + COOLING
MAKES: 10 SERVINGS

- 1¼ pounds fresh beets
- 1 tablespoon balsamic vinegar
- 1½ teaspoons honey
- 1½ teaspoons Dijon mustard
- ¼ teaspoon salt
- ¼ teaspoon pepper
- ¼ cup olive oil
- 5 cups fresh baby spinach
- 2 ounces fresh goat cheese, crumbled
- ½ cup chopped walnuts, toasted
  Additional pepper, optional

1. Scrub beets and trim tops to 1 in. Place in a Dutch oven and cover with water. Bring to a boil. Reduce heat; cover and simmer for 30-60 minutes or until tender. Remove from the water; cool. Peel beets and cut into 1-in. pieces.
2. In a small bowl, whisk the vinegar, honey, mustard, salt and pepper. Slowly whisk in oil until blended.
3. Place spinach in salad bowl. Drizzle with dressing; toss to coat. Top with beets, goat cheese and walnuts. Sprinkle with additional pepper if desired.

Tropical Chicken Salad

PREP: 10 MIN. + CHILLING
MAKES: 4-6 SERVINGS

- 2 cups cubed cooked chicken
- 1 cup chopped celery
- 1 cup mayonnaise
- ½ to 1 teaspoon curry powder
- 1 can (20 ounces) chunk pineapple, drained
- 2 large firm bananas, sliced
- 1 can (11 ounces) mandarin oranges, drained
- ½ cup flaked coconut
  Salad greens, optional
- ¾ cup salted peanuts or cashew halves

1. Place chicken and celery in a large bowl. Combine the mayonnaise and curry powder; add to chicken mixture and mix well. Cover and chill for at least 30 minutes.
2. Before serving, add the pineapple, bananas, oranges and coconut; toss gently. Serve on salad greens if desired. Sprinkle with nuts.

GRAND PRIZE WINNER ★★★★

Shrimp Salad with Peaches

Trying to change my husband's taste for meat and potatoes is easy when I serve him this flavorful shrimp dish, complete with healthy fruit and greens.

—GILDA LESTER MILLSBORO, DE

PREP: 25 MIN. • **GRILL:** 10 MIN.
MAKES: 4 SERVINGS

- ¾ **pound uncooked large shrimp**
- ½ **cup hoisin sauce**
- 6 **tablespoons olive oil, divided**
- ¼ **cup lemon juice, divided**
- 1 **teaspoon hot pepper sauce**
- ½ **teaspoon ground cumin**
- 4 **medium peaches, halved**
- ¼ **teaspoon salt**
- 8 **cups fresh arugula**
- ½ **cup fresh cilantro leaves**
- ½ **cup crumbled goat cheese**
- 1 **medium lemon, quartered**

1. Peel and devein the shrimp, leaving tails on. In a large resealable plastic bag, combine the hoisin sauce, 2 tablespoons oil, 2 tablespoons lemon juice, hot sauce and cumin. Add the shrimp; seal the bag and turn to coat. Refrigerate for up to 30 minutes. Drain and discard the marinade.

2. Thread shrimp on four metal or soaked wooden skewers. Moisten a paper towel with cooking oil; using long-handled tongs, rub on the grill rack to coat lightly. Brush peach halves with 1 tablespoon oil.

3. Grill shrimp and peaches, covered, over medium heat or broil 4 in. from the heat for 6-8 minutes or until shrimp turn pink, turning once.

4. In a large bowl, combine salt with the remaining oil and lemon juice. Add the arugula and cilantro; toss to coat. Divide among four plates. Top with peaches, shrimp and goat cheese. Squeeze lemon over salads.

Tuna-Stuffed Jumbo Shells

These light, fresh-tasting stuffed shells really star as part of a luncheon menu. I came up with this distinctive combination of ingredients by accident one day using leftovers from other recipes. It's a cool summer main dish.

—PHY BRESSE LUMBERTON, NC

PREP: 25 MIN. + CHILLING
MAKES: 5 SERVINGS

- 10 **jumbo pasta shells**
- ½ **cup mayonnaise**
- 2 **tablespoons sugar**
- 1 **can (12 ounces) tuna, drained**
- 1 **cup diced celery**
- ½ **cup diced green onions**
- ½ **cup diced green pepper**
- ½ **cup shredded carrot**
- 2 **tablespoons minced fresh parsley**

CREAMY CELERY DRESSING

- ¼ **cup sour cream**
- ¼ **cup sugar**
- ¼ **cup cider vinegar**
- 2 **tablespoons mayonnaise**
- 1 **teaspoon celery seed**
- 1 **teaspoon onion powder**
  Lettuce leaves and red onion rings, optional

1. Cook pasta according to package directions; rinse in cold water and drain. In a bowl, combine mayonnaise and sugar. Stir in the tuna, celery, onions, green pepper, carrot and parsley. Spoon into pasta shells; cover and refrigerate.

2. For the dressing, combine sour cream, sugar, vinegar, mayonnaise, celery seed and onion powder.

3. Arrange lettuce and onion rings, if desired, along with shells on a serving platter; drizzle with dressing.

Glazed Salmon Salad

Honey and smoked paprika lend delightful flavors and a bright color to this beautiful dish. It feels special, but it's quick enough for weeknights, too.

—**ELIZABETH DEHART** WEST JORDAN, UT

PREP: 20 MIN. • **BAKE:** 20 MIN.
MAKES: 4 SERVINGS

- 4 salmon fillets (4 ounces each)
- 1 tablespoon olive oil
- 2 teaspoons smoked paprika
- 2 teaspoons honey
- 1 garlic clove, minced
- ½ teaspoon salt
- ½ teaspoon pepper
- ¼ teaspoon crushed red pepper flakes

SALAD

- 4 cups fresh baby spinach
- ½ cup shredded carrot
- ¼ cup chopped red onion
- ¼ cup olive oil
- 2 tablespoons cider vinegar
- 1½ teaspoons finely chopped shallot
- 1 teaspoon Dijon mustard

1. Place salmon in an 11x7-in. baking dish coated with cooking spray.
2. In a small bowl, combine the oil, paprika, honey, garlic, salt, pepper and pepper flakes; brush over salmon. Bake, uncovered, at 350° for 20-25 minutes or until fish flakes easily with a fork. Cut salmon into 1-in. pieces.
3. In a large bowl, combine the spinach, carrot and onion. Divide among four serving plates; top with salmon. In a small bowl, combine the oil, vinegar, shallot and mustard; drizzle over salads. Serve immediately.

Almond Chicken Salad

My mother used to prepare this salad for an evening meal during the hot summer months. It also serves well as a delicious but quick luncheon or potluck dish. You can't beat the tasty combination of chicken, grapes and almonds.

—**KATHY KITTELL** LENEXA, KS

START TO FINISH: 15 MIN.
MAKES: 6-8 SERVINGS

- 4 cups cubed cooked chicken
- 1½ cups seedless green grapes, halved
- 1 cup chopped celery
- ¾ cup sliced green onions
- 3 hard-cooked large eggs, chopped
- ½ cup Miracle Whip
- ¼ cup sour cream
- 1 tablespoon prepared mustard
- 1 teaspoon salt
- ½ teaspoon pepper
- ¼ teaspoon onion powder
- ¼ teaspoon celery salt
- ⅛ teaspoon ground mustard
- ⅛ teaspoon paprika
- ½ cup slivered almonds, toasted
- 1 kiwifruit, peeled and sliced, optional

1. In a large bowl, combine chicken, grapes, celery, onions and eggs. In another bowl, combine the next nine ingredients; stir until smooth.
2. Pour over the chicken mixture and toss gently. Stir in almonds and serve immediately, or refrigerate and add the almonds just before serving. Garnish with kiwi if desired.

FUN BITE

Have picky eaters at your house? Try serving chicken, egg or tuna salad in an ice cream cone instead of between bread. Kids love this crunchy lunch that resembles dessert.

—**SUZANNE M.** LYONS, GA

Olive Caprese Salad

When heirloom tomatoes arrive, feature them with red onions, green olives and a surprising twist: star anise.

—JULIE MERRIMAN SEATTLE, WA

PREP: 35 MIN. • **COOK:** 5 MIN. + MARINATING
MAKES: 10 SERVINGS

- 1 cup plus 2 tablespoons red wine vinegar, divided
- ½ cup sugar
- 1 whole star anise
- ¾ cup thinly sliced red onion (about ½ medium)
- 2 pounds medium heirloom tomatoes, cut into wedges
- 2 cups heirloom cherry tomatoes, halved
- 1 cup pitted green olives, halved
- 8 ounces fresh mozzarella cheese, sliced and halved
- 1 tablespoon each minced fresh basil, tarragon, mint and cilantro
- 1 serrano pepper, thinly sliced
- ¼ cup olive oil
- 2 tablespoons lime juice
- 1½ teaspoons grated lime peel
- ¼ teaspoon salt, optional

1. In a small saucepan, combine 1 cup vinegar, sugar and star anise. Bring to a boil, stirring to dissolve sugar. Remove from the heat. Cool slightly; stir in onion. Let stand for 30 minutes.

2. In a large bowl, combine the tomatoes, olives, cheese, herbs and serrano pepper. Remove star anise from onion mixture; drain onion, reserving 2 tablespoons marinade. (Discard remaining marinade or save for other use.) Add onion to tomato mixture.

3. In a small bowl, whisk the oil, lime juice and peel and remaining vinegar; pour over tomato mixture. Drizzle with reserved marinade; toss gently to coat. Season with salt if desired. Serve immediately.

NOTE *Wear disposable gloves when cutting hot peppers; the oils can burn skin. Avoid touching your face.*

Spicy Pepper Slaw

In addition to making a great side, this slaw can be piled on top of a chicken sandwich or burger. Jalapenos give it just the right kick.

—CHERYL MCCLEARY KANSAS CITY, KS

PREP: 20 MIN. + CHILLING
MAKES: 8 SERVINGS

- 3 cups shredded cabbage
- 2 celery ribs, chopped
- 1 medium green pepper, julienned
- 1 cup cut fresh green beans (1-inch pieces)
- 1 cup cut fresh asparagus (1-inch pieces)
- 1 bunch green onions, chopped
- 1 banana pepper, seeded and chopped
- 2 jalapeno peppers, seeded and chopped
- 2 serrano peppers, seeded and chopped
- ½ cup cider vinegar
- 3 tablespoons olive oil
- 1 tablespoon lime juice
- 1 tablespoon minced fresh thyme
- 1 tablespoon snipped fresh dill
- 1 tablespoon minced fresh cilantro
- 1 teaspoon salt
- 1 teaspoon pepper

In a large bowl, combine the first nine ingredients. In a small bowl, whisk the remaining ingredients; pour over salad and toss to coat. Refrigerate salad for at least 1 hour before serving.

NOTE *Wear disposable gloves when cutting hot peppers; the oils can burn skin. Avoid touching your face.*

PER SERVING *1 cup equals 76 cal., 5 g fat (1 g sat. fat), 0 chol., 314 mg sodium, 6 g carb., 3 g fiber, 2 g pro.* **Diabetic Exchanges:** *1 vegetable, 1 fat.*

Roasted Red Potato Salad

PREP: 55 MIN.
MAKES: 8 SERVINGS

- 2 pounds small red potatoes, quartered
- ¼ cup olive oil
- ¾ teaspoon salt, divided
- ½ teaspoon pepper, divided
- 3 ounces cream cheese, softened
- ½ cup sour cream
- 1 can (4 ounces) chopped green chilies
- 1 teaspoon smoked Spanish paprika
- ½ teaspoon garlic powder
- 1 can (15¼ ounces) whole kernel corn, drained
- 1 small red onion, finely chopped
- 1 small sweet red pepper, finely chopped
- ⅓ cup minced fresh cilantro

1. Toss potatoes with oil, ½ teaspoon salt and ¼ teaspoon pepper; place in a greased 15x10x1-in. baking pan. Bake at 400° for 30-35 minutes or until tender, stirring once. Cool slightly.

2. For dressing, in a small bowl, beat the cream cheese and sour cream until smooth. Stir in the chilies, paprika, garlic powder and remaining salt and pepper.

3. In a large bowl, combine the corn, onion, red pepper and potatoes. Add 1 cup dressing and cilantro; toss to coat (save remaining dressing for another use). Serve immediately.

❝My love for Southwestern flavors led me to create this perfect dish. I discovered that smoked paprika is an ideal addition to this recipe.❞

—**KELLY FAUST** LOUISVILLE, KY

Cheddar Ham Chowder, page 48

49

55

67

Soups & Sandwiches

The savory combination of soup and sandwich is a longtime duo that **always hits the spot!** Turn here for 38 steaming soups, piled-high sandwiches and simple wraps. Whether you pair them together or enjoy them individually, **a lip-smacking meal** is certainly in store. Give them a try tonight!

Italian Sausage Minestrone

My family asks for this soup every year after the cold weather sets in. I like to serve it with crusty French bread to dip into the broth.

—ELIZABETH RENTERIA VANCOUVER, WA

PREP: 20 MIN. + FREEZING • **COOK:** 1¼ HOURS
MAKES: 13 SERVINGS (3¾ QUARTS)

- 1 **pound bulk Italian sausage**
- 2 **large carrots, chopped**
- 2 **celery ribs, chopped**
- 1 **medium onion, chopped**
- 6 **garlic cloves, minced**
- 3 **tablespoons olive oil**
- 7 **cups reduced-sodium chicken broth**
- 2 **cans (15 ounces each) cannellini or white kidney beans, rinsed and drained**
- 2 **cans (14½ ounces each) fire-roasted diced tomatoes, undrained**
- 2 **bay leaves**
- 1 **tablespoon Italian seasoning**
- 1 **tablespoon tomato paste**
- 1 **cup ditalini or other small pasta**
  Shredded or shaved Parmesan cheese

1. In a Dutch oven, cook sausage over medium heat until no longer pink; drain.

2. In the same pan, saute the carrots, celery, onion and garlic in oil until tender. Stir in the broth, beans, tomatoes, bay leaves, Italian seasoning, tomato paste and sausage. Bring to a boil. Reduce heat; cover and simmer for 30 minutes, adding pasta during the last 6-8 minutes. Cook, uncovered, until pasta is tender.

FREEZE OPTION *Before adding pasta, cool soup. Freeze soup and cheese separately in freezer containers for up to 3 months. To use, partially thaw in refrigerator overnight. Place in a Dutch oven. Bring to a boil. Stir in pasta; return to a boil. Reduce heat; cook, uncovered, for 6-8 minutes or until pasta is tender. Serve with cheese.*

Thai Shrimp Soup

This tasty, crowd-pleasing soup comes together in minutes, and I like the fact that the ingredients are always available in my little local grocery store.

—JESSIE GREARSON-SAPAT FALMOUTH, ME

PREP: 20 MIN. • **COOK:** 20 MIN.
MAKES: 8 SERVINGS (2 QUARTS)

- 1 **medium onion, chopped**
- 1 **tablespoon olive oil**
- 3 **cups reduced-sodium chicken broth**
- 1 **cup water**
- 1 **tablespoon brown sugar**
- 1 **tablespoon minced fresh gingerroot**
- 1 **tablespoon fish sauce or soy sauce**
- 1 **tablespoon red curry paste**
- 1 **lemon grass stalk**
- 1 **pound uncooked large shrimp, peeled and deveined**
- 1½ **cups frozen shelled edamame**
- 1 **can (13.66 ounces) light coconut milk**
- 1 **can (8¾ ounces) whole baby corn, drained and cut in half**
- ½ **cup bamboo shoots**
- ¼ **cup fresh basil leaves, torn**
- ¼ **cup minced fresh cilantro**
- 2 **tablespoons lime juice**
- 1½ **teaspoons grated lime peel**
- 1 **teaspoon curry powder**

1. In a Dutch oven, saute onion in oil until tender. Add the broth, water, brown sugar, ginger, fish sauce, curry paste and lemon grass. Bring to a boil. Reduce heat; carefully stir in shrimp and edamame. Cook, uncovered, for 5-6 minutes or until shrimp turn pink.

2. Add the coconut milk, corn, bamboo shoots, basil, cilantro, lime juice, lime peel and curry powder; heat through. Discard lemon grass.

PER SERVING *1 cup equals 163 cal., 7 g fat (3 g sat. fat), 69 mg chol., 505 mg sodium, 9 g carb., 2 g fiber, 14 g pro.*
***Diabetic Exchanges:** 2 lean meat, 1 vegetable, 1 fat.*

Bacon Popper Burgers

What do you get when you combine a jalapeno popper and a great burger? This fantastic recipe! It takes the classic components of a popper and encases them in a juicy patty for a burst of flavor in every bite.

—JO DAVISON NAPLES, FL

PREP: 30 MIN. • **GRILL:** 15 MIN.
MAKES: 4 SERVINGS

- 3 **jalapeno peppers, halved lengthwise and seeded**
- 1 **teaspoon olive oil**
- 6 **bacon strips, cooked and crumbled**
- 1 **package (3 ounces) cream cheese, softened**
- 2 **garlic cloves, minced**
- 1 **teaspoon salt**
- 1 **teaspoon lemon-pepper seasoning**
- ½ **teaspoon pepper**
- ¼ **teaspoon paprika**
- 2 **pounds ground beef**
- 4 **slices pepper Jack cheese**
- 4 **hamburger buns, split**
- 4 **lettuce leaves**
- 1 **large tomato, sliced**
- ¾ **cup guacamole**

1. Brush jalapenos with oil. Grill, covered, over medium heat for 3-5 minutes or until tender, turning occasionally. When cool enough to handle, finely chop. In a small bowl, combine the bacon, cream cheese and chopped jalapeno until blended.

2. In a large bowl, combine the garlic, salt, lemon pepper, pepper and paprika. Crumble beef over mixture and mix well. Shape into eight thin patties. Spoon bacon mixture onto center of four patties; top with remaining patties and press edges firmly to seal.

3. Grill burgers, covered, over medium heat or broil 4 in. from heat for 6-7 minutes on each side or until a meat thermometer reads 160° and juices run clear. Top with pepper Jack cheese. Cover and cook 1-2 minutes longer or until pepper Jack cheese is melted.

4. Grill hamburger buns, cut side down, over medium heat for 30-60 seconds or until toasted. Serve burgers on buns with lettuce, tomato and guacamole.

NOTE *Wear disposable gloves when cutting hot peppers; the oils can burn skin. Avoid touching your face.*

Cheddar Ham Chowder

Life on a farm can get hectic. Along with my husband's four brothers, we custom-feed 5,000 head of cattle and grow 5,000 acres of crops. So I often freeze this soup and thaw it for a fast, easy meal. Since it's hearty, all I need to add are rolls or bread and a salad, and dinner is ready!

—**ANN HEINE** MISSION HILL, SD

PREP: 20 MIN. • **COOK:** 25 MIN.
MAKES: 6-8 SERVINGS (2 QUARTS)

- 2 **cups water**
- 2 **cups cubed peeled potatoes**
- ½ **cup sliced carrots**
- ½ **cup sliced celery**
- ¼ **cup chopped onion**
- 1 **teaspoon salt**
- ¼ **teaspoon pepper**
- ¼ **cup butter**
- ¼ **cup all-purpose flour**
- 2 **cups milk**
- 2 **cups (8 ounces) shredded sharp cheddar cheese**
- 1 **can (15¾ ounces) whole kernel corn, drained**
- 1½ **cups cubed fully cooked ham**

1. In a large saucepan, bring the water, potatoes, carrots, celery, onion, salt and pepper to a boil. Reduce heat; cover and simmer for 8-10 minutes or until vegetables are just tender. Remove from the heat; do not drain.

2. Meanwhile, in another saucepan, melt the butter. Stir in flour until smooth; gradually add milk. Bring to a boil; cook and stir for 2 minutes or until thickened.

3. Add cheese and stir until melted. Stir into the undrained vegetables; return large saucepan to the heat. Add corn and ham; heat through, stirring occasionally.

Turkey Sandwich with Pineapple Salsa

This is the first recipe I created on my own. The pineapple brightens the flavor of the turkey mixture. Feel free to use rolls in place of the French bread.

—**ANDREA BOYER** LENORE, ID

PREP: 25 MIN. • **BAKE:** 15 MIN.
MAKES: 6 SERVINGS

- 1¼ **cups finely chopped fresh pineapple**
- 2 **plum tomatoes, finely chopped**
- ½ **cup finely chopped onion**
- ⅓ **cup minced fresh cilantro**
- 1 **loaf (1 pound) French bread**
- 1 **pound thinly sliced cooked turkey**
- 6 **slices part-skim mozzarella cheese**

AIOLI
- ¾ **cup mayonnaise**
- 2 **tablespoons lemon juice**
- 2 **garlic cloves, minced**
- ½ **teaspoon pepper**

1. In a small bowl, combine the pineapple, tomatoes, onion and cilantro; set aside.

2. Cut bread in half horizontally; place cut sides up on an ungreased baking sheet. Bake at 350° for 4-5 minutes or until toasted; remove top half from pan. Layer bottom half with turkey and cheese. Bake 10-13 minutes longer or until turkey is heated through and cheese is melted.

3. Meanwhile, combine the aioli ingredients in a small bowl. Carefully spread over cheese; top with salsa. Replace bread top; cut into six slices.

Mom's Italian Beef Sandwiches

My mom made the best Italian beef. I've added to it over the years, but it's still her recipe. She made this for family reunions, and there were never leftovers.

—**MARY MCVEY** COLFAX, NC

PREP: 20 MIN. • **COOK:** 8 HOURS
MAKES: 16 SERVINGS

- 1 boneless beef rump roast or bottom round roast (2 pounds), halved
- 1 boneless beef chuck roast (2 pounds), halved
- 1 beef sirloin tip roast (1 pound)
- 2 tablespoons canola oil
- 2 cups water
- 1 medium onion, chopped
- 4 garlic cloves, minced
- 2 envelopes Italian salad dressing mix
- 1 envelope zesty Italian salad dressing mix
- 1 envelope (0.87 ounce) brown gravy mix
- 1 to 2 tablespoons crushed red pepper flakes
- 1 tablespoon Italian seasoning
- 2 teaspoons Worcestershire sauce
- 16 hoagie buns, split
  Sliced provolone cheese, optional
  Giardiniera, optional

1. In a large skillet, brown each roast in oil on all sides. Drain. Transfer meat to a 7-qt. slow cooker. Combine the water, onion, garlic, salad dressing and gravy mixes, pepper flakes, Italian seasoning and Worcestershire sauce; pour over beef. Cover and cook on low for 8-10 hours or until meat is tender.
2. Remove beef; cool slightly. Skim fat from cooking juices. Pour juices into a large bowl. Shred beef with two forks; add to bowl. Using a slotted spoon, place ½ cup on each bun. Top with cheese and giardiniera if desired.
FREEZE OPTION *Cool meat and juices; transfer to freezer containers. Freeze for up to 3 months. To use, thaw in the refrigerator overnight. Place in a Dutch oven; heat through. Using a slotted spoon, place ½ cup on each bun. Top with cheese and giardiniera if desired.*

> Pears give this harvest soup a pleasant sweetness and nice velvety finish, while curry and ginger provide delightful flavor.
>
> —SARAH VASQUES MILFORD, NH

Butternut Squash & Pear Soup

PREP: 1¼ HOURS • **COOK:** 45 MIN.
MAKES: 9 SERVINGS

- 1 medium butternut squash (about 3 pounds)
- 1 medium onion, chopped
- 2 tablespoons canola oil
- 1 tablespoon curry powder
- 2 garlic cloves, minced
- 2 teaspoons minced fresh gingerroot
- 1 teaspoon salt
- 4 cups reduced-sodium chicken broth
- 4 medium pears, peeled and chopped
- ½ cup heavy whipping cream
  Balsamic vinegar and snipped chives, optional

1. Cut squash in half; discard seeds. Place squash cut side down in a 15x10x1-in. baking pan coated with cooking spray. Bake at 400° for 40-50 minutes or until tender. Cool slightly; scoop out pulp and set aside.

2. In a Dutch oven, saute onion in oil until tender. Add the curry, garlic, ginger and salt; cook 1 minute longer. Stir in the broth, pears and squash. Bring to a boil. Reduce heat; simmer, uncovered, for 30 minutes. Cool slightly.

3. In a blender, process soup in batches until smooth. Return all to the pan; add cream and heat through. Top with balsamic vinegar and chives if desired.

PER SERVING ¾ cup equals 190 cal., 8 g fat (3 g sat. fat), 18 mg chol., 527 mg sodium, 29 g carb., 7 g fiber, 4 g pro. *Diabetic Exchanges: 2 starch, 1 fat.*

PERFECT PEARS

To ripen pears, place them in a paper bag at room temperature. When pears give in slightly to pressure, store in the refrigerator. Pears used for cooking should be a little more firm. Before cooking pears, use a vegetable peeler or paring knife to remove the skin, which turns tough when exposed to heat.

Turkey Meatball Gyros

My whole family loves these winning meatballs, and I appreciate how quick and easy they are. The meatballs can be made the night before or made in a big batch to freeze and use as needed.

—JENNIFER CODUTO KENT, OH

START TO FINISH: 30 MIN.
MAKES: 4 SERVINGS

- ½ cup seasoned bread crumbs
- 1 large egg
- 1 teaspoon garlic powder
- ½ teaspoon salt
- ¼ teaspoon pepper
- 1 pound lean ground turkey
- ¾ cup (6 ounces) reduced-fat plain yogurt
- ½ cup finely chopped peeled cucumber
- 2 tablespoons finely chopped onion
- 1½ teaspoons lemon juice
- 8 whole wheat pita pocket halves
- 2 cups shredded lettuce
- 1 cup chopped tomatoes

1. In a large bowl, combine the bread crumbs, egg and seasonings. Crumble turkey over mixture and mix well. Shape into 16 balls.

2. Place the meatballs on a rack coated with cooking spray in a shallow baking pan. Bake, uncovered, at 400° for 15-20 minutes or until no longer pink.

3. Meanwhile, in a small bowl, combine the yogurt, cucumber, onion and lemon juice. Line pitas with lettuce and tomatoes; add meatballs and drizzle with yogurt sauce.

Mojito Pulled Pork

PREP: 20 MIN. • **COOK:** 7 HOURS
MAKES: 16 SERVINGS

- 1 **boneless pork shoulder roast (4 to 5 pounds)**
- 2 **teaspoons salt**
- 2 **teaspoons dried oregano**
- 2 **teaspoons each ground cumin, paprika and pepper**
- 1 **bunch fresh cilantro, divided**
- 2 **medium onions, halved and sliced**
- ¼ **cup canned chopped green chilies**
- 4 **garlic cloves, minced**
- 2 **cans (14½ ounces each) reduced-sodium chicken broth**
- ⅔ **cup orange juice**
- ½ **cup lime juice**
- 16 **sandwich buns, split**
   Barbecue sauce

1. Cut roast in half. Combine the salt, oregano, cumin, paprika and pepper; rub over pork. Place in a 4- or 5-qt. slow cooker.

2. Mince cilantro to measure ¼ cup; set aside. Trim remaining cilantro, discarding stems. Add the whole cilantro leaves, onions, chilies and garlic to the slow cooker. Combine the broth, orange juice and lime juice; pour over roast. Cover and cook on low for 7-9 hours or until meat is tender.

3. Remove roast; cool slightly. Skim fat from cooking juices; set aside 3 cups juices. Discard remaining juices. Shred pork with two forks and return to slow cooker. Stir in minced cilantro and reserved cooking juices; heat through. Spoon ½ cup of the meat onto each bun. Serve with barbecue sauce.

PER SERVING *1 bun with ½ cup pork mixture (calculated without barbecue sauce) equals 418 cal., 16 g fat (5 g sat. fat), 67 mg chol., 916 mg sodium, 40 g carb., 2 g fiber, 29 g pro.* **Diabetic Exchanges:** *3 medium-fat meat, 2 starch.*

❝This fork-tender pulled pork tastes fabulous on a bun, in a wrap or in a tortilla. My kids like to eat the pork and its citrus-flavored juices spooned over rice.❞

—**MINDY OSWALT** WINNETKA, CA

Hearty Vegetarian Chili

Packed with mushrooms, beans, sun-dried tomatoes and more, this quick chili is so satisfying, you won't even miss the meat!

—PAM IVBULS OMAHA, NE

START TO FINISH: 30 MIN.
MAKES: 9 SERVINGS (2¼ QUARTS)

- 1¾ cups chopped baby portobello mushrooms
- 1 medium onion, finely chopped
- ½ cup chopped sun-dried tomatoes (not packed in oil)
- 2 tablespoons olive oil
- 2 garlic cloves, minced
- 1 package (12 ounces) frozen vegetarian meat crumbles
- 2 cans (16 ounces each) chili beans, undrained
- 2 cans (14½ ounces each) no-salt-added diced tomatoes
- ½ cup water
- ½ cup vegetable broth
- 4½ teaspoons chili powder
- 2 teaspoons brown sugar
- ½ teaspoon celery salt
- ½ teaspoon ground cumin
- 1 medium ripe avocado, peeled and finely chopped
- 9 tablespoons reduced-fat sour cream

1. In a Dutch oven, saute the mushrooms, onion and sun-dried tomatoes in oil until tender. Add garlic; cook 1 minute longer. Add meat crumbles; heat through.

2. Stir in the chili beans, tomatoes, water, broth, chili powder, brown sugar, celery salt and cumin. Bring to a boil. Reduce heat; simmer, uncovered, for 10 minutes. Ladle chili into bowls. Top each with avocado and sour cream.

NOTE *Vegetarian meat crumbles are a nutritious protein source made from soy. Look for them in the natural foods freezer section.*

PER SERVING *1 serving equals 275 cal., 10 g fat (2 g sat. fat), 5 mg chol., 768 mg sodium, 37 g carb., 12 g fiber, 17 g pro.* **Diabetic Exchanges:** *2 lean meat, 2 vegetable, 1½ starch, 1 fat.*

Fresh Fruit Soup

Entertaining is a big part of a military wife's life—my husband was a career Army man—so this soup recipe got a lot of use! It's a great cooldown after Mexican food, but I've also served it with butter cookies at a baby shower.

—JENNY SAMPSON LAYTON, UT

PREP: 20 MIN. + CHILLING
MAKES: 8-10 SERVINGS (ABOUT 2½ QUARTS)

- 1 can (12 ounces) frozen orange juice concentrate, thawed
- 1½ cups sugar
- 1 cinnamon stick (2 inches)
- 6 whole cloves
- ¼ cup cornstarch
- 2 tablespoons lemon juice
- 2 cups sliced fresh strawberries
- 2 medium bananas, sliced
- 2 cups halved green grapes

1. In a large saucepan, mix orange juice with water according to package directions. Remove ½ cup of juice; set aside. Add sugar, cinnamon stick and cloves to saucepan; bring to a boil. Reduce heat and simmer for 5 minutes.

2. Combine cornstarch and reserved orange juice until smooth; stir into pan. Bring to a boil; cook and stir for 2 minutes or until thickened. Remove from the heat and stir in lemon juice.

3. Pour into a large bowl; cover and chill. Just before serving, remove the spices and stir in fruit.

3. Cut chicken into strips. Fill each pita half with chicken, cucumber, tomatoes, onion and cheese; drizzle with sauce.
PER SERVING *2 filled pita halves equals 428 cal., 14 g fat (6 g sat. fat), 85 mg chol., 801 mg sodium, 41 g carb., 3 g fiber, 33 g pro.* **Diabetic Exchanges:** *3 starch, 3 lean meat, 1 fat.*

Onion Italian Sausage

When my five children were all still at home, this was one of their most-requested meals. I've long had this recipe among my standbys and, like all cooks who improvise and experiment, I've changed it as our tastes have changed. It comes together in no time, and it's a great change of pace from usual dinnertime fare.
—**RUTH VAN DER LEEST** LYNDON, IL

START TO FINISH: 30 MIN.
MAKES: 6 SERVINGS

- 6 **medium onions, peeled and sliced ¼ inch thick**
- 2 **tablespoons butter**
- 6 **Italian sausage links**
- 1 **small green pepper, chopped**
- 1½ **tablespoons Italian seasoning**
  - **Dash reduced-sodium soy sauce**

1. In a large skillet, saute onions in butter until lightly browned. Remove from pan; set aside. In the same skillet, lightly brown sausage, turning frequently. Remove; set aside with onions.
2. Add more butter to skillet if necessary; saute pepper until crisp-tender. Add the onions, sausages, Italian seasonings and soy sauce. Add water to 1-in. depth and simmer until a thermometer inserted in the sausages reads 140° and water is cooked away. Serve on buns.

Greek Grilled Chicken Pitas

I switched up my mom's recipe to create this tasty variation. It's delicious and perfect for warm days. It takes advantage of fresh summer veggies and keeps my kitchen cool.
—**BLAIR LONERGAN** ROCHELLE, VA

PREP: 20 MIN. + MARINATING • **GRILL:** 10 MIN.
MAKES: 4 SERVINGS

- ½ **cup balsamic vinaigrette**
- 1 **pound boneless skinless chicken breast halves**

CUCUMBER SAUCE
- 1 **cup plain Greek yogurt**
- ½ **cup finely chopped cucumber**
- ¼ **cup finely chopped red onion**
- 1 **tablespoon minced fresh parsley**
- 1 **tablespoon lime juice**
- 1 **garlic clove, minced**
- ¼ **teaspoon salt**
- ⅛ **teaspoon pepper**

PITAS
- 8 **pita pocket halves**
- ½ **cup sliced cucumber**
- ½ **cup grape tomatoes, chopped**
- ½ **cup sliced red onion**
- ½ **cup crumbled feta cheese**

1. Pour vinaigrette into a large resealable plastic bag. Add the chicken; seal bag and turn to coat. Refrigerate for at least 4 hours or overnight. In a small bowl, combine the cucumber sauce ingredients; chill until serving.
2. Drain and discard marinade. If grilling the chicken, moisten a paper towel with cooking oil; using long-handled tongs, lightly coat the grill rack. Grill chicken, covered, over medium heat or broil 4 in. from the heat for 4-7 minutes on each side or until a thermometer reads 170°.

PINCH OF THIS

A pinch is thought to be the amount of a dry ingredient that can be held between your thumb and forefinger. A dash is a very small amount of seasoning added with a quick downward stroke of the hand. A pinch or a dash of an ingredient is usually somewhere between $\frac{1}{16}$ and a scant $\frac{1}{8}$ teaspoon.

Big Red Soup

We're Nebraska football fans, and on game day, I make up a big pot of this soup that boasts a dash of Mexican flavor. The whole family gathers around the TV to eat this award winner while we watch the game and cheer on our team.

—**SHELLY KORELL** BAYARD, NE

PREP: 20 MIN. • **COOK:** 8 HOURS
MAKES: 12 SERVINGS (3 QUARTS)

- 2 **pounds beef stew meat, cut into 1-inch cubes**
- 2 **tablespoons canola oil**
- ¾ **cup chopped onion**
- 2 **cloves garlic, minced**
- 2 **cans (14½ ounces each) diced tomatoes in sauce**
- 1 **can (10½ ounces) condensed beef broth, undiluted**
- 1 **can (10½ ounces) condensed chicken broth, undiluted**
- 1 **can (10¾ ounces) condensed tomato soup, undiluted**
- ¼ **cup water**
- 1 **teaspoon ground cumin**
- 1 **teaspoon chili powder**
- 1 **teaspoon salt**
- ½ **teaspoon lemon-pepper seasoning**
- 2 **teaspoons Worcestershire sauce**
- ⅓ **cup picante sauce**
- 8 **corn tortillas, cut into quarters**
- 1 **cup (4 ounces) shredded cheddar cheese**

1. In a large skillet, brown beef in oil. Transfer to a 5-qt. slow cooker; add the remaining ingredients except for tortillas and cheese. Cover and cook on low for 8-10 hours or until meat is tender.

2. To serve, place enough tortilla quarters to cover the bottom of each bowl. Pour soup over tortilla pieces; sprinkle with cheese.

Roasted Tomato Soup

Every year, after we gather up all of the tomatoes from my mom's garden, we create this flavor-packed soup. Although it sounds like a lot of garlic, when it's roasted, the garlic becomes mellow and almost sweet.

—**KAITLYN LERDAHL** MADISON, WI

PREP: 25 MIN. • **COOK:** 40 MIN.
MAKES: 6 SERVINGS

- 15 **large tomatoes (5 pounds), seeded and quartered**
- ¼ **cup plus 2 tablespoons canola oil, divided**
- 8 **garlic cloves, minced**
- 1 **large onion, chopped**
- 2 **cups water**
- 1 **teaspoon salt**
- ½ **teaspoon crushed red pepper flakes, optional**
- ½ **cup heavy whipping cream**
  Fresh basil leaves, optional

1. Preheat oven to 400°. Place tomatoes in a greased 15x10x1-in. baking pan. Combine ¼ cup oil and garlic; drizzle over tomatoes. Toss to coat. Bake 15-20 minutes or until softened, stirring occasionally. Remove and discard the skins.

2. Meanwhile, in a Dutch oven, saute onion in remaining oil until tender. Add tomatoes, water, salt and, if desired, pepper flakes. Bring to a boil. Reduce heat; cover and simmer 30 minutes or until flavors are blended. Cool soup slightly.

3. In a blender, process soup in batches until smooth. Return to pan. Stir in cream and heat through. Sprinkle with basil if desired.

Pepperoni Pizza Chili

Pizza and chili go together like fans and football in this must-try halftime food that always delivers.

—JENNIFER GELORMINO PITTSBURGH, PA

PREP: 20 MIN. • **COOK:** 30 MIN.
MAKES: 12 SERVINGS (3 QUARTS)

- 2 **pounds ground beef**
- 1 **pound bulk hot Italian sausage**
- 1 **large onion, chopped**
- 1 **large green pepper, chopped**
- 4 **garlic cloves, minced**
- 1 **jar (16 ounces) salsa**
- 1 **can (16 ounces) hot chili beans, undrained**
- 1 **can (16 ounces) kidney beans, rinsed and drained**
- 1 **can (12 ounces) pizza sauce**
- 1 **package (8 ounces) sliced pepperoni, halved**
- 1 **cup water**
- 2 **teaspoons chili powder**
- ½ **teaspoon salt**
- ½ **teaspoon pepper**
- 3 **cups (12 ounces) shredded part-skim mozzarella cheese**

1. In a Dutch oven, cook the beef, sausage, onion, green pepper and garlic over medium heat until meat is no longer pink; drain.

2. Stir in the salsa, beans, pizza sauce, pepperoni, water, chili powder, salt and pepper. Bring to a boil. Reduce heat; cover and simmer for 20 minutes or until heated through. Sprinkle servings with cheese.

FREEZE OPTION *Before adding cheese, cool chili. Freeze chili in freezer containers. To use, partially thaw in refrigerator overnight. Heat through in a saucepan, stirring occasionally and adding a little water if necessary. Sprinkle each serving with cheese.*

Meat-atarian Sub

GRAND PRIZE

This recipe started out as amped-up garlic bread and turned into an unforgettable football-day sandwich.

—**SHANON MAYER** EVANSTON, WY

PREP: 20 MIN. • **BAKE:** 25 MIN.
MAKES: 6 SERVINGS

- 1 cup (4 ounces) shredded part-skim mozzarella cheese
- ½ cup grated Parmesan cheese
- ½ cup butter, softened
- ½ cup mayonnaise
- 2 garlic cloves, minced
- 1 teaspoon Italian seasoning
- ¼ teaspoon crushed red pepper flakes
- ¼ teaspoon pepper
- 1 loaf (1 pound) French bread, halved lengthwise
- 1 pound sliced deli ham
- 2 packages (2.1 ounces each) ready-to-serve fully cooked bacon, warmed
- 4 ounces sliced pepperoni
- ½ cup pizza sauce

1. Preheat oven to 350°. In a small bowl, combine first eight ingredients. Spread over cut sides of bread. Layer with ham, bacon, pepperoni and pizza sauce; replace top.
2. Wrap in foil; place on a large baking sheet. Bake 25-30 minutes or until heated through. Cut into slices.

Jalapeno Popper Mega Burgers

If you like a little spice in your food, these big stuffed burgers are for you. Just be sure to have plenty of frosty cold drinks on hand to serve with them.

—**KRIS SWIHART** PERRYSBURG, OH

PREP: 25 MIN. • **GRILL:** 15 MIN.
MAKES: 4 SERVINGS

- 1 medium ripe avocado, peeled and cubed
- 1 medium tomato, finely chopped
- 1 small onion, finely chopped
- 1 can (4 ounces) diced jalapeno peppers, drained, divided
- 1 tablespoon lime juice
- 1 garlic clove, minced
- 2 pounds ground beef
- 4 ounces reduced-fat cream cheese
- 1 cup (4 ounces) shredded Monterey Jack cheese
- 1 tablespoon steak seasoning
- 4 kaiser rolls, split
- 4 Bibb lettuce leaves

1. In a small bowl, combine the avocado, tomato, onion, ¼ cup jalapenos, lime juice and garlic; set aside.
2. Shape beef into eight patties. In another bowl, combine the cheeses and remaining jalapenos. Spoon onto the center of four patties. Top with remaining patties and press edges firmly to seal; sprinkle burgers with steak seasoning.
3. Grill burgers, covered, over medium heat for 6-7 minutes on each side or until a thermometer reads 160°. Serve on rolls with lettuce leaves and avocado mixture.
NOTE *This recipe was tested with McCormick Montreal Steak Seasoning. Look for it in the spice aisle.*

Veggie Tortellini Soup

Italian cuisine has more to offer than just spaghetti and pizza. Wait until you taste this sensational soup! I have served it to company for years, and they usually ask for a copy of the recipe before they leave.

—**PRISCILLA GILBERT** INDIAN HARBOUR BEACH, FL

PREP: 15 MIN. • **COOK:** 20 MIN.
MAKES: 7 SERVINGS

3 medium carrots, chopped
1 large onion, chopped
1 tablespoon olive oil
4 garlic cloves, minced
2 cans (14½ ounces each) vegetable broth
2 medium zucchini, chopped
4 plum tomatoes, chopped
2 cups refrigerated cheese tortellini
⅓ cup chopped fresh spinach
1 teaspoon minced fresh rosemary or ¼ teaspoon dried rosemary, crushed
¼ teaspoon pepper
1 tablespoon red wine vinegar

1. In a Dutch oven, saute carrots and onion in oil until onion is tender. Add garlic; cook 1 minute longer.
2. Stir in the broth, zucchini, tomatoes, tortellini, spinach, rosemary and pepper. Bring to a boil. Reduce heat; cover and simmer for 8-10 minutes or until tortellini are tender. Just before serving, stir in vinegar.
PER SERVING *1 cup equals 155 cal., 5 g fat (2 g sat. fat), 13 mg chol., 693 mg sodium, 24 g carb., 3 g fiber, 6 g pro. Diabetic Exchanges: 1 starch, 1 vegetable, ½ fat.*

> "The meat for these sandwiches comes out of the slow cooker tender and flavorful. Living as we do in the foothills of the Cascades, we frequently have deer and elk in the freezer. I sometimes substitute that in this recipe, and it never tastes like game."

—**BERNICE MUILENBURG** MOLALLA, OR

Teriyaki Sandwiches

PREP: 30 MIN. • **COOK:** 7 HOURS
MAKES: 8 SERVINGS

2 pounds boneless beef chuck steak
¼ cup soy sauce
1 tablespoon brown sugar
1 teaspoon ground ginger
1 garlic clove, minced
4 teaspoons cornstarch
2 tablespoons water
8 French rolls, split
¼ cup butter, melted
Pineapple rings
Chopped green onions

1. Cut steak into thin bite-size slices. In a 3-qt. slow cooker, combine the soy sauce, sugar, ginger and garlic. Add steak. Cover and cook on low for 7-9 hours or until meat is tender.
2. Remove meat with a slotted spoon; set aside. Carefully pour liquid into a 2-cup measuring cup; skim fat. Add water to liquid to measure 1½ cups.
3. Pour into a large saucepan. Combine cornstarch and water until smooth; add to pan. Cook and stir until thick and bubbly, about 2 minutes. Add meat and heat through.
4. Brush the rolls with butter; broil 4-5 in. from the heat for 2-3 minutes or until lightly toasted. Fill with meat, pineapple and green onions.

Chipotle-Black Bean Chili

This thick slow-cooked chili is special to me because it cooks on its own while I'm at work. My family and friends love it. It's really terrific served with corn bread.

—**PATRICIA NIEH** PORTOLA VALLEY, CA

PREP: 15 MIN. • **COOK:** 7 HOURS
MAKES: 8 SERVINGS (2½ QUARTS)

- 2 **cans (15 ounces each) black beans, rinsed and drained**
- 2 **cans (14½ ounces each) fire-roasted diced tomatoes, undrained**
- 1 **large onion, finely chopped**
- 1 **medium green pepper, finely chopped**
- 2 **chipotle peppers in adobo sauce, finely chopped**
- 2 **tablespoons adobo sauce**
- 2 **garlic cloves, minced**
- 1 **boneless beef chuck roast (2 pounds), cut into 1-inch cubes**
- 1 **tablespoon ground cumin**
- 1 **tablespoon dried oregano**
- ½ **teaspoon salt**
- ½ **teaspoon pepper**
  Optional toppings: shredded Monterey Jack cheese, reduced-fat sour cream, minced fresh cilantro and lime wedges

1. In a large bowl, combine the beans, tomatoes, onion, green pepper, chipotle peppers, adobo sauce and garlic. In another bowl, combine the beef, cumin, oregano, salt and pepper.
2. Pour half of the tomato mixture into a 4- or 5-qt. slow cooker; add the beef. Top with remaining tomato mixture. Cover and cook on low for 7-9 hours or until meat is tender. Serve with toppings of your choice.

FREEZE OPTION *Before adding toppings, cool chili. Freeze chili in freezer containers. To use, partially thaw in refrigerator overnight. Heat through in a saucepan, stirring occasionally and adding a little broth if necessary. Sprinkle with toppings.*
NOTE *If your family's taste runs more toward mild flavors, simply omit the chipotle peppers and adobo sauce. Add 1 can (4 ounces) drained diced green chilies and 1 teaspoon chili powder.*

Curried Tuna Sandwiches

If you're looking for a change from traditional tuna sandwiches, try this recipe. It includes my favorite ingredients from a few different tuna salad recipes, including apples, raisins and curry. The first time I combined them, I loved the results!

—**LORENE CORBETT** TRYON, NE

START TO FINISH: 10 MIN.
MAKES: 2 SERVINGS

- ¼ **cup chopped apple**
- 2 **tablespoons raisins**
- 2 **tablespoons mayonnaise**
- ¼ **teaspoon onion salt**
- ⅛ **teaspoon curry powder**
- 1 **can (6 ounces) tuna, drained and flaked**
- 2 **sandwich rolls, split**
  Additional mayonnaise, optional
  Lettuce leaves

In a small bowl, combine the first five ingredients; add tuna and mix well. Spread rolls with additional mayonnaise if desired; top each with ½ cup tuna mixture and lettuce.
PER SERVING *1 sandwich (prepared with low-sodium tuna and fat-free mayonnaise; calculated without roll) equals 170 cal., 375 mg sodium, 15 mg chol., 15 g carb., 26 g pro, 1 g fat.* **Diabetic Exchanges:** *3 lean meat, 1 fruit.*

Cuban-Style Pork Sandwiches

Loaded with tangy flavor, this is a lighter version of a favorite restaurant-style sandwich. If you don't have a panini maker, tuck the sandwiches under the broiler until the bread is browned and the cheese melted.

—ROBIN HAAS CRANSTON, RI

PREP: 20 MIN. • **COOK:** 6 HOURS + STANDING
MAKES: 10 SERVINGS

- 1 **large onion, cut into wedges**
- ¾ **cup reduced-sodium chicken broth**
- 1 **cup minced fresh parsley**
- 7 **garlic cloves, minced and divided**
- 2 **tablespoons cider vinegar**
- 1 **tablespoon plus 1½ teaspoons lemon juice, divided**
- 2 **teaspoons ground cumin**
- 1 **teaspoon ground mustard**
- 1 **teaspoon dried oregano**
- ½ **teaspoon salt**
- ½ **teaspoon pepper**
- 1 **boneless pork shoulder butt roast (3 to 4 pounds)**
- 1¼ **cups fat-free mayonnaise**
- 2 **tablespoons Dijon mustard**
- 10 **whole wheat hamburger buns, split**
- 1¼ **cups (5 ounces) shredded reduced-fat Swiss cheese**
- 1 **medium onion, thinly sliced and separated into rings**
- 2 **whole dill pickles, sliced**

1. Place onion wedges and broth in a 5-qt. slow cooker. In a small bowl, combine the parsley, 5 garlic cloves, vinegar, 1 tablespoon lemon juice, cumin, mustard, oregano, salt and pepper; rub over pork. Add to slow cooker. Cover and cook on low for 6-8 hours or until meat is tender.

2. Remove meat; let stand for 10 minutes before slicing. In another small bowl, combine the mayonnaise, mustard and remaining garlic and lemon juice; spread over buns. Layer bun bottoms with pork, cheese, sliced onion and pickles; replace tops.

3. Cook on a panini maker or indoor grill for 2-3 minutes or until buns are browned and cheese is melted.

TEARY TIP

To reduce tears while cutting onions, freeze them for 20 minutes before chopping. Also, use a very sharp knife and chop quickly. You can save both time and tears by chopping many onions at once. Freeze the extras in an airtight container for up to 3 months.

Chilled Corn and Shrimp Soup

Hot days call for cool foods like this refreshing, delicately spiced soup. It's so pretty and unique, your guests are sure to remember it.

—MARY LEVERETTE COLUMBIA, SC

PREP: 30 MIN. + CHILLING
MAKES: 4 SERVINGS

- ½ cup chopped sweet onion
- 3 tablespoons olive oil
- 1½ pounds uncooked small shrimp, peeled and deveined
- 2 garlic cloves, minced
- 1 teaspoon curry powder
- 2 cups buttermilk
- 1 package (16 ounces) frozen shoe-peg corn, thawed, divided
- 1 cup (8 ounces) reduced-fat sour cream
- 1 teaspoon hot pepper sauce
- 1 teaspoon salt
- ½ teaspoon coarsely ground pepper
- 2 tablespoons minced chives

1. In a large skillet, saute onion in oil until tender. Add the shrimp, garlic and curry; saute 4-6 minutes longer or until shrimp turn pink. Remove from the heat and set aside.
2. In a blender, combine the buttermilk, 2 cups corn, sour cream, pepper sauce, salt and pepper. Cover and process until smooth; transfer to a large bowl. Add remaining corn and shrimp mixture. Cover and refrigerate for at least 3 hours. Garnish servings with chives.

Hearty Split Pea Soup

We started a 39-day soup challenge, figuring if *Survivor* contestants could last for 39 days on little food, surely we could survive on soup! This was a family favorite.

—DEBRA KEIL OWASSO, OK

PREP: 30 MIN. • **COOK:** 7 HOURS
MAKES: 6 SERVINGS (2¼ QUARTS)

- 1 large onion, chopped
- 1 cup chopped celery
- 1 cup chopped fresh carrots
- 2 tablespoons olive oil
- 1 teaspoon dried thyme
- 1 package (16 ounces) dried green split peas, rinsed
- 4 cups vegetable broth
- 2 cups water
- 6 ounces Canadian bacon, chopped
- ¼ teaspoon pepper

1. In a large skillet, saute the onion, celery and carrots in oil until tender. Add thyme; cook 1 minute longer.
2. Transfer to a 5-qt. slow cooker. Add the peas, broth and water. Cover and cook on low for 7-8 hours or until the peas are tender.
3. Cool slightly. In a blender, process half of the soup until smooth. Return all to the slow cooker. Add bacon and pepper; heat through.

Open-Faced Chicken Avocado Burgers

A creamy avocado spread and thick slices of fresh mozzarella make these chicken sandwiches true contest winners. They're delightful in summer when tomatoes are at their very best.

—LISA HUNDLEY ABERDEEN, NC

PREP: 30 MIN. • **COOK:** 15 MIN.
MAKES: 4 SERVINGS PLUS ¼ CUP LEFTOVER SPREAD

- 1 tablespoon lemon juice
- ¼ teaspoon Worcestershire sauce
- ½ medium ripe avocado, peeled
- ½ cup mayonnaise
- ¼ cup sour cream
- 4 green onions, coarsely chopped
- ½ teaspoon salt
- ½ teaspoon cayenne pepper

BURGERS

- ¼ cup shredded Parmesan cheese
- 2 tablespoons prepared pesto
- 3 garlic cloves, minced
- ¼ teaspoon salt
- 1 pound ground chicken
- 4 tablespoons olive oil, divided
- ½ pound fresh mozzarella cheese, cut into 4 slices
- 4 slices Italian bread (¾ inch thick)
- 2 cups fresh arugula or baby spinach
- 8 slices tomato
- ¼ teaspoon dried basil
- ¼ teaspoon pepper

1. In a blender, combine the first eight ingredients; cover and process until smooth. Chill until serving. For burgers, in a small bowl, combine the Parmesan cheese, pesto, garlic and salt. Crumble chicken over mixture and mix well. Shape into four patties.

2. In a large skillet over medium heat, cook burgers in 2 tablespoons oil for 5-7 minutes on each side or until a thermometer reads 165° and juices run clear. Top with cheese; cover and cook 1 minute longer.

3. Meanwhile, brush bread with remaining oil; place on a baking sheet. Broil 3-4 in. from the heat for 1-2 minutes on each side or until toasted.

4. Spread each slice of toast with 2 tablespoons avocado spread (refrigerate remaining spread for another use). Top with arugula, a burger and sliced tomato. Sprinkle with basil and pepper.

Island Sausage Wraps

The filling in these wraps is loaded with bold flavors that all work together. In fact, the filling is so good you could eat it with a fork or simply serve it alongside some tortilla or pita chips.

—FELICE BOGUS RALEIGH, NC

PREP: 20 MIN. • **COOK:** 15 MIN.
MAKES: 6 SERVINGS

- ½ cup mango chutney
- ½ cup barbecue sauce
- 1 package (12 ounces) fully cooked chorizo chicken sausage links or flavor of your choice, cut into ½-inch slices
- 2 tablespoons olive oil
- 1 medium sweet red pepper, sliced
- 2 cups cooked jasmine rice
- 2 cups sliced peeled mangoes
- 1 medium red onion, sliced
- 1 cup unsweetened pineapple chunks, well drained
- ¼ cup minced fresh cilantro
- 6 whole wheat tortillas (8 inches), room temperature

1. In a small saucepan, combine chutney and barbecue sauce. Bring to a boil. Reduce heat; simmer, uncovered, for 8-10 minutes or until slightly thickened. Cool to room temperature.

2. Meanwhile, in a large skillet, brown chicken sausage in oil; remove meat and keep warm. In the same skillet, saute red pepper until tender.

3. Spoon the rice, red pepper, mangoes, onion, pineapple, cilantro, sauce mixture and chicken sausage down the center of each tortilla; roll up.

MANGO MUSTS

When buying mangoes, look for ones with unblemished green to yellow skin tinged with red. Ripe mangoes will feel fairly firm when gently pressed and have a sweet, fruity aroma.

Mushroom Onion Soup

Even folks who don't like mushrooms have a hard time resisting this specialty! I've found it's a great first course when I have friends over for dinner.

—NANCY KUCZYNSKI HOLMEN, WI

PREP: 10 MIN. • **COOK:** 25 MIN.
MAKES: 4 SERVINGS (ABOUT 1½ QUARTS)

- 2 cups (8 ounces) fresh mushrooms
- 3 tablespoons butter
- 2 medium onions, chopped
- 2 tablespoons all-purpose flour
- 5 cups chicken broth
- ½ teaspoon salt, optional
  Dash pepper
- ⅓ cup uncooked long grain rice
- 1 bay leaf
- 2 tablespoons chopped fresh parsley

1. Trim mushroom stems level with the caps; finely chop stems and thinly slice caps.
2. In a large saucepan, melt butter; add the mushrooms and onions. Cook and stir over low heat for 5 minutes. Blend in flour; add broth, salt if desired, and pepper.
3. Cook and stir until mixture comes to a boil. Reduce heat. Add the long grain rice and bay leaf; cover and simmer for 15-20 minutes or until the rice is tender. Discard bay leaf. Sprinkle with parsley.

CLEANING CUES

Gently remove dirt from mushrooms with a mushroom brush or a damp paper towel. Or quickly rinse them under cold water, then drain and pat dry with paper towels. Do not peel mushrooms. Trim the stems. For shiitake mushrooms, remove and discard stems. For enoki, trim the base and separate the stems.

Steak House Burgers

When I asked my brothers to come over for barbecue, they laughed. So I came up with this. After it won a contest, they don't laugh anymore!

—BONNIE GEAVARAS-BOOTZ SCOTTSDALE, AZ

PREP: 25 MIN. • **GRILL:** 10 MIN.
MAKES: 4 SERVINGS

- 5 tablespoons mayonnaise
- 4½ teaspoons prepared horseradish
- ¼ cup shredded Parmesan cheese
- 3 tablespoons butter, softened, divided
- ½ teaspoon garlic powder
- 4 hamburger buns, split
- 1½ pounds ground beef
- ¼ cup steak sauce
- 4½ teaspoons onion soup mix
- 4 slices Swiss cheese
- 1½ pounds sliced fresh mushrooms
- 2 green onions, chopped
- ¼ cup French-fried onions
  Sliced tomato and lettuce, optional

1. In a small bowl, combine mayonnaise and horseradish; cover and refrigerate until serving. In another small bowl, combine Parmesan cheese, 1 tablespoon butter and garlic powder; spread over bun tops. Set aside.
2. In a large bowl, combine the beef, steak sauce and onion soup mix. Shape into four patties.
3. Moisten a paper towel with cooking oil; using long-handled tongs, lightly coat the grill rack. Grill burgers, covered, over medium heat or broil 4 in. from the heat for 4-5 minutes on each side or until a thermometer reads 160° and juices run clear.
4. Top with Swiss cheese; cover and grill 1-2 minutes longer or until cheese is melted. Place hamburger buns, cut side down, on grill for 1-2 minutes or until toasted.
5. Meanwhile, in a large skillet, saute the mushrooms and green onions in the remaining butter until tender. Serve burgers on buns; top with horseradish sauce, French-fried onions, mushroom mixture and, if desired, tomato and lettuce.

Stuffing Dumpling Soup

I've always loved turkey, dumplings and stuffing, so I combined them and added a punch of Creole flavor. My family loves it, even my little ones. It's got some kick, but a dollop of sour cream mellows that out.

—RELINA SHIRLEY RENO, NV

PREP: 20 MIN. • **COOK:** 25 MIN.
MAKES: 5 SERVINGS

- 1 **cup sliced fresh mushrooms**
- 1 **medium onion, chopped**
- 1 **tablespoon olive oil**
- 3 **garlic cloves, minced**
- 4 **cups reduced-sodium chicken broth**
- 1½ **cups chopped fresh carrots**
- 2 **teaspoons Creole seasoning**
- 2 **large eggs**
- ½ **cup all-purpose flour**
- 2 **cups cooked stuffing**
- 2 **cups cubed cooked turkey**
- 1½ **cups cut fresh green beans**

1. In a Dutch oven, saute mushrooms and onion in oil until tender. Add garlic; cook 1 minute longer. Add the broth, carrots and Creole seasoning. Bring to a boil. Reduce heat; simmer, uncovered for 5-8 minutes or until carrots are tender.

2. Meanwhile, in a large bowl, whisk eggs and flour until smooth. Crumble stuffing over mixture; mix well. If necessary, add water, 1 teaspoon at a time, until mixture holds its shape.

3. Add the turkey and green beans to soup; return to a boil. Drop stuffing mixture by heaping tablespoonfuls onto simmering soup. Cover and simmer for 8-10 minutes or until a toothpick inserted in a dumpling comes out clean (do not lift the cover while simmering).

NOTE *The following spices may be substituted for 1 teaspoon Creole seasoning: 1/4 teaspoon each salt, garlic powder and paprika; and a pinch each of dried thyme, ground cumin and cayenne pepper.*

PER SERVING *1 1/4 cups equals 390 cal., 15 g fat (3 g sat. fat), 127 mg chol., 1,252 mg sodium, 38 g carb., 6 g fiber, 27 g pro.* **Diabetic Exchanges:** *2 lean meat, 1 starch, 1 vegetable, 1 fat.*

Easy Minestrone

This recipe is special because it's one of the few dinners my entire family loves. And I can feel good about serving it because it's full of nutrition and low in fat.

—LAUREN BRENNAN HOOD RIVER, OR

PREP: 25 MIN. • **COOK:** 40 MIN.
MAKES: 11 SERVINGS (2¾ QUARTS)

- 2 **large carrots, diced**
- 2 **celery ribs, chopped**
- 1 **medium onion, chopped**
- 1 **tablespoon olive oil**
- 1 **tablespoon butter**
- 2 **garlic cloves, minced**
- 2 **cans (14½ ounces each) reduced-sodium chicken broth**
- 2 **cans (8 ounces each) no-salt-added tomato sauce**
- 1 **can (16 ounces) kidney beans, rinsed and drained**
- 1 **can (15 ounces) garbanzo beans or chickpeas, rinsed and drained**
- 1 **can (14½ ounces) diced tomatoes, undrained**
- 1½ **cups shredded cabbage**
- 1 **tablespoon dried basil**
- 1½ **teaspoons dried parsley flakes**
- 1 **teaspoon dried oregano**
- ½ **teaspoon pepper**
- 1 **cup uncooked whole wheat elbow macaroni**
- 11 **teaspoons grated Parmesan cheese**

1. In a large saucepan, saute the carrots, celery and onion in oil and butter until tender. Add the garlic cloves; cook 1 minute longer.

2. Stir in the broth, tomato sauce, beans, tomatoes, cabbage, basil, parsley, oregano and pepper. Bring to a boil. Reduce heat; cover and simmer for 20 minutes. Meanwhile, cook pasta according to package directions; drain.

3. Return soup to a boil. Stir in pasta; heat through. Ladle into bowls. Sprinkle with cheese.

FREEZE OPTION *Before adding Parmesan cheese, freeze cooled soup in freezer containers. To use, partially thaw in refrigerator overnight. Heat through in a saucepan, stirring occasionally and adding a little broth or water if necessary.*

PER SERVING *1 cup equals 180 cal., 4 g fat (1 g sat. fat), 4 mg chol., 443 mg sodium, 29 g carb., 7 g fiber, 8 g pro.* **Diabetic Exchanges:** *2 starch, 1 lean meat.*

Orange Chicken Wraps

Oranges give these cool and crunchy wraps a pleasant change of pace. The tasty handhelds come together in a snap. Enjoy them as a simple weeknight meal or weekend lunch. What a great way to use leftover chicken!

—JAMIE JONES MADISON, GA

START TO FINISH: 20 MIN.
MAKES: 8 SERVINGS

- 4 **cups coleslaw mix**
- 2 **cans (11 ounces each) mandarin oranges, drained**
- 1½ **cups fresh broccoli florets**
- 1 **medium sweet yellow pepper, thinly sliced**
- ¼ **cup chopped celery**
- 1 **tablespoon sunflower kernels**
- 1 **teaspoon grated orange peel**
- ⅓ **cup coleslaw salad dressing**
- 2 **packages (6 ounces each) ready-to-serve roasted chicken breast strips, chopped**
- ¾ **cup honey barbecue sauce**
- 8 **flour tortillas (10 inches)**

1. In a large bowl, combine the first seven ingredients. Add salad dressing; toss to coat. In another bowl, combine chicken and barbecue sauce.

2. Spoon ¾ cup coleslaw mixture down the center of each tortilla; top with ¼ cup chicken mixture. Roll up.

Nutty Chicken Pita Sandwiches

When company is coming for lunch, this is my favorite sandwich to make, since it looks and tastes a bit fancy. Even kids like it because of the crunchy nuts and creamy filling.
—GLENDA SCHWARZ MORDEN, MB

PREP: 15 MIN. + CHILLING
MAKES: 6 SERVINGS

- 1 package (8 ounces) cream cheese, softened
- 3 tablespoons milk
- 1 tablespoon lemon juice
- 2 cups cubed cooked chicken
- ½ cup chopped green pepper
- 2 tablespoons chopped green onions
- 1 teaspoon ground mustard
- ½ teaspoon dried thyme
- ½ teaspoon salt
- ⅛ teaspoon pepper
- ¼ cup chopped walnuts
- 6 pita pocket halves

1. In a large bowl, beat the cream cheese, milk and lemon juice until smooth. Stir in the chicken, green pepper, onions, mustard, thyme, salt and pepper; refrigerate.
2. Just before serving, stir in walnuts. Spoon about ½ cup filling into each pita half.

FAST FREEZER TIP

When chicken pieces are on sale, consider purchasing several packages. You can bake all the chicken at once. When the meat is cool enough to handle, cube and freeze it in 1-cup portions to use in soups, sandwiches, casseroles and other quick meals.

Tex-Mex Chili

I dreamed up this hearty chili with a Tex-Mex twist years ago. It's still everyone's favorite and the go-to recipe in our family cookbook.
—MARTHA HOOK TYLER, TX

PREP: 20 MIN. • **COOK:** 4 HOURS
MAKES: 9 SERVINGS

- 1½ pounds ground beef
- 1 medium onion, chopped
- 5 garlic cloves, minced
- 1 can (14½ ounces) diced tomatoes, undrained
- 1 cup water
- 1 cup V8 juice
- ¼ cup brewed coffee
- 2 envelopes chili seasoning
- 1 can (16 ounces) refried beans
- 1 can (15 ounces) Ranch Style beans (pinto beans in seasoned tomato sauce)
- 2 tablespoons ground cumin
- 2 tablespoons chili powder
- ¼ teaspoon lemon juice

1. In a large skillet, cook beef and onion over medium heat until the meat is no longer pink. Add garlic; cook 1 minute longer. Drain. Stir in the tomatoes, water, juice, coffee and chili seasoning.
2. Transfer to a 4-qt. slow cooker. Stir in remaining ingredients. Cover and cook on low for 4-5 hours to allow flavors to blend.

❝The slow cooker makes these sandwiches a convenient option for busy weeknights. The apricot preserves lend a sweet flavor to the pork.❞

—**MEGAN KLIMKEWICZ** KAISER, MO

Sweet & Tangy Pulled Pork

PREP: 15 MIN. • **COOK:** 8 HOURS
MAKES: 12 SERVINGS

- 1 **boneless pork shoulder butt roast (3 to 4 pounds)**
- 1 **jar (18 ounces) apricot preserves**
- 1 **large onion, chopped**
- 2 **tablespoons reduced-sodium soy sauce**
- 2 **tablespoons Dijon mustard Hamburger buns, split, optional**

1. Cut pork roast in half; place in a 4- or 5-qt. slow cooker. Combine the preserves, onion, soy sauce and mustard; pour over roast. Cover and cook on low for 8-10 hours or until meat is tender.

2. Remove meat; cool slightly. Skim fat from cooking juices. Shred pork with two forks and return to slow cooker; heat through. Serve on buns, if desired.

PER SERVING *½ cup (calculated without buns) equals 296 cal., 11 g fat (4 g sat. fat), 67 mg chol., 248 mg sodium, 29 g carb., trace fiber, 20 g pro.* ***Diabetic Exchanges:*** *3 lean meat, 2 starch.*

Sweet & Spicy Fusion Burgers

These burgers combine some of my favorite flavors and textures, and you can do most of the work ahead of time. You'll find naan, an Indian flatbread, in the international or bread section of your grocery store.

—JAMIE BROWN-MILLER NAPA, CA

PREP: 25 MIN. • **GRILL:** 10 MIN.
MAKES: 4 SERVINGS

- 2 cups shredded cabbage
- 2 teaspoons sesame seeds
- 2 teaspoons lemon juice
- 2 teaspoons Dijon mustard
- 2 teaspoons sesame oil
- 2 tablespoons Sriracha Asian hot chili sauce
- 2 tablespoons soy sauce
- 2 tablespoons honey
- 1 tablespoon red wine vinegar
- ¼ teaspoon salt
- ¼ teaspoon pepper
- 1 pound ground turkey
- 4 naan flatbreads, warmed
- ½ medium cucumber, thinly sliced
- ½ cup julienned sweet red pepper
- 1 package (5.3 ounces) fresh goat cheese

1. Place cabbage in a small bowl. In another small bowl, combine the sesame seeds, lemon juice, mustard and oil; pour over cabbage and toss to coat.

2. In a large bowl, combine the chili sauce, soy sauce, honey, vinegar, salt and pepper. Crumble turkey over mixture and mix well. Shape into four patties.

3. Moisten a paper towel with cooking oil; using long-handled tongs, lightly coat the grill rack. Grill burgers, covered, over medium heat or broil 4 in. from the heat for 5-7 minutes on each side or until a meat thermometer reads 165° and juices run clear.

4. Serve on naan with cabbage mixture, cucumber, red pepper and cheese.

Andouille-Shrimp Cream Soup

Inspired by southern Louisiana corn stew, this soup features a wonderful blend of andouille sausage, shrimp and subtle spices.

—JUDY ARMSTRONG PRAIRIEVILLE, LA

PREP: 20 MIN. • **COOK:** 30 MIN.
MAKES: 7 SERVINGS

- ½ pound fully cooked andouille sausage links, thinly sliced
- 1 medium onion, chopped
- 2 celery ribs, thinly sliced
- 1 medium sweet red pepper, chopped
- 1 medium green pepper, chopped
- 1 jalapeno pepper, seeded and chopped
- ¼ cup butter, cubed
- 3 garlic cloves, minced
- 2 cups fresh or frozen corn, thawed
- 4 plum tomatoes, chopped
- 1 cup vegetable broth
- 2 tablespoons minced fresh thyme or 2 teaspoons dried thyme
- 1 teaspoon chili powder
- ½ teaspoon salt
- ½ teaspoon pepper
- ¼ to ½ teaspoon cayenne pepper
- 1 pound uncooked medium shrimp, peeled and deveined
- 1 cup heavy whipping cream

1. In a large skillet, saute the first six ingredients in butter until vegetables are tender. Add garlic; cook 1 minute longer. Add the corn, tomatoes, broth, thyme, chili powder, salt, pepper and cayenne. Bring to a boil. Reduce heat; simmer, uncovered, for 10 minutes.

2. Stir in shrimp and cream. Bring to a gentle boil. Simmer, uncovered, for 8-10 minutes or until shrimp turn pink.

NOTE *Wear disposable gloves when cutting hot peppers; the oils can burn skin. Avoid touching your face.*

Chicken Chorizo Posole

I first tasted posole while visiting a friend in Santa Fe. It was a revelation! I have since been experimenting with many versions, and this one has become a much-loved tradition for my family.
—**JENNIFER BECKMAN** FALLS CHURCH, VA

PREP: 40 MIN. • **COOK:** 40 MIN.
MAKES: 9 SERVINGS

- 1 **pound tomatillos, husks removed, cut in half**
- 1 **large onion, quartered**
- 2 **jalapeno peppers, halved and seeded**
- 4 **garlic cloves, peeled**
- 4 **cups water**
- 1 **cup reduced-sodium chicken broth**
- 1 **whole garlic bulb, loose paper removed, cut in half**
- 5 **whole cloves**
- 2 **bay leaves**
- 2 **boneless skinless chicken breast halves (6 ounces each)**
- 1 **pound uncooked chorizo or bulk spicy pork sausage**
- 2 **cans (15 ounces each) hominy, rinsed and drained**
- 3 **teaspoons lime juice, divided**
- 1 **teaspoon dried oregano**
- 1 **teaspoon ground cumin**
- ½ **teaspoon salt, divided**
- 1 **cup minced fresh cilantro, divided**

SALSA
- 1 **medium mango, peeled and cubed**
- 1 **medium ripe avocado, peeled and cubed**
- 5 **radishes, chopped**

GARNISH
- 6 **cups tortilla chips**

1. Place the tomatillos, onion, jalapenos and garlic cloves on a greased baking sheet. Bake at 425° for 25-30 minutes or until tomatillos are tender. Cool slightly. Transfer to a food processor; cover and process until blended.

2. In a Dutch oven, bring the water, broth, garlic bulb, cloves and bay leaves to a boil. Reduce heat; add chicken breasts and poach, uncovered, for 15-20 minutes or until no longer pink.

3. Remove the chicken from the broth and shred. Strain broth, discarding seasonings. Crumble the chorizo into Dutch oven; cook over medium heat for 6-8 minutes or until fully cooked. Drain. Return broth to Dutch oven. Stir in the hominy, 2 teaspoons lime juice, oregano, cumin, ¼ teaspoon salt, tomatillo mixture and shredded chicken; heat through. Stir in ½ cup cilantro.

4. For salsa, in a small bowl, combine the mango, avocado, radishes and remaining cilantro, lime juice and salt. Serve with soup. Garnish with chips.

FREEZE OPTION *Freeze cooled soup in freezer containers. To use, partially thaw in refrigerator overnight. Heat through in a saucepan, stirring occasionally and adding a little broth if necessary. Prepare salsa and serve with soup.*

NOTE *Wear disposable gloves when cutting hot peppers; the oils can burn skin. Avoid touching your face.*

Brie & Sausage Brunch Bake, page 88

81

83

91

Breakfast & Brunch

Rise and shine! It's time to wake up and tackle the day with these **blue-ribbon delights.** Whether you're looking to surprise your family one morning or you need a dish for a **Sunday brunch,** the eye openers found here are sure to fit the bill.

Crab Quiche

Rich and elegant, this party-pretty quiche is flecked with minced parsley, chives and cilantro. It's ideal for a weekend brunch but would also be wonderful as a late-night supper.

—**LORI WARDOCLIP** GIBSONIA, PA

PREP: 30 MIN. • **BAKE:** 40 MIN. + STANDING
MAKES: 6 SERVINGS

- 1   **sheet refrigerated pie pastry**
- 4   **large eggs**
- 2   **cups heavy whipping cream**
- 2   **tablespoons minced chives**
- 2   **tablespoons minced fresh cilantro**
- 2   **tablespoons minced fresh parsley or 2 teaspoons dried parsley flakes**
- ½   **teaspoon salt**
- ½   **teaspoon seafood seasoning**
- ¼   **teaspoon pepper**
- ⅛   **teaspoon ground nutmeg**
- 1   **can (6½ ounces) lump crabmeat, drained**
- ½   **cup shredded Swiss cheese**
- ½   **cup shredded Monterey Jack cheese**
  Fresh chives, optional

1. Unroll pastry into a 9-in. pie plate; flute edges. Line unpricked pastry with a double thickness of heavy-duty foil. Bake at 450° for 8 minutes. Remove foil; bake for 5-7 minutes longer or until lightly browned. Cool on a wire rack.

2. In a large bowl, whisk the eggs, cream, chives, cilantro, parsley, salt, seafood seasoning, pepper and nutmeg; stir in the crabmeat and cheeses. Pour into crust.

3. Bake at 375° for 40-45 minutes or until a knife inserted near the center comes out clean. Let stand for 15 minutes before cutting. Garnish with fresh chives if desired.

Breakfast Biscuit Cups

The first time I made these cups, my husband and his assistant coach came into the kitchen as I pulled the pan from the oven. They devoured the hearty biscuits!

—**DEBRA CARLSON** COLUMBUS JUNCTION, IA

PREP: 30 MIN. • **BAKE:** 20 MIN.
MAKES: 8 SERVINGS

- ⅓   **pound bulk pork sausage**
- 1   **tablespoon all-purpose flour**
- ⅛   **teaspoon salt**
- ½   **teaspoon pepper, divided**
- ¾   **cup plus 1 tablespoon 2% milk, divided**
- ½   **cup frozen cubed hash brown potatoes, thawed**
- 1   **tablespoon butter**
- 2   **large eggs**
- ⅛   **teaspoon garlic salt**
- 1   **can (16.3 ounces) large refrigerated flaky biscuits**
- ½   **cup shredded Colby-Monterey Jack cheese**

1. In a large skillet, cook sausage over medium heat until no longer pink; drain. Stir in the flour, salt and ¼ teaspoon pepper until blended; gradually add ¾ cup milk. Bring to a boil; cook and stir for 2 minutes or until thickened. Remove from the heat and set aside.

2. In another large skillet over medium heat, cook potatoes in butter until tender. Whisk the eggs, garlic salt and remaining milk and pepper; add to skillet. Cook and stir until almost set.

3. Press each biscuit onto the bottom and up the sides of eight ungreased muffin cups. Spoon the egg mixture, half the cheese, and sausage into cups; sprinkle with remaining cheese.

4. Bake at 375° for 18-22 minutes or until golden brown. Cool for 5 minutes before removing from pan.

FREEZE OPTION *Freeze cooled pastries in a freezer container, separating layers with waxed paper. To use, microwave one frozen biscuit cup on high for 50-60 seconds or until heated through.*

Strawberry Puff Pancake

This recipe serves four, but if there are just two of you, prepare it using 2 eggs and ½ cup milk. It's yummy with either a strawberry or blueberry topping.

—BRENDA MORTON HALE CENTER, TX

START TO FINISH: 30 MIN.
MAKES: 4 SERVINGS

- 2 **tablespoons butter**
- 3 **large eggs**
- ¾ **cup fat-free milk**
- 1 **teaspoon vanilla extract**
- ¾ **cup all-purpose flour**
- ⅛ **teaspoon salt**
- ⅛ **teaspoon ground cinnamon**
- ¼ **cup sugar**
- 1 **tablespoon cornstarch**
- ½ **cup water**
- 1 **cup sliced fresh strawberries**
  Confectioners' sugar

1. Place butter in a 9-in. pie plate; place in a 400° oven for 4-5 minutes or until melted. Meanwhile, in a small bowl, whisk the eggs, milk and vanilla. In another small bowl, combine the flour, salt and cinnamon; whisk into egg mixture until blended.

2. Pour into prepared pie plate. Bake for 15-20 minutes or until sides are crisp and golden brown.

3. In a small saucepan, combine sugar and cornstarch. Stir in water until smooth; add strawberries. Cook and stir over medium heat until thickened. Coarsely mash strawberries. Serve with pancake. Dust with confectioners' sugar.

PER SERVING *1 slice with ⅓ cup sauce (calculated without confectioners' sugar) equals 277 cal., 10 g fat (5 g sat. fat), 175 mg chol., 187 mg sodium, 38 g carb., 2 g fiber, 9 g pro. Diabetic Exchanges: 2½ starch, 1 medium-fat meat, 1 fat.*

Southwestern Quiche

I first made this dish when I was hosting a brunch. The Southwestern flavors really pop when served with salsa and a dollop of sour cream.

—CYNTHIA STACKHOUSE PAPILLION, NE

PREP: 20 MIN. • **BAKE:** 40 MIN. + STANDING
MAKES: 6 SERVINGS

- 4 flour tortillas (8 inches)
- 1 pound uncooked chorizo
- ½ pound sliced fresh mushrooms
- 1 tablespoon butter
- 1 green onion, thinly sliced
- ¼ teaspoon salt
- ¼ teaspoon pepper
- 4 large eggs, beaten
- 1 cup (4 ounces) shredded sharp cheddar cheese, divided
- 1 cup heavy whipping cream
- 1 medium tomato, seeded and chopped
- ½ teaspoon garlic powder
- ½ teaspoon ground cumin
  Salsa and cubed avocado, optional

1. In a greased 9-in. pie plate, arrange tortillas in an overlapping pattern so that they cover sides and bottom of pie plate, forming a crust. Set aside.
2. In a large skillet, cook chorizo over medium heat until fully cooked; drain and set aside. In the same skillet, saute mushrooms in butter until tender. Add onion, salt and pepper; cook 2 minutes longer.
3. In a large bowl, combine the eggs, half of the cheese, chorizo, cream, tomato, garlic powder and cumin. Stir in mushroom mixture. Pour into pie plate; top with remaining cheese. Cover edges of quiche with foil so tortillas do not burn.
4. Bake at 350° for 40-45 minutes or until a knife inserted near the center comes out clean. Let stand for 10 minutes before cutting. Serve with salsa and avocado if desired.

GRAND PRIZE WINNER ★★★★

Southwest Breakfast Tart

Give a hungry breakfast crowd something that will really stick to their ribs. This cheesy tart is packed with hearty sausage, plenty of heat, bright colors and Tex-Mex flavor.

—PAMELA SHANK PARKERSBURG, WV

PREP: 30 MIN. • **BAKE:** 25 MIN. + STANDING
MAKES: 6 SERVINGS

- ½ pound bulk spicy pork sausage
- 4 teaspoons chopped seeded jalapeno pepper
- 1 tablespoon finely chopped red onion
- 1 can (4 ounces) chopped green chilies
- 1 sheet refrigerated pie pastry
- 1¼ cups shredded Monterey Jack cheese, divided
- 6 large eggs
- ⅓ cup half-and-half cream
- ½ teaspoon salt
- ¼ teaspoon pepper
- 1 tablespoon finely chopped sweet red pepper
- 1 tablespoon finely chopped green pepper
  Optional toppings: sour cream, salsa, chopped tomatoes and sliced green onions

1. In a large skillet, cook the sausage, jalapeno and onion over medium heat until meat is no longer pink; drain. Stir in chilies.
2. Press pastry onto the bottom and up the sides of an ungreased 9-in. tart pan with removable bottom; trim edges. Sprinkle ½ cup cheese over crust; top with sausage mixture.
3. In a large bowl, whisk the eggs, cream, salt and pepper. Pour over sausage mixture. Sprinkle with red and green peppers and ½ cup cheese.
4. Bake at 350° for 25-30 minutes or until eggs are set and a knife inserted near the center comes out clean. Sprinkle with remaining cheese. Let stand for 10 minutes before cutting. Serve with toppings of your choice.

FREEZE OPTION *Before adding the reserved cheese and toppings, securely wrap and freeze the cooled quiche in plastic wrap and foil. To use, partially thaw in the refrigerator overnight. Remove from refrigerator 30 minutes before baking. Preheat oven to 350°. Unwrap quiche; reheat in oven until heated through and a thermometer inserted in center reads 165°. Top with cheese and toppings as directed.*

NOTE *Wear disposable gloves when cutting hot peppers; the oils can burn skin. Avoid touching your face.*

Spring Morning Casserole

My mom gave me this recipe, and it has quickly become my favorite breakfast casserole. I love that it can be made the night before and popped in the oven for a special breakfast.

—MELODY HOLLAND LEBANON, PA

PREP: 25 MIN. + CHILLING
BAKE: 40 MIN. + STANDING
MAKES: 12 SERVINGS

- 2 cups cut fresh asparagus (1-inch pieces)
- 1 small sweet red pepper, chopped
- 1 small onion, chopped
- 3 tablespoons butter
- 8 cups cubed day old French bread
- 1 cup cubed fully cooked ham
- 2 cups (8 ounces) shredded cheddar cheese
- 8 large eggs, beaten
- 2 cups 2% milk
- ⅓ cup honey
- ½ teaspoon salt
- ½ teaspoon pepper

1. In a large skillet, saute the asparagus, red pepper and onion in butter until tender; set aside.

2. Place bread in a greased 13x9-in. baking dish. Layer with cooked ham, 1 cup cheese and vegetable mixture. Sprinkle with remaining cheese. In a large bowl, combine the eggs, milk, honey, salt and pepper. Pour over the top. Cover and refrigerate overnight.

3. Remove from the refrigerator 30 minutes before baking. Bake, uncovered, at 350° for 40-45 minutes or until a knife inserted near the center comes out clean. Let stand for 10 minutes before cutting.

Apricot & White Chocolate Coffee Cake

Here's a luscious make-and-take recipe for those holiday brunches you're invited to. It couldn't be simpler or quicker to prepare, and you can vary the preserves to any flavor you might have on hand.

—**HOLLY BAUER** WEST BEND, WI

PREP: 15 MIN. • **BAKE:** 20 MIN.
MAKES: 12 SERVINGS

- 2 cups biscuit/baking mix
- 2 tablespoons sugar
- 1 large egg
- ⅔ cup 2% milk
- 2 tablespoons canola oil
- ½ cup white baking chips
- ½ cup apricot preserves

TOPPING
- ⅓ cup biscuit/baking mix
- ⅓ cup sugar
- 2 tablespoons cold butter

1. In a large bowl, combine the biscuit mix and sugar. Whisk the egg, milk and oil; stir into dry ingredients just until moistened. Fold in chips. Pour into a greased 9-in. round baking pan.
2. Drop preserves by teaspoonfuls over batter. Cut through batter with a knife to swirl the preserves.
3. For topping, combine biscuit mix and sugar in small bowl; cut in butter until crumbly. Sprinkle over batter.
4. Bake at 400° for 20-25 minutes or until golden brown. Serve warm.

Baked Fruit Compote

A splash of Madeira wine gives canned fruit a fancy, festive mood. This quick compote brightens any winter brunch. Mix and match canned fruits to suit your family's tastes.

—**MYRT PFANNKUCHE** PELL CITY, AL

START TO FINISH: 30 MIN.
MAKES: 11 SERVINGS

- 1 can (29 ounces) sliced peaches, drained
- 1 can (20 ounces) pineapple chunks, drained
- 2 cans (8 ounces each) grapefruit sections, drained
- 1 can (15¼ ounces) sliced pears, drained
- 1 can (11 ounces) mandarin oranges, drained
- 1 cup pitted dried plums
- ½ cup butter, cubed
- ½ cup packed brown sugar
- ¼ cup Madeira wine, optional
  Fresh mint leaves, optional

1. Preheat oven to 350°. In a 13x9-in. baking dish, combine the first six ingredients.
2. In a small saucepan, combine butter and brown sugar. Bring to a boil over medium heat; cook and stir 2-3 minutes or until sugar is dissolved. Remove from heat; stir in wine if desired. Pour over fruit and toss to coat.
3. Bake, uncovered, 20-25 minutes or until heated through. Garnish with mint if desired.

Italian Brunch Bake

This is a great overnight entree to make when you have company coming over for brunch. I often make it during the holidays. When I wake up, all I have to do is pop it into the oven, and in no time, the troops are fed.

—VIVIAN TAYLOR MIDDLEBURG, FL

PREP: 30 MIN. + CHILLING • **BAKE:** 55 MIN. + STANDING
MAKES: 12 SERVINGS

- 1 pound bulk Italian sausage
- 1 pound baby portobello mushrooms, quartered
- 1 large onion, chopped
- 1 medium sweet red pepper, chopped
- 1 medium green pepper, chopped
- 2 garlic cloves, minced
- 2 packages (6 ounces each) fresh baby spinach
- 8 slices Italian bread (1 inch thick)
- 12 large eggs
- 1 cup 2% milk
- 1 teaspoon Italian seasoning
- ½ teaspoon salt
- ½ teaspoon pepper
- ¼ teaspoon ground nutmeg
- 4 cups (16 ounces) shredded Italian cheese blend

1. In a large skillet, cook sausage, mushrooms, onion, peppers and garlic over medium heat until meat is no longer pink; drain and set aside.
2. In a large skillet coated with cooking spray, saute spinach until wilted. Place bread on a baking sheet. Broil 2-3 in. from heat for 1-2 minutes or until lightly browned. Transfer to a greased 13x9-in. baking dish.
3. In a large bowl, combine eggs, milk, Italian seasoning, salt, pepper and nutmeg. Layer sausage mixture and spinach over bread; pour egg mixture over top. Sprinkle with cheese; cover and refrigerate overnight.
4. Remove from refrigerator 30 minutes before baking. Preheat oven to 350°. Cover and bake for 50 minutes. Uncover; bake 5-10 minutes longer or until a knife inserted near the center comes out clean. Let stand 10 minutes before cutting.

Hash Brown Pancetta Casserole

Eggs, hash browns, cheese, spinach, pancetta and fabulous flavor—this casserole has everything! You could also substitute provolone or Swiss cheese for the fontina.

—GILDA LESTER MILLSBORO, DE

PREP: 25 MIN. • **BAKE:** 30 MIN. + STANDING
MAKES: 8 SERVINGS

- 1 large onion, finely chopped
- 1 tablespoon olive oil
- 2 garlic cloves, minced
- 1 package (10 ounces) frozen chopped spinach, thawed and squeezed dry
- ¼ teaspoon salt
- ¼ teaspoon pepper
- 2 ounces sliced pancetta or bacon, finely chopped
- 3 cups frozen shredded hash brown potatoes, thawed
- 8 large eggs
- 2 cups 2% milk
- 1 cup (4 ounces) shredded fontina cheese, divided
- 1 cup (4 ounces) shredded cheddar cheese, divided
- ¼ cup minced fresh parsley
- 1 tablespoon Worcestershire sauce
- 1 teaspoon ground mustard
- ¼ teaspoon ground nutmeg
  Freshly ground pepper and additional fresh parsley, optional

1. In a large skillet, saute onion in oil until tender. Add garlic; cook 1 minute longer. Stir in the spinach, salt and pepper. Remove from the heat.
2. In another skillet, cook pancetta over medium heat until crisp. Remove to paper towels with a slotted spoon; drain.
3. In a greased 13x9-in. baking dish, layer the hash browns, spinach mixture and pancetta. In a large bowl, whisk the eggs, milk, ½ cup fontina cheese, ½ cup cheddar cheese, parsley, Worcestershire sauce, mustard and nutmeg; pour over casserole. Sprinkle with remaining cheeses.
4. Bake, uncovered, at 350° for 30-35 minutes or until a knife inserted near the center comes out clean. Let stand for 10 minutes before cutting. If desired, sprinkle with freshly ground pepper and garnish with additional parsley.

Here's a smart way to use up leftover potatoes and veggies, if you have them. Use 2½ cups leftover mashed potatoes and whatever cooked vegetables you have on hand. You can also use ½ pound of Italian sausage instead of bacon.

—**HEATHER KING** FROSTBURG, MD

Spinach Quiche with Potato Crust

PREP: 25 MIN. • **BAKE:** 55 MIN. + STANDING
MAKES: 8 SERVINGS

- 1 package (24 ounces) refrigerated mashed potatoes
- 2 tablespoons olive oil, divided
- 8 ounces sliced fresh mushrooms
- 2 garlic cloves, minced
- 5 ounces frozen chopped spinach, thawed and squeezed dry (about ½ cup)
- 6 bacon strips, cooked and crumbled or ⅓ cup bacon bits
- 2 teaspoons minced fresh rosemary or ½ teaspoon dried rosemary, crushed
- 4 large eggs
- 1 cup 2% milk
- ¼ teaspoon pepper
- 1 cup (4 ounces) shredded cheddar cheese

1. Preheat oven to 350°. Press mashed potatoes onto bottom and up sides of a greased 9-in. deep-dish pie plate. Brush with 1 tablespoon oil. Bake 30 minutes or until edges are golden brown.

2. Meanwhile, in a large skillet, heat remaining oil over medium-high heat. Add mushrooms; cook and stir for 3-4 minutes or until tender. Add garlic; cook 1 minute longer. Remove from heat. Stir in spinach, bacon and rosemary; spoon over crust. In a small bowl, whisk eggs, milk and pepper until blended; stir in cheese. Pour over the mushroom mixture.

3. Bake 25-30 minutes longer or until golden brown and a knife inserted near the center comes out clean. Let stand 10 minutes before cutting.

Cranberry Orange Pancakes

As special as Christmas morning itself, these fluffy pancakes are drop-dead gorgeous, ready in just minutes and brimming with sweet, tart and tangy flavor. Seconds, anyone?

—NANCY ZIMMERMAN CAPE MAY COURT HOUSE, NJ

PREP: 20 MIN. • **COOK:** 5 MIN./BATCH
MAKES: 12 PANCAKES (1¼ CUPS SYRUP)

SYRUP
- 1 cup fresh or frozen cranberries
- ⅔ cup orange juice
- ½ cup sugar
- 3 tablespoons maple syrup

PANCAKES
- 2 cups biscuit/baking mix
- 2 tablespoons sugar
- 2 teaspoons baking powder
- 2 large eggs
- 1 large egg yolk
- 1 cup evaporated milk
- 2 tablespoons orange juice
- 1 teaspoon grated orange peel
- ½ cup chopped fresh or frozen cranberries
  Orange peel strips, optional

1. In a small saucepan, bring the cranberries, orange juice and sugar to a boil. Reduce heat; simmer, uncovered, for 5 minutes. Cool slightly. With a slotted spoon, remove ¼ cup cranberries; set aside.

2. In a blender, process cranberry mixture until smooth. Transfer to a small bowl; stir in maple syrup and reserved cranberries. Keep warm.

3. In a large bowl, combine the biscuit mix, sugar and baking powder. In another bowl, whisk the eggs, egg yolk, milk, orange juice and peel. Stir into dry ingredients just until blended. Fold in chopped cranberries.

4. Drop batter by ¼ cupfuls onto a greased hot griddle; turn when bubbles form on top. Cook until second side is golden brown. Serve with syrup. Garnish with orange peel strips if desired.

FRESH IS BEST

Fresh cranberries are in season from early fall through December. When buying, look for packages with shiny, bright red (light or dark) berries. Avoid berries that are bruised, shriveled or have brown spots. Always rinse fresh berries before using.

Breakfast Tortas

My husband likes these ciabatta rolls served with pickled jalapenos. Try substituting leftover taco meat, ham, grilled steak or chicken for the bacon.

—CAROLYN KUMPE EL DORADO, CA

PREP: 25 MIN. • **BAKE:** 15 MIN.
MAKES: 4 SERVINGS

- 4 ciabatta rolls
- ¾ cup refried black beans
- ⅓ cup sour cream
- ¼ cup minced fresh cilantro
- 2 teaspoons lime juice
- 3 to 5 drops chipotle hot pepper sauce
- ⅛ teaspoon salt
- 4 large eggs
- ½ cup shredded Monterey Jack cheese
- 1 teaspoon olive oil
- 4 cooked bacon strips, halved
- ½ medium ripe avocado, peeled and sliced
- ½ cup salsa
- 2 green onions, chopped

1. Cut the top third off each ciabatta roll; hollow out bottom, leaving a ½-in. shell (discard removed bread or save for another use). Place roll bottoms on an ungreased baking sheet.

2. In a small bowl, combine the refried beans, sour cream, cilantro, lime juice, pepper sauce and salt. Spread ¼ cup inside each roll. Break an egg into each roll. Bake at 400° for 10 minutes.

3. Sprinkle cheese over eggs. Brush roll tops with olive oil; place on the baking sheet. Bake 5-8 minutes longer or until egg whites are completely set and yolks begin to thicken but are not firm. Top each with bacon, avocado, salsa and onions. Replace roll tops.

Blue Cheese Quiche with Caramelized Pears

The flavors of sweet sauteed onions, pears and blue cheese come together in this decadent version of a brunch classic. Pop it in the oven, and you'll have just enough time to whip up a fruit salad or a side to pair with it.

—MAGGIE CARRICK GAITHERSBURG, MD

PREP: 25 MIN. • **BAKE:** 30 MIN.
MAKES: 8 SERVINGS

- 1 sheet frozen puff pastry, thawed
- 8 turkey bacon strips, diced
- 1 cup (4 ounces) crumbled blue cheese
- 8 large eggs
- 1 cup heavy whipping cream
- ½ cup shredded Parmesan cheese
- ¾ teaspoon salt
- ½ teaspoon ground nutmeg
- ½ teaspoon pepper

TOPPING

- 1 medium onion, thinly sliced
- 2 teaspoons olive oil
- 3 medium pears, thinly sliced
- 1 tablespoon brown sugar

1. Unfold puff pastry; press into a greased 9-in. fluted tart pan with removable bottom. In a large skillet, cook bacon over medium heat until crisp. Spoon bacon into crust and sprinkle with blue cheese. In a large bowl, whisk the eggs, cream, Parmesan cheese, salt, nutmeg and pepper; pour over top.

2. Bake at 350° for 30-35 minutes or until a knife inserted near the center comes out clean. Meanwhile, in a large skillet, saute onion in oil until tender. Add pears and brown sugar; cook 4 minutes longer. Serve with quiche.

4. For syrup, in a small saucepan, mix sugar and cornstarch; stir in water until smooth. Stir in ¼ cup blueberries. Bring to a boil; cook and stir until berries pop, about 3 minutes. Remove from heat; stir in butter, lemon juice and remaining berries. Serve warm with French toast.

Scrambled Egg Casserole

PREP: 20 MIN. + CHILLING • **BAKE:** 30 MIN.
MAKES: 10-12 SERVINGS

CHEESE SAUCE
  2 **tablespoons butter**
7½ **teaspoons all-purpose flour**
  2 **cups milk**
  ½ **teaspoon salt**
  ⅛ **teaspoon pepper**
  1 **cup cubed process cheese (Velveeta)**
  1 **cup cubed fully cooked ham**
  ¼ **cup chopped green onions**
  3 **tablespoons butter, melted**
12 **large eggs, beaten**
  1 **can (4 ounces) mushroom stems and pieces, drained**
TOPPING
  ¼ **cup melted butter**
2¼ **cups soft bread crumbs**

1. To make cheese sauce, in a large skillet, melt butter; stir in flour and cook for 1 minute. Gradually stir in milk. Bring to a boil; cook and stir for 1-2 minutes or until thickened. Add the salt, pepper and cheese; stir until cheese melts. Set aside.
2. In a small skillet, saute ham and green onion in 3 tablespoons butter until onion is tender. Add eggs and cook over medium heat until eggs are set; stir in mushrooms and cheese sauce.
3. Spoon eggs into greased 13x9-in. baking pan. Combine topping ingredients; spread evenly over egg mixture. Cover; chill overnight. Uncover; bake at 350° for 30 minutes.

> **❝This has become the brunch dish I'm known for. The recipe combines the favorite flavors of hearty, old-time country breakfasts with the ease of a modern, make-ahead dish.❞**
>
> —**MARY ANNE MCWHIRTER** PEARLAND, TX

Slow-Cooked Blueberry French Toast

Your slow cooker can be your best friend on a busy Saturday or Sunday morning. Just get this recipe going, run some errands and come back to the aroma of French toast ready to eat.
—**ELIZABETH LORENZ** PERU, IN

PREP: 30 MIN. + CHILLING • **COOK:** 3 HOURS
MAKES: 12 SERVINGS (2 CUPS SYRUP)

  8 **large eggs**
  ½ **cup plain yogurt**
  ⅓ **cup sour cream**
  1 **teaspoon vanilla extract**
  ½ **teaspoon ground cinnamon**
  1 **cup 2% milk**
  ⅓ **cup maple syrup**
  1 **loaf (1 pound) French bread, cubed**
1½ **cups fresh or frozen blueberries**
12 **ounces cream cheese, cubed**
BLUEBERRY SYRUP
  1 **cup sugar**
  2 **tablespoons cornstarch**
  1 **cup cold water**
  ¾ **cup fresh or frozen blueberries, divided**
  1 **tablespoon butter**
  1 **tablespoon lemon juice**

1. In a large bowl, whisk eggs, yogurt, sour cream, vanilla and cinnamon. Gradually whisk in milk and maple syrup until blended.
2. Place half of the bread in a greased 5- or 6-qt. slow cooker; layer with half of the blueberries, cream cheese and egg mixture. Repeat layers. Refrigerate, covered, overnight.
3. Remove from refrigerator 30 minutes before cooking. Cook, covered, on low 3-4 hours or until a knife inserted near the center comes out clean.

Ultimate Bacon-Maple French Toast

A savory update on baked French toast, this is an easy make-ahead dish that's excellent for brunches and showers. The combination of maple syrup, bacon and pecans makes it impressive and satisfying.

—**JOHN WHITEHEAD** GREENVILLE, SC

PREP: 30 MIN. + CHILLING
BAKE: 40 MIN. + STANDING
MAKES: 10 SERVINGS

- 8 **large eggs**
- 2 **cups half-and-half cream**
- 1 **cup 2% milk**
- 1 **tablespoon sugar**
- 1 **tablespoon brown sugar**
- 1 **teaspoon vanilla extract**
- ½ **teaspoon ground cinnamon**
- ¼ **teaspoon ground nutmeg**
  Dash salt
  Dash cayenne pepper
- 1 **loaf (1 pound) French bread, cut into 1-inch slices**

TOPPING

- 6 **thick-sliced bacon strips, cooked and crumbled**
- 1 **cup butter, melted**
- 1 **cup packed brown sugar**
- ½ **cup chopped pecans, toasted**
- 2 **tablespoons corn syrup**
- 1 **teaspoon ground cinnamon**
- ½ **teaspoon ground nutmeg**
- ¼ **teaspoon ground cloves**
  Maple syrup

1. Grease a 13x9-in. baking dish; set aside.

2. In a large shallow bowl, whisk the first 10 ingredients. Dip each slice of bread into egg mixture. Arrange slices into prepared dish. Pour remaining egg mixture over top. Cover and refrigerate overnight.

3. Remove from the refrigerator 30 minutes before baking. Preheat oven to 350°. In a small bowl, combine the first eight topping ingredients. Spread over the top.

4. Bake, uncovered, 40-45 minutes or until a knife inserted near center comes out clean. Let stand 10 minutes before serving. Drizzle with syrup.

Crustless Quiche Bake

Chock-full of veggies, cheese, bacon and eggs, this yummy recipe would be great served with fresh muffins or toasted breads and fruit!

—**JUNE MARIE RACUS** SUN CITY WEST, AZ

PREP: 30 MIN. • **BAKE:** 40 MIN. + STANDING
MAKES: 12 SERVINGS

- 14 **bacon strips, chopped**
- 1 **pound sliced fresh mushrooms**
- ½ **cup chopped green pepper**
- 8 **green onions, thinly sliced**
- 1 **jar (2 ounces) diced pimientos, drained**
- 2 **tablespoons sherry, optional**
- 12 **large eggs**
- 1½ **cups 2% milk**
- ¾ **teaspoon dried thyme**
- ¾ **teaspoon seasoned salt**
- ½ **teaspoon ground mustard**
  Dash dill weed
- 4 **cups (16 ounces) shredded Gruyere or Swiss cheese, divided**

1. In a large skillet, cook bacon over medium heat until crisp. Remove to paper towels with a slotted spoon; drain, reserving 2 tablespoons drippings.

2. In the drippings, saute the mushrooms, green pepper and onions until tender. Add pimientos and, if desired, sherry; cook until liquid is evaporated.

3. In a large bowl, whisk the eggs, milk, thyme, seasoned salt, mustard and dill. Add the bacon, mushroom mixture and 3 cups cheese. Transfer to a greased 13x9-in. baking dish.

4. Bake, uncovered, at 350° for 35 minutes. Sprinkle with the remaining cheese. Bake 5-10 minutes longer or until a knife inserted near the center comes out clean and cheese is melted. Let stand for 10 minutes before cutting.

FREEZE OPTION *Freeze unbaked quiche and remaining cheese separately in freezer containers. To use, remove from freezer 30 minutes before baking (do not thaw). Preheat oven to 350°. Bake quiche as directed, increasing time as necessary for a knife inserted near the center to come out clean.*

Old-Fashioned Tomato Gravy

This is my mother-in-law's favorite breakfast. My family and I also enjoy it for a light supper. On a cold day, it's great with warm peach cobbler or bread pudding.

—**LAURIE FISHER** GREELEY, CO

START TO FINISH: 30 MIN.
MAKES: 6-8 SERVINGS

- ½ **pound bacon strips, diced**
- 1 **small onion, chopped**
- 2 **tablespoons all-purpose flour**
- ⅛ **teaspoon salt**
  Pinch pepper
- 1 **can (14½ ounces) diced tomatoes, undrained**
- 3 **cups tomato juice**
- 6 **to 8 hot biscuits, split**

In a skillet, cook bacon until crisp. Remove to paper towels to drain; discard all but 2 tablespoons drippings. Cook onion in drippings until tender. Stir in flour, salt and pepper; cook and stir over low heat until mixture is golden brown. Gradually add tomatoes and tomato juice; stir well. Bring to a boil over medium heat. Cook and stir for 2 minutes. Reduce heat; simmer, uncovered, for 10-15 minutes or until thickened, stirring occasionally. Stir in bacon. Serve over biscuits.

BRUNCH BASICS

Planning a brunch buffet for a crowd? Consider offering two entrees—one egg based and one featuring a starch, such as a French toast bake. Add at least two side dishes to your lineup. Include a light option, such as a colorful fruit salad, which works well served with both savory dishes and dessert options. In addition to coffee and fruit juice, be sure to make water available to your guests.

Cinnamon Roll Coffee Cake

Ready in a snap, this fresh-from-the-oven treat will be a sensational no-fuss addition to any weekend or holiday brunch. Guests will never guess how easy it is to whip up.

—TERESA MAAG LEIPSIC, OH

PREP: 20 MIN. • **BAKE:** 25 MIN. + STANDING
MAKES: 12 SERVINGS

- 1 tube (17½ ounces) large refrigerated cinnamon rolls with cream cheese icing
- 2 packages (8 ounces each) cream cheese, softened
- 3 large eggs
- ½ cup sugar
- 1 teaspoon vanilla extract
- ½ cup chopped pecans
- ¼ cup all-purpose flour
- ¼ cup quick-cooking oats
- ¼ cup packed brown sugar
- 1 teaspoon ground cinnamon
- 3 tablespoons butter, melted
  Whipped cream and additional ground cinnamon, optional

1. Unroll the tube of cinnamon rolls into one long rectangle. Press onto the bottom of a greased 13x9-in. baking dish; seal perforations. Set aside icing packet from cinnamon rolls.

2. In a large bowl, beat the cream cheese, eggs, sugar and vanilla extract until smooth. Pour over crust. In a small bowl, combine the chopped pecans, flour, oats, brown sugar and cinnamon; stir in the butter. Sprinkle over the cream cheese layer.

3. Bake at 350° for 25-30 minutes or until a toothpick inserted near the center comes out clean. Drizzle with contents of icing packet; let stand for 15 minutes before serving. If desired, serve with a dollop of whipped cream sprinkled with additional cinnamon.

Flaky Egg Bake

Phyllo dough adds a touch of elegance and layers of crispy, buttery goodness to this company-special breakfast bake.

—CRYSTAL JO BRUNS ILIFF, CO

PREP: 40 MIN. + FREEZING • **BAKE:** 40 MIN.
MAKES: 12 SERVINGS

- ¾ pound bulk Italian sausage
- 1 cup sliced fresh mushrooms
- 1 medium onion, finely chopped
- 1 medium sweet red pepper, chopped
- 1 medium green pepper, chopped
- 6 large eggs, divided use
- 1½ cups (6 ounces) shredded Havarti cheese
- 1 package (10 ounces) frozen chopped spinach, thawed and squeezed dry
- 1 cup ricotta cheese
- ⅓ cup grated Parmesan cheese
- 2 tablespoons minced fresh basil or 2 teaspoons dried basil

- 1 cup butter, melted
- 30 sheets phyllo dough (14 inches x 9 inches)

1. In a large skillet, cook sausage, mushrooms, onion and peppers over medium heat until meat is no longer pink and vegetables are tender; drain. Return sausage mixture to skillet. Whisk five eggs; add to skillet. Cook and stir over medium-high heat until set; stir in the Havarti cheese. Set aside.

2. In a small bowl, combine the spinach, ricotta cheese, Parmesan cheese, basil and remaining egg. Brush a 13x9-in. baking pan with butter. Unroll phyllo dough; trim to fit into the pan.

3. Layer 10 sheets in prepared pan, brushing each sheet with butter. (Keep remaining phyllo covered with plastic wrap and a damp towel to prevent it from drying out.) Top with half of the sausage mixture.

4. Layer with 10 additional phyllo sheets, brushing each with butter; spread with ricotta mixture. Layer with five phyllo sheets, brushing again with butter; top with remaining sausage mixture. Layer with remaining phyllo and butter. Using a sharp knife, cut into 12 rectangles. Bake at 350°, uncovered, 30-40 minutes or until golden brown.

FREEZE OPTION *Cover and freeze unbaked casserole up to 3 months. Thaw in refrigerator overnight. Remove from refrigerator 30 minutes before baking. Bake, uncovered, at 350° for 40-50 minutes or until golden brown.*

NOTE *Look for phyllo dough in the frozen pastry section.*

Gingerbread Scones
with Lemon Butter

Busy morning? Fill your kitchen with the warm aroma of these tender gingerbread scones. Then slather on some lip-smacking lemon butter and relax with a steaming cup of coffee. Yum!

—SHARON DELANEY-CHRONIS SOUTH MILWAUKEE, WI

START TO FINISH: 30 MIN.
MAKES: 16 SCONES

2¼ cups all-purpose flour
1 teaspoon baking powder
1 teaspoon ground cinnamon
½ teaspoon ground ginger
¼ teaspoon salt
¼ teaspoon baking soda
¼ teaspoon ground allspice
¼ teaspoon ground nutmeg
½ cup cold butter
¾ cup heavy whipping cream
⅓ cup molasses
½ cup dried currants
LEMON BUTTER
¼ cup butter, softened
¼ cup confectioners' sugar
1 tablespoon lemon juice
1 teaspoon grated lemon peel

1. In a large bowl, combine the first eight ingredients. Cut in butter until mixture resembles coarse crumbs. Whisk cream and molasses; stir into crumb mixture just until moistened. Stir in currants.
2. Turn onto a floured surface; knead 10 times. Pat or roll out to ½-in. thickness; cut with a floured 2-in. biscuit cutter.

3. Place 2 in. apart on a lightly greased baking sheet. Bake at 425° for 8-10 minutes or until golden brown.
4. Meanwhile, in a small bowl, beat the softened butter, confectioners' sugar, lemon juice and peel until combined. Serve with warm scones.

Slow Cooker Ham & Eggs

This dish is great anytime of the year, but I love serving it on holiday mornings. It's basically a hands-free recipe that helps me create a fun meal for the family.

—ANDREA SCHAAK JORDAN, MN

PREP: 15 MIN. • **COOK:** 3 HOURS
MAKES: 6 SERVINGS

6 large eggs
1 cup biscuit/baking mix
⅔ cup 2% milk
⅓ cup sour cream
2 tablespoons minced fresh parsley
2 garlic cloves, minced
½ teaspoon salt
½ teaspoon pepper
1 cup cubed fully cooked ham
1 cup (4 ounces) shredded Swiss cheese
1 small onion, finely chopped
⅓ cup shredded Parmesan cheese

1. In a large bowl, whisk the first eight ingredients until blended; stir in remaining ingredients. Pour into a greased 3- or 4-qt. slow cooker.
2. Cook, covered, on low 3-4 hours or until eggs are set. Cut into wedges.

Brie & Sausage Brunch Bake

I've frequently made this for holidays and special weekends, and I always get requests for the recipe. It's make-ahead convenient, reheats well and even tastes great the next day.

—**BECKY HICKS** FOREST LAKE, MN

PREP: 30 MIN. + CHILLING • **BAKE:** 50 MIN. + STANDING
MAKES: 12 SERVINGS

- 1 pound bulk Italian sausage
- 1 small onion, chopped
- 8 cups cubed day-old sourdough bread
- ½ cup chopped roasted sweet red peppers
- ½ pound Brie cheese, rind removed, cubed
- ⅔ cup grated Parmesan cheese
- 2 tablespoons minced fresh basil or 2 teaspoons dried basil
- 8 large eggs
- 2 cups heavy whipping cream
- 1 tablespoon Dijon mustard
- 1 teaspoon pepper
- ½ teaspoon salt
- ¾ cup shredded part-skim mozzarella cheese
- 3 green onions, sliced

1. In a large skillet, cook sausage and onion over medium heat until meat is no longer pink; drain.

2. Place bread cubes in a greased 13x9-in. baking dish. Layer with sausage mixture, red peppers, Brie and Parmesan cheeses and basil. In a large bowl, whisk eggs, cream, mustard, pepper and salt; pour over top. Cover and refrigerate overnight.

3. Remove from the refrigerator 30 minutes before baking. Preheat oven to 350°. Bake, uncovered, 45-50 minutes or until a knife inserted near the center comes out clean.

4. Sprinkle with mozzarella cheese. Bake 4-6 minutes or until cheese is melted. Let stand 10 minutes before cutting. Sprinkle with green onions.

Molasses-Pecan Sticky Buns

As much as I like making yeast breads, I enjoy watching others enjoying my baking even more. These soft, tender rolls are loaded with the gooey goodness of molasses.

—**SHIRLEY SAYLOR** FELTON, PA

PREP: 45 MIN. + RISING • **BAKE:** 25 MIN.
MAKES: 12 SERVINGS

- 3½ to 4 cups all-purpose flour
- 3 tablespoons sugar
- 2 packages (¼ ounce each) quick-rise yeast
- 1 teaspoon salt
- 1 cup 2% milk
- ½ cup water
- ¼ cup butter, cubed

FILLING

- ¼ cup butter, softened
- 1½ teaspoons ground cinnamon

TOPPING

- ½ cup butter, cubed
- 1 cup packed brown sugar
- ⅔ cup chopped pecans
- ½ cup molasses

1. In a large bowl, combine 2 cups flour, sugar, yeast and salt. In a small saucepan, heat the milk, water and butter to 120°-130°. Add to dry ingredients; beat just until moistened. Stir in enough remaining flour to form a soft dough (dough will be sticky).

2. Turn dough onto a floured surface; knead until smooth and elastic, about 6-8 minutes. Cover and let rest for 10 minutes.

3. Roll into a 14x12-in. rectangle. Spread butter to within ½ in. of edges; sprinkle with cinnamon. Roll up jelly-roll style, starting with a long side; pinch seams to seal. Cut into 12 rolls.

4. In a small saucepan, melt remaining butter. Stir in the brown sugar, pecans and molasses; pour into a greased 13x9-in. baking dish. Place rolls, cut side down, in dish.

5. Cover and let rise in a warm place until doubled, about 15 minutes. Bake at 375° for 25-30 minutes or until golden brown. Immediately invert buns onto a serving platter. Serve warm.

EASY IDEA

If you find it difficult to slice cinnamon roll dough with a knife, try this trick. Place a piece of unflavored dental floss under the rolled dough, 1 in. from the end. Bring the floss up around the dough and cross it over the top, cutting through the dough and filling. Repeat at 1-in. intervals.

Mushroom-Herb Stuffed French Toast

PREP: 25 MIN. • **COOK:** 5 MIN./BATCH
MAKES: 8 SERVINGS

- 1 **pound thinly sliced baby portobello mushrooms**
- 4 **tablespoons butter, divided**
- 1 **package (8 ounces) reduced-fat cream cheese**
- 2 **cups (8 ounces) shredded Gruyere or Swiss cheese, divided**
- 4 **tablespoons minced chives, divided**
- 1 **tablespoon minced fresh tarragon or 1 teaspoon dried tarragon**
- 1 **garlic clove, minced**
- ⅛ **teaspoon salt**
- ⅛ **teaspoon pepper**
- 16 **slices Texas toast**
- 4 **large eggs**
- 2 **cups 2% milk**
- 2 **tablespoons butter, melted**

1. In a large skillet, saute mushrooms in 1 tablespoon butter until tender; set aside.

2. In a small bowl, beat the cream cheese, 1 cup Gruyere cheese, 2 tablespoons chives, tarragon, garlic, salt and pepper until blended. Spread over bread slices. Spoon mushrooms over half of the slices; place remaining bread slices over the top, spread side down.

3. In a shallow bowl, whisk the eggs, milk and melted butter. Dip both sides of sandwiches into egg mixture.

4. In a large skillet, toast sandwiches in remaining butter in batches for 2-3 minutes on each side or until golden brown. Sprinkle with remaining cheese and chives.

❝This recipe transforms French toast into a savory delight with mushrooms and cheese. Its ooey-gooey texture is irresistible!❞

—LISA HUFF WILTON, CT

Tiramisu Crepes

Delicate crepes, filled with creamy mascarpone cheese and laced with vanilla and a hint of coffee liqueur, always make for a mouthwatering morning treat. They're special in every way.
—**KAREN SHELTON** COLLIERVILLE, TN

PREP: 30 MIN. + CHILLING • **COOK:** 5 MIN./BATCH
MAKES: 22 CREPES

- 4 **large eggs**
- ¾ **cup 2% milk**
- ¼ **cup club soda**
- 3 **tablespoons butter, melted**
- 2 **tablespoons strong brewed coffee**
- 1 **teaspoon vanilla extract**
- 1 **cup all-purpose flour**
- 3 **tablespoons sugar**
- 2 **tablespoons baking cocoa**
- ¼ **teaspoon salt**

FILLING

- 1 **carton (8 ounces) mascarpone cheese**
- 1 **package (8 ounces) cream cheese, softened**
- 1 **cup sugar**
- ¼ **cup coffee liqueur or strong brewed coffee**
- 2 **tablespoons vanilla extract**
  Optional toppings: chocolate syrup, whipped cream and baking cocoa

1. In a large bowl, beat the eggs, milk, soda, butter, coffee and vanilla. Combine the flour, sugar, cocoa and salt; add to milk mixture and mix well. Cover and refrigerate for 1 hour.
2. Heat a lightly greased 8-in. nonstick skillet over medium heat; pour 2 tablespoons batter into the center of skillet. Lift and tilt pan to coat bottom evenly. Cook until top appears dry; turn and cook 15-20 seconds longer. Remove to a wire rack. Repeat with remaining batter, greasing skillet as needed. When cool, stack crepes with waxed paper or paper towels in between.
3. For filling, in a large bowl, beat the cheeses and sugar until fluffy. Add liqueur and vanilla; beat until smooth. Spoon about 2 tablespoons filling down the center of each crepe; roll up. Top with chocolate syrup, whipped cream and cocoa if desired.

Cinnamon Bagels with Crunchy Topping

Once you get the hang of it, you won't believe how simple it is to make these bakery-quality bagels right in your kitchen.
—**KRISTEN STREEPEY** GENEVA, IL

PREP: 40 MIN. + RISING • **BAKE:** 15 MIN. + COOLING
MAKES: 1 DOZEN

- 2 **teaspoons active dry yeast**
- 1½ **cups warm water (110° to 115°)**
- 4 **tablespoons brown sugar, divided**
- 3 **teaspoons ground cinnamon**
- 1½ **teaspoons salt**
- 2¾ to 3¼ **cups all-purpose flour**

TOPPING

- ¼ **cup sugar**
- ¼ **cup packed brown sugar**
- 3 **teaspoons ground cinnamon**

1. In a large bowl, dissolve yeast in warm water. Add 3 tablespoons brown sugar, cinnamon and salt; mix well. Stir in enough flour to form a soft dough.
2. Turn onto a lightly floured surface; knead until smooth and elastic, about 6-8 minutes. Place in a bowl coated with cooking spray, turning once to coat the top. Cover and let rise in a warm place until doubled, about 1 hour.
3. Punch dough down. Shape into 12 balls. Push thumb through each center to form a 1½-in. hole. Stretch and shape dough to form an even ring. Place on a floured surface. Cover and let rest for 10 minutes.
4. Fill a Dutch oven two-thirds full with water and remaining brown sugar; bring to a boil. Drop bagels, two at a time, into boiling water. Cook for 45 seconds; turn and cook 45 seconds longer. Remove with a slotted spoon; drain well on paper towels.
5. In a small bowl, mix topping ingredients; sprinkle over bagels. Place 2 in. apart on baking sheets coated with cooking spray. Bake at 400° for 15-20 minutes or until golden brown. Remove to wire racks to cool.

Meatball Pie, page 103

99

102

113

Beef & Pork Entrees

Big appetites have met their match! In this chapter, you'll find the **meatiest main dishes** to fill the hungriest diners at your table. Page through and choose from a **variety of favorites,** from savory steaks, pot roast and stew to fork-tender ribs, chops and ham.

Grilled Ribeyes with Herb Butter

Here's my go-to entree for special occasions. The tantalizing fragrance of the herbes de Provence lets everyone know they're in for a real treat. Try the seasoning and herb butter with filet mignon, T-bones and steak strips, too.

—JOHN BARANSKI BALDWIN CITY, KS

PREP: 25 MIN. + MARINATING • **GRILL:** 10 MIN.
MAKES: 4 SERVINGS

- ¼ cup olive oil
- ¼ cup dry red wine
- 1 tablespoon minced fresh rosemary or 1 teaspoon dried rosemary, crushed
- 1 tablespoon red wine vinegar
- 1 tablespoon Dijon mustard
- 1 teaspoon coarsely ground pepper
- 1 teaspoon Worcestershire sauce
- 2 garlic cloves, minced
- 4 beef ribeye steaks (¾ pound each)

STEAK SEASONINGS
- 2 teaspoons kosher salt
- 1 teaspoon sugar
- 1 teaspoon herbes de Provence
- 1 teaspoon coarsely ground pepper

HERB BUTTER
- ¼ cup butter, softened
- 1 tablespoon minced fresh parsley
- 1 teaspoon prepared horseradish

1. In a large resealable plastic bag, combine the first eight ingredients. Add the steaks; seal the bag and turn to coat. Refrigerate overnight.
2. Drain and discard the marinade. Combine the steak seasonings; sprinkle over steaks.
3. Grill the steaks, covered, over medium heat or broil 3-4 in. from the heat for 5-7 minutes on each side or until the meat reaches the desired doneness (for medium-rare, a thermometer should read 145°; medium, 160°; well-done, 170°).

4. For herb butter, in a small bowl, beat the butter, parsley and horseradish until blended. Spoon 1 tablespoon herb butter over each steak.
NOTE *Look for herbes de Provence in the spice aisle.*

Mushroom Pot Roast

Packed with wholesome veggies and tender beef, this home-style dinner always goes over well. The wine-warmed flavors make it a standout! Add a scoop of mashed potatoes on the side so you can enjoy every last drop of rich, savory gravy.

—ANGIE STEWART TOPEKA, KS

PREP: 25 MIN. • **COOK:** 6 HOURS
MAKES: 10 SERVINGS

- 1 boneless beef chuck roast (3 to 4 pounds)
- ½ teaspoon salt
- ¼ teaspoon pepper
- 1 tablespoon canola oil
- 1½ pounds sliced fresh shiitake mushrooms
- 2½ cups thinly sliced onions
- 1½ cups reduced-sodium beef broth
- 1½ cups dry red wine or additional reduced-sodium beef broth
- 1 can (8 ounces) tomato sauce
- ¾ cup chopped peeled parsnips
- ¾ cup chopped celery
- ¾ cup chopped carrots
- 8 garlic cloves, minced
- 2 bay leaves
- 1½ teaspoons dried thyme
- 1 teaspoon chili powder
- ¼ cup cornstarch
- ¼ cup water
  Mashed potatoes

1. Sprinkle the roast with salt and pepper. In a Dutch oven, brown roast in oil on all sides. Transfer to a 6-qt. slow cooker. Add the mushrooms, onions, broth, wine, tomato sauce, parsnips, celery, carrots, garlic, bay leaves, thyme and chili powder. Cover and cook on low for 6-8 hours or until the meat is tender.
2. Remove the meat and vegetables to a serving platter; keep warm. Discard the bay leaves. Skim the fat from the cooking juices; transfer to a small saucepan. Bring the liquid to a boil. Combine the cornstarch and water until smooth; gradually stir into the pan. Bring to a boil; cook and stir for 2 minutes or until thickened. Serve with the mashed potatoes, meat and vegetables.
PER SERVING *4 ounces cooked beef with ⅔ cup vegetables and ½ cup gravy (calculated without the potatoes) equals 310 cal., 14 g fat (5 g sat. fat), 89 mg chol., 363 mg sodium, 14 g carb., 3 g fiber, 30 g pro.* **Diabetic Exchanges:** *4 lean meat, 2 vegetable, 1½ fat.*

Beef Stew with Cheddar Dumplings

This cozy, comforting stew is popular not only with my family, but also with guests. They especially like the fluffy dumplings flecked with cheddar cheese.

—JACKIE RILEY GARRETTSVILLE, OH

PREP: 25 MIN. • **COOK:** 1½ HOURS
MAKES: 6-8 SERVINGS

- ½ cup all-purpose flour
- ½ teaspoon salt
- ½ teaspoon pepper
- 2 to 3 pounds beef stew meat, cut into 1-inch pieces
- 2 tablespoons canola oil
- 5 cups water
- 5 teaspoons beef bouillon granules
- 1 tablespoon browning sauce, optional
- ½ teaspoon onion salt
- ½ teaspoon garlic salt
- 4 medium carrots, sliced
- 1 medium onion, cut into wedges
- 1 can (14½ ounces) cut green beans, drained

DUMPLINGS

- 2 cups biscuit/baking mix
- 1 cup (4 ounces) shredded cheddar cheese
- ⅔ cup milk

1. In a large resealable plastic bag, combine the flour, salt and pepper. Add beef, a few pieces at a time, and shake to coat. In a Dutch oven, brown beef in oil in batches.

2. Stir in the water, beef bouillon, browning sauce if desired, onion salt and garlic salt. Bring to a boil. Reduce heat; cover and simmer for 1 hour.

3. Add the carrots and onion. Cover and simmer 10-15 minutes longer or until the vegetables are tender. Stir in green beans.

4. For the dumplings, combine the biscuit mix and shredded cheddar cheese. Stir in enough milk to form a soft dough. Drop by tablespoonfuls onto the simmering stew. Cover and simmer for 10-12 minutes (do not lift the cover) or until a toothpick inserted in a dumpling comes out clean. Serve immediately.

Sour Cream Swiss Steak

I spent a year looking for new and different beef recipes. This discovery is the one my family raves about. It's a great change from the usual Swiss steak.

—BARB BENTING GRAND RAPIDS, MI

PREP: 50 MIN. • **BAKE:** 1½ HOURS
MAKES: 6-8 SERVINGS

- ⅓ cup all-purpose flour
- 1½ teaspoons each salt, pepper, paprika and ground mustard
- 3 pounds beef top round steak, cut into serving-size pieces
- 3 tablespoons canola oil
- 3 tablespoons butter
- 1½ cups water
- 1½ cups (12 ounces) sour cream
- 1 cup finely chopped onion
- 2 garlic cloves, minced
- ⅓ cup soy sauce
- ¼ to ⅓ cup packed brown sugar
- 3 tablespoons all-purpose flour
  Additional paprika, optional

1. In a shallow bowl, combine flour, salt, pepper, paprika and mustard; dredge the steak.
2. In a large skillet, heat the oil and butter. Cook steak on both sides until browned. Carefully add the water; cover and simmer for 30 minutes.
3. In a bowl, combine the sour cream, onion, garlic, soy sauce, brown sugar and flour; stir until smooth. Transfer steak to a greased 2½-qt. baking dish; add sour cream mixture.
4. Cover; bake at 325° for 1½ hours or until tender. Sprinkle steak with paprika if desired.

SAVE THE PASTE

A tablespoon or two of tomato paste adds richness and color to many savory dishes. Here's a tip for storing leftover tomato paste. Mound it in 1-tablespoon portions on a waxed paper-lined baking sheet. Freeze the paste until firm, then transfer it to a resealable freezer bag. The next time you need some, simply remove the desired amount.

Hungarian Goulash

My grandmother used to prepare goulash for my mother. Paprika and caraway add wonderful flavor, and sour cream gives it that traditional richness.

—MARCIA DOYLE POMPANO, FL

PREP: 20 MIN. • **COOK:** 7 HOURS
MAKES: 12 SERVINGS

- 3 medium onions, chopped
- 2 medium carrots, chopped
- 2 medium green peppers, chopped
- 3 pounds beef stew meat, cut into 1-inch cubes
- ¾ teaspoon salt, divided
- ¾ teaspoon pepper, divided
- 2 tablespoons olive oil
- 1½ cups reduced-sodium beef broth
- ¼ cup all-purpose flour
- 3 tablespoons paprika
- 2 tablespoons tomato paste
- 1 teaspoon caraway seeds
- 1 garlic clove, minced
  Dash sugar
- 12 cups uncooked whole wheat egg noodles
- 1 cup (8 ounces) reduced-fat sour cream

1. Place the onions, carrots and green peppers in a 5-qt. slow cooker. Sprinkle the meat with ½ teaspoon salt and ½ teaspoon pepper. In a large skillet, brown meat in oil in batches. Transfer to slow cooker.
2. Add the beef broth to the skillet, stirring to loosen browned bits from pan. Combine flour, paprika, tomato paste, caraway seeds, garlic, sugar and remaining salt and pepper; stir into skillet. Bring to a boil; cook and stir for 2 minutes or until thickened. Pour over meat. Cover and cook on low for 7-9 hours or until meat is tender.
3. Cook the egg noodles according to package directions. Stir sour cream into the slow cooker. Drain noodles; serve with goulash.
PER SERVING *⅔ cup goulash with 1 cup noodles equals 388 cal., 13 g fat (4 g sat. fat), 78 mg chol., 285 mg sodium, 41 g carb., 7 g fiber, 31 g pro.* ***Diabetic Exchanges:*** *3 lean meat, 2 starch, 1 vegetable, 1 fat.*

When we tried marinating vegetables in a bourbon sauce and serving them hot off the grill with bratwurst, the recipe quickly made our VIP tailgate party list.

—**MARY LEVERETTE** COLUMBIA, SC

Bourbon Brat Skewers

PREP: 20 MIN. + MARINATING
GRILL: 15 MIN.
MAKES: 6 SKEWERS

- ½ **cup reduced-sodium soy sauce**
- ½ **cup bourbon**
- 3 **tablespoons brown sugar**
- 1 **teaspoon seasoned salt**
- ¼ **teaspoon cayenne pepper**
- 2 **cups whole mushrooms**
- 2 **medium sweet red peppers, cut into 1-inch pieces**
- 1 **medium green pepper, cut into 1-inch pieces**
- 1 **medium onion, cut into wedges**
- 1 **package (16 ounces) uncooked bratwurst links, cut into 1-inch slices**

1. In a large resealable plastic bag, combine the first five ingredients. Add the vegetables; seal bag and turn to coat. Refrigerate for at least 1 hour.

2. Drain and reserve marinade. On six metal or soaked wooden skewers, alternately thread the vegetables and bratwurst.

3. Spoon some reserved marinade over the vegetables and bratwurst. Grill, covered, over medium heat for 15-20 minutes or until bratwurst is no longer pink and vegetables are tender, turning and basting frequently with the reserved marinade during the last 5 minutes.

Smoky Cranberry Ribs

Living near New Jersey's cranberry bogs inspires me to use the tangy red berries in my cooking. These sweet and savory grilled ribs make a winning main course any time I serve them.
—**CHRISTINE WENDLAND** BROWNS MILLS, NJ

PREP: 25 MIN. + CHILLING • **GRILL:** 2 HOURS
MAKES: 6 SERVINGS

- 4½ teaspoons paprika
- 4 teaspoons salt
- 2 teaspoons fennel seed
- 1½ teaspoons pepper
- 1 teaspoon onion powder
- 1 teaspoon caraway seeds
- 1 teaspoon ground allspice
- ½ teaspoon garlic powder
- ½ teaspoon rubbed sage
- 6 pounds pork baby back ribs

SAUCE
- 1½ cups fresh or frozen cranberries, thawed
- 1½ cups packed dark brown sugar
- 1 cup cider vinegar
- 1 small sweet onion, chopped
- ¼ cup ketchup

1. In a spice grinder or with a mortar and pestle, combine the first nine ingredients; grind until fennel and caraway seeds are crushed. Set aside 4 teaspoons for sauce.
2. Rub the remaining spice mixture over ribs. Cover and refrigerate for at least 1 hour.
3. Wrap the ribs in a large piece of heavy-duty foil (about 28x18 in.); seal tightly. Prepare the grill for indirect heat, using a drip pan. Place ribs over drip pan and grill, covered, over indirect medium heat for 1½-2 hours or until tender.

4. In a small saucepan, combine the cranberries, brown sugar, vinegar, onion and reserved spice mixture. Cook over medium heat until the cranberries pop, about 15 minutes; cool slightly. Transfer to a blender; add ketchup. Cover and process until smooth. Set aside 1 cup sauce for serving.
5. Moisten a paper towel with cooking oil; using long-handled tongs, lightly coat grill rack. Carefully remove the ribs from the foil. Place over direct heat; baste the ribs with some of the sauce. Grill, covered, over medium heat for 20-30 minutes or until browned, turning and basting occasionally. Serve with the reserved sauce.

Crescent Cheeseburger Pie

Mom gave me her famous cheeseburger pie recipe shortly before my wedding. Today, more than three decades later, my husband, children and grandchildren are enjoying it!
—**ELINORE DUMONT** DRUMHELLER, AB

PREP: 30 MIN. • **BAKE:** 40 MIN. + STANDING
MAKES: 6 SERVINGS

- 1 pound ground beef
- ½ cup chopped onion
- 1 can (8 ounces) tomato sauce
- 1 can (4 ounces) mushroom stems and pieces, drained
- ¼ cup minced fresh parsley
- ¼ teaspoon salt
- ¼ teaspoon dried oregano
- ⅛ teaspoon pepper
- 2 tubes (8 ounces each) refrigerated crescent rolls
- 2 large eggs
- 1 large egg, separated
- 6 slices process American cheese
- 1 tablespoon water

1. Preheat oven to 350°. In a large skillet, cook beef and onion over medium heat until the meat is no longer pink; drain. Stir in the tomato sauce, mushrooms, parsley, salt, oregano and pepper; set aside.
2. Unroll 1 tube of crescent dough and separate dough into eight triangles. Arrange in a single layer in a lightly greased 9-in. pie plate. Press into dish to form a crust and seal the seams. In a small bowl, whisk eggs and 1 egg white.
3. Pour half of the beaten egg mixture over the pie shell. Spoon the meat mixture into shell; arrange cheese slices on top. Spread with remaining beaten egg. Mix water and remaining egg yolk; set aside.
4. Unroll second tube of crescent dough; place four sections of dough together to form a 12x6-in. rectangle. Press the perforations to seal; roll dough into a 12-in. square.
5. Brush edges of bottom crust with some of the egg yolk mixture; place dough on top of filling. Trim, seal and flute edges. Cut slits in top. Brush top with remaining egg yolk mixture.
6. Bake for 40 minutes, tenting with foil after 15 minutes if necessary. Let stand for 10 minutes before serving.

Big Daddy's BBQ Ribs

Now you see them, now you don't! These are gone in a flash when I set out a platter for my co-workers. Plenty of spices and brown sugar combine for an excellent rub.
—**ERIC BRZOSTEK** EAST ISLIP, NY

PREP: 30 MIN. + CHILLING • **BAKE:** 1½ HOURS
MAKES: 8 SERVINGS

> ¾ cup packed brown sugar
> 2 tablespoons mesquite seasoning
> 4½ teaspoons garlic powder
> 4½ teaspoons paprika
> 1 tablespoon dried minced onion
> 1 tablespoon seasoned salt
> 1 tablespoon ground cinnamon
> 1 tablespoon ground cumin
> 1 tablespoon pepper
> 1 teaspoon salt
> 8 pounds pork spareribs, cut into serving size pieces
> 3½ cups barbecue sauce

1. In a small bowl, combine the first 10 ingredients. Rub over the ribs; cover and refrigerate overnight.
2. Place the ribs bone side down on a rack in a shallow roasting pan. Cover and bake at 350° for 1 hour; drain. Brush some of the barbecue sauce over the ribs. Bake, uncovered, for 30-45 minutes or until tender, basting occasionally with barbecue sauce.

No-Fuss Beef Roast

Jazz up your roast with convenient canned mushroom soup, tomatoes and just a few other ingredients. The gravy is tasty over a scoop of mashed potatoes.
—**JEANIE BEASLEY** TUPELO, MS

PREP: 10 MIN. • **COOK:** 6 HOURS
MAKES: 8 SERVINGS

> 1 boneless beef chuck roast (3 to 4 pounds)
> 1 can (14½ ounces) stewed tomatoes, cut up
> 1 can (10¾ ounces) condensed cream of mushroom soup, undiluted
> 1 envelope Lipton beefy onion soup mix
> ¼ cup cornstarch
> ½ cup cold water

1. Cut the roast in half. Transfer to a 5-qt. slow cooker. In a small bowl, combine the tomatoes, soup and soup mix; pour over the meat. Cover and cook on low for 6-8 hours or until meat is tender.
2. Remove meat to a serving platter; keep warm. Skim fat from cooking juices; transfer to a large saucepan. Bring the liquid to a boil. Combine cornstarch and cold water until smooth; stir into the pan. Bring to a boil; cook and stir for 2 minutes or until thickened. Serve with roast.

Rice-Stuffed Peppers

When we were expecting company, my mother often fixed her beefy stuffed peppers. The cheese sauce really sets them apart.

—**LISA EASLEY** LONGVIEW, TX

PREP: 40 MIN. • **BAKE:** 1 HOUR
MAKES: 8 SERVINGS

- 2 **pounds ground beef**
- 1 **medium onion, chopped**
- 1 **small green pepper, chopped**
- 2 **garlic cloves, minced**
- 1½ **teaspoons salt**
- ½ **teaspoon pepper**
- 3¾ **cup water**
- 1 **can (14½ ounces) diced tomatoes, undrained**
- 1 **can (10 ounces) diced tomatoes and green chilies, undrained**
- 1 **can (15 ounces) tomato sauce**
- 1 **tablespoon ground cumin**
- 3 **cups uncooked instant rice**
- 4 **medium green peppers**

CHEESE SAUCE

- 1½ **pounds process American cheese, cubed**
- 1 **can (10 ounces) diced tomatoes and green chilies, undrained**

1. In a Dutch oven, cook the beef, onion, chopped green pepper, garlic, salt and pepper over medium heat until the beef is no longer pink, breaking beef into crumbles; drain. Add water, tomatoes, tomato sauce and cumin. Bring to a boil. Reduce heat; simmer, uncovered, for 10 minutes.

2. Stir in rice; simmer, uncovered, for 5 minutes. Remove from the heat; cover and let stand for 5 minutes.

3. Remove the tops and seeds from the green peppers; cut in half widthwise. Place in a large pan of boiling water; boil for 4 minutes.

4. Drain the peppers and stuff with meat mixture. Place remaining meat mixture in an ungreased 13x9-in. baking dish; top with the stuffed peppers, pressing down gently. Cover; bake at 350° for 1 hour. In a saucepan, heat sauce ingredients until cheese is melted. Serve over peppers.

HASH IT OUT

For a hearty hash, cube leftover beef roast and combine it with sliced red potatoes and chopped onion in a skillet with a little olive oil, salt and pepper. Fry until the potatoes are tender.

—**ROBYN S.** RONALD, WA

Hearty New England Dinner

This favorite slow-cooker recipe came from one of my friends. At first, my husband was skeptical about a roast that wasn't made in the oven. But the horseradish gravy and old-fashioned goodness of this dinner won him over.

—**CLAIRE MCCOMBS** SAN DIEGO, CA

PREP: 20 MIN. • **COOK:** 7½ HOURS
MAKES: 6-8 SERVINGS

- 2 **medium carrots, sliced**
- 1 **medium onion, sliced**
- 1 **celery rib, sliced**
- 1 **boneless beef chuck roast (about 3 pounds)**
- 1 **teaspoon salt, divided**
- ¼ **teaspoon pepper**
- 1 **envelope onion soup mix**
- 2 **cups water**
- 1 **tablespoon white vinegar**
- 1 **bay leaf**
- ½ **small head cabbage, cut into wedges**
- 3 **tablespoons butter**
- 2 **tablespoons all-purpose flour**
- 1 **tablespoon dried minced onion**
- 2 **tablespoons prepared horseradish**

1. Place the carrots, onion and celery in a 5-qt. slow cooker. Cut the roast in half. Place the roast over vegetables; sprinkle with ½ teaspoon salt and pepper. Add onion soup mix, water, vinegar and bay leaf. Cover and cook on low for 7-9 hours
or until beef is tender.

2. Remove the beef and keep warm; discard bay leaf. Add the cabbage. Cover and cook on high for 30-40 minutes or until cabbage is tender.

3. Meanwhile, melt the butter in a small saucepan; stir in the flour and onion. Skim fat from the cooking liquid in the slow cooker. Add 1½ cups cooking liquid to the saucepan. Stir in horseradish and remaining salt; bring to a boil. Cook and stir for 2 minutes or until thickened and bubbly. Serve with the roast and vegetables.

Shepherd's Pie Twice-Baked Potatoes

This spin on stuffed potatoes makes a satisfying meal. Pair the spuds with a green side salad—satisfaction is guaranteed!

—CYNTHIA GERKEN NAPLES, FL

PREP: 1¾ HOURS • **BAKE:** 25 MIN.
MAKES: 6 SERVINGS

- 6 large russet potatoes
- 2 tablespoons olive oil
- 1 pound ground beef
- 1 medium onion, chopped
- 1 medium green pepper, chopped
- 1 medium sweet red pepper, chopped
- 4 garlic cloves, minced
- 1 package (16 ounces) frozen mixed vegetables
- 3 tablespoons Worcestershire sauce
- 1 tablespoon tomato paste
- 1 tablespoon steak seasoning
- ¼ teaspoon salt
- ⅛ teaspoon pepper
  Dash cayenne pepper
- 2 teaspoons paprika, divided
- ½ cup butter, cubed
- ¾ cup heavy whipping cream
- ¼ cup sour cream
- 1 cup shredded Monterey Jack cheese
- 1 cup shredded cheddar cheese
- ¼ cup shredded Parmesan cheese
- 2 tablespoons minced chives

TOPPINGS

- 1 teaspoon paprika
- ½ cup shredded cheddar cheese
- 1 tablespoon minced chives

1. Scrub and pierce potatoes; rub with oil. Bake at 375° for 1 hour or until tender.
2. In a large skillet, cook the beef, onion, peppers and garlic over medium heat until the beef is no longer pink, breaking the beef into crumbles; drain. Add the mixed vegetables, Worcestershire sauce, tomato paste, steak seasoning, salt, pepper, cayenne and 1 teaspoon paprika. Cook and stir until vegetables are tender.

3. When cool enough to handle, cut a thin slice off the top of each baked potato and discard. Scoop out the pulp, leaving thin shells.
4. In a large bowl, mash the pulp with the butter. Add the whipping cream, sour cream, cheeses and chives. Mash the potatoes until combined. Spoon 1 cup meat mixture into each potato shell; top with ½ cup potato mixture. Sprinkle with remaining paprika.
5. Place on a baking sheet. Bake at 375° for 20 minutes. Sprinkle with the cheddar cheese; bake 5 minutes longer or until melted. Sprinkle with chives.

Merlot Filet Mignon

Use just a handful of ingredients to prepare an extra-special entree for two. The rich sauce adds a touch of elegance.

—JAUNEEN HOSKING WATERFORD, WI

START TO FINISH: 20 MIN.
MAKES: 2 SERVINGS

- 2 beef tenderloin steaks (8 ounces each)
- 3 tablespoons butter, divided
- 1 tablespoon olive oil
- 1 cup merlot
- 2 tablespoons heavy whipping cream
- ⅛ teaspoon salt

1. In a small skillet, cook the steaks in 1 tablespoon butter and olive oil over medium heat for 4-6 minutes on each side or until meat reaches desired doneness (for medium-rare, a thermometer should read 145°; medium, 160°; well-done, 170°). Remove and keep warm.
2. In the same skillet, add the wine, stirring to loosen the browned bits from the pan. Bring to a boil; cook until the liquid is reduced to ¼ cup. Add the heavy whipping cream, salt and remaining butter; bring to a boil. Cook and stir for 1-2 minutes or until slightly thickened and butter is melted. Serve with steaks.

Meatball Pie

As a child growing up on a farm, I took part in 4-H Club cooking activities. I still love to serve classic, wholesome recipes like my from-scratch meatball and veggie pie.

—SUSAN KEITH FORT PLAIN, NY

PREP: 30 MIN. • **BAKE:** 45 MIN. + STANDING
MAKES: 6 SERVINGS

- 1 **pound ground beef**
- ¾ **cup soft bread crumbs**
- ¼ **cup chopped onion**
- 2 **tablespoons minced fresh parsley**
- 1 **teaspoon salt**
- ½ **teaspoon dried marjoram**
- ⅛ **teaspoon pepper**
- ¼ **cup milk**
- 1 **large egg, lightly beaten**
- 1 **can (14½ ounces) stewed tomatoes**
- 1 **tablespoon cornstarch**
- 2 **teaspoons beef bouillon granules**
- 1 **cup frozen peas**
- 1 **cup sliced carrots, cooked**

CRUST
- 2⅔ **cups all-purpose flour**
- ½ **teaspoon salt**
- 1 **cup shortening**
- 7 **to 8 tablespoons ice water**
  Half-and-half cream

1. In a large bowl, combine the first nine ingredients (the mixture will be soft). Divide into fourths; shape each portion into 12 small meatballs. Brown the meatballs, a few at a time, in a large skillet; drain and set aside.
2. Drain tomatoes, reserving liquid. Combine liquid with cornstarch; pour into skillet. Add tomatoes and bouillon; bring to a boil over medium heat, stirring constantly. Stir in peas and carrots. Remove from the heat and set aside.
3. Preheat oven to 400°. For crust, in a large bowl, combine flour and salt. Cut in shortening until mixture resembles coarse crumbs. Add the ice water, 1 tablespoon at a time,

tossing lightly with a fork. Transfer to a lightly floured surface. Knead gently to form a dough. (The mixture will be very crumbly at first, but will come together and form a dough as it's kneaded.) Divide dough in half.
4. Roll each half of dough between two pieces of lightly floured waxed paper to a ⅛-in.-thick circle. Remove the top piece of waxed paper from one pastry circle; invert onto a 10-in. pie plate. Remove the remaining waxed paper. Trim pastry even with the rim. Add the meatballs; spoon tomato mixture over top.
5. Remove top piece of waxed paper from remaining pastry circle; invert onto the pie. Remove remaining waxed paper. Trim, seal and flute edge. Cut slits in top; brush with cream.
6. Bake 45-50 minutes or until the crust is golden brown. Cover the edges loosely with foil during the last 10 minutes if needed to prevent overbrowning. Let stand 10 minutes before cutting.

Tangy Pork Chops

When my husband and I had our first child, this pork chop recipe was so convenient. I could start it during nap time, and we'd enjoy an easy but delicious dinner that night.

—KAROL HINES KITTY HAWK, NC

PREP: 15 MIN. • **COOK:** 5½ HOURS
MAKES: 4 SERVINGS

- 4 **bone-in pork loin chops**
- ½ **teaspoon salt, optional**
- ⅛ **teaspoon pepper**
- 2 **medium onions, chopped**
- 2 **celery ribs, chopped**
- 1 **large green pepper, sliced**
- 1 **can (14½ ounces) stewed tomatoes**
- ½ **cup ketchup**
- 2 **tablespoons cider vinegar**
- 2 **tablespoons brown sugar**
- 2 **tablespoons Worcestershire sauce**
- 1 **tablespoon lemon juice**
- 1 **teaspoon beef bouillon granules**
- 2 **tablespoons cornstarch**
- 2 **tablespoons cold water**
  Hot cooked rice, optional

1. Place the chops in a 3-qt. slow cooker; sprinkle with salt if desired and pepper. Add the onions, celery, green pepper and tomatoes. Combine the ketchup, vinegar, brown sugar, Worcestershire sauce, lemon juice and bouillon; pour over the vegetables. Cover and cook on low for 5-6 hours or until meat is tender.
2. Mix cornstarch and water until smooth; stir into liquid in slow cooker. Cover and cook on high for 30 minutes or until thickened. Serve with rice if desired.
PER SERVING *One serving (prepared with reduced-sodium bouillon and no-salt-added stewed tomatoes and ketchup; without salt and rice) equals 227 cal., 4 g fat (0 sat. fat), 37 mg chol., 183 mg sodium, 34 g carb., 0 fiber, 16 g pro.*
Diabetic Exchanges: *2 lean meat, 2 vegetable, 1 starch.*

Cola Barbecue Ribs

Too cold to fire up the grill? You can enjoy the smoky goodness of a summer barbecue all year long by preparing these tender ribs in your slow cooker.

—**KAREN SHUCK** EDGAR, NE

PREP: 10 MIN. • **COOK:** 9 HOURS
MAKES: 4 SERVINGS

  ¼ cup packed brown sugar
  2 garlic cloves, minced
  1 teaspoon salt
  ½ teaspoon pepper
  3 tablespoons liquid smoke, optional
  4 pounds pork spareribs, cut into serving-size pieces
  1 medium onion, sliced
  ½ cup cola
  1½ cups barbecue sauce

1. In a small bowl, combine the brown sugar, garlic, salt, pepper and, if desired, liquid smoke; rub over ribs.
2. Layer ribs and onion in a greased 5- or 6-qt. slow cooker; pour cola over ribs. Cover and cook on low for 8-10 hours or until the ribs are tender. Drain the liquid. Pour sauce over ribs and cook 1 hour longer.

Festive Glazed Ham

For as long as I can remember, my favorite room has been the kitchen. Once when my parents were visiting, I cooked a Sunday ham with this glaze. I've been doing it the same way ever since.

—**BECKY MAGEE** CHANDLER, AZ

PREP: 10 MIN. + MARINATING • **BAKE:** 2 HOURS
MAKES: 10-16 SERVINGS

  1 bone-in fully cooked ham (5 to 8 pounds)
  1½ cups orange juice
  1¼ cups packed brown sugar
  1 tablespoon grated orange peel
  1 teaspoon ground mustard
  ¼ teaspoon ground cloves

1. Score the surface of the ham, making diamond shapes ½ in. deep. Place in a large baking dish.
2. In a bowl, mix the remaining ingredients; pour over the ham. Cover and refrigerate overnight, turning the ham occasionally.
3. Reserving the glaze, remove ham to a rack in a shallow roasting pan. Insert meat thermometer. Bake, uncovered, at 325° until thermometer registers 140° about 2-4 hours, brushing occasionally with glaze.

Chipotle-Honey Grilled T-Bones

Want to kick things up a notch on the grill? Here's the steak for you! The marinade makes T-bones absolutely mouthwatering. My husband even makes this recipe in a Dutch oven, and the meat just sizzles.

—DONNA GOUTERMONT SEQUIM, WA

PREP: 20 MIN. + MARINATING • **GRILL:** 10 MIN.
MAKES: 4 SERVINGS

- ½ cup minced fresh cilantro
- ½ cup lime juice
- ½ cup honey
- 2 tablespoons adobo sauce
- 1 tablespoon chopped chipotle pepper in adobo sauce
- 3 garlic cloves, minced
- 1 teaspoon salt
- 1 teaspoon ground cumin
- ½ teaspoon ground allspice
- ½ teaspoon pepper
- ¼ teaspoon Dijon mustard
- 4 beef T-bone steaks (12 ounces each)

1. In a small bowl, combine the first 11 ingredients. Pour ½ cup marinade into a large resealable plastic bag. Add the steaks; seal the bag and turn to coat. Refrigerate for up to 1 hour. Cover and refrigerate remaining marinade.

2. Drain and discard marinade. Grill steaks, covered, over medium heat or broil 4 in. from the heat for 5-6 minutes on each side or until the meat reaches the desired doneness (for medium-rare, a meat thermometer should read 145°; medium, 160°; well-done, 170°), basting occasionally with ½ cup reserved marinade. Serve with remaining marinade.

Tater Tot Casseroles

With ground beef, cheese and plenty of Tater Tots, this homey casserole is a sure crowd-pleaser. Cayenne pepper and hot Italian sausage give it an extra punch of flavor.

—RYAN JONES CHILLICOTHE, IL

PREP: 25 MIN. • **BAKE:** 45 MIN.
MAKES: 2 CASSEROLES (6 SERVINGS EACH)

- ¾ pound bulk hot Italian sausage
- ¾ pound lean ground beef (90% lean)
- 1 small onion, chopped
- 2 cans (10¾ ounces each) condensed cream of celery soup, undiluted
- 2 cups frozen cut green beans, thawed
- 1 can (15¼ ounces) whole kernel corn, drained
- 2 cups (8 ounces) shredded Colby-Monterey Jack cheese, divided
- ½ cup 2% milk
- 1 teaspoon garlic powder
- ¼ teaspoon seasoned salt
- ¼ to ½ teaspoon cayenne pepper
- 1 package (32 ounces) frozen Tater Tots

1. In a Dutch oven, cook the sausage, beef and onion over medium heat until meat is no longer pink, breaking meat into crumbles; drain. Add soup, beans, corn, 1 cup cheese, milk, garlic powder, seasoned salt and cayenne. Transfer to two greased 11x7-in. baking dishes. Top with Tater Tots; sprinkle with remaining cheese.

2. Cover and freeze one casserole for up to 3 months. Cover and bake the remaining casserole at 350° for 40 minutes. Uncover and bake 5-10 minutes longer or until bubbly.

TO USE FROZEN CASSEROLE *Thaw in the refrigerator overnight. Remove from the refrigerator 30 minutes before baking. Cover and bake at 350° for 50 minutes. Uncover and bake 5-10 minutes longer or until bubbly.*

Sizzling Ancho Ribeyes

My family loves to add Southwestern flavor to all kinds of foods, including these simple ribeyes from the grill. You won't want to skip the delectable chipotle butter.

—ANGELA SPENGLER TAMPA, FL

START TO FINISH: 25 MIN.
MAKES: 6 SERVINGS

- 4 **teaspoons salt**
- 4 **teaspoons ground ancho chili pepper**
- 1 **teaspoon pepper**
- 6 **beef ribeye steaks (¾ pound each)**
- 6 **tablespoons butter, softened**
- 6 **chipotle peppers in adobo sauce**

1. In a small bowl, combine the salt, ancho chili pepper and pepper; rub over the steaks. In another small bowl, beat the butter and chipotle peppers until blended.

2. Grill steaks, covered, over medium heat or broil 4 in. from the heat for 5-7 minutes on each side or until the meat reaches desired doneness (for medium-rare, a thermometer should read 145°; medium, 160°; well-done, 170°). Serve with chipotle butter.

SAY CHIPOTLE

A chipotle is a dried jalapeno pepper that has a smoky, slightly sweet, lightly fruity flavor. With a heat level of mild to medium, it's often used for sauces, soups (such as chili) and stews. Canned chipotles in adobo sauce have a spicy flavor and are available in the ethnic food aisle of most grocery stores.

Burrito Pie

Layer after layer of meat sauce, cheese and flour tortillas create an irresistible Mexican dish people of all ages dig in to. The recipe makes two casseroles, so you can eat one tonight and freeze one for an easy meal another time.

—**RENEE STARRET** BENTON, LA

PREP: 40 MIN. • **BAKE:** 30 MIN.
MAKES: 2 CASSEROLES (6 SERVINGS EACH)

- 2 **pounds ground beef**
- 1 **medium onion, chopped**
- 2 **garlic cloves, minced**
- 2 **cans (15 ounces each) Ranch Style beans (pinto beans in seasoned tomato sauce)**
- 1 **bottle (16 ounces) taco sauce**
- 1 **can (10 ounces) diced tomatoes and green chilies, undrained**
- 1 **can (4 ounces) chopped green chilies**
- 1 **can (3.8 ounces) sliced ripe olives, drained**
- 12 **flour tortillas (8 inches), halved**
- 4 **cups (16 ounces) shredded Colby-Monterey Jack cheese**

1. In a large skillet, cook beef and onion over medium heat until meat is no longer pink, breaking meat into crumbles. Add garlic; cook 1 minute longer. Drain. Stir in beans, taco sauce, tomatoes, green chilies and ripe olives. Bring to a boil. Reduce heat; simmer, uncovered, for 20-25 minutes or until slightly thickened.

2. Spread 1 cup mixture in each of two greased 11x7-in. baking dishes. Layer with 4 tortilla halves, 1 cup mixture and ⅔ cup cheese. Repeat twice.

3. Cover and freeze one casserole for up to 3 months. Cover and bake the remaining casserole at 350° for 20 minutes. Uncover and bake 10-15 minutes longer or until bubbly and cheese is melted. Let stand for 5 minutes before serving.

TO USE FROZEN CASSEROLE *Thaw in refrigerator overnight. Remove from refrigerator 30 minutes before baking. Cover and bake at 350° for 25 minutes. Uncover; bake 10-15 minutes longer or until bubbly and cheese is melted. Let stand for 5 minutes before serving.*

Sweet and Savory Pulled Beef Dinner

This saucy pulled beef is great served over egg noodles. Or pile it on your favorite hard rolls for casual party sandwiches.

—**PATTY MANOCCHI** GLENVILLE, NY

PREP: 25 MIN. • **COOK:** 6 HOURS
MAKES: 6 SERVINGS

- 1 **teaspoon salt**
- 1 **teaspoon ground mustard**
- 1 **teaspoon barbecue seasoning**
- 1 **teaspoon paprika**
- 1 **teaspoon chili powder**
- ½ **teaspoon pepper**
- 1 **boneless beef chuck roast (3 pounds)**
- 3 **tablespoons olive oil**
- 1 **large onion, halved and sliced**
- 1 **large sweet red pepper, sliced**

SAUCE
- 1 **can (8 ounces) tomato sauce**
- ⅓ **cup packed brown sugar**
- 3 **tablespoons honey**
- 2 **tablespoons Dijon mustard**
- 2 **tablespoons Worcestershire sauce**
- 2 **tablespoons soy sauce**
- 5 **garlic cloves, minced**
- 4 **teaspoons balsamic vinegar**
- ¾ **teaspoon salt**
  Cooked egg noodles

1. Combine the first six ingredients. Cut roast in half; rub with seasonings. In a large skillet, brown the beef in olive oil on all sides. Transfer to a 4- or 5-qt. slow cooker. Top with the onion and red pepper.

2. In a small bowl, combine the tomato sauce, brown sugar, honey, mustard, Worcestershire sauce, soy sauce, garlic, balsamic vinegar and salt; pour over vegetables. Cover and cook on low for 6-8 hours or until the meat is tender.

3. Remove the roast; cool slightly. Strain cooking juices, reserving the vegetables and 1¼ cups juices; skim fat from the reserved juices. Shred the beef with two forks and return to the slow cooker. Stir in the reserved vegetables and cooking juices; heat through. Serve with egg noodles.

Brown Bag Burritos

This recipe made it past the pickiest taste testers I know: my kids! They always say they won't eat beans, but they love these plump burritos, which I can easily freeze, pull out and microwave.

—**MINDY CULVER** POST FALLS, ID

PREP: 35 MIN. + FREEZING • **COOK:** 5 MIN./BATCH
MAKES: 16 SERVINGS

- 2 **pounds ground beef**
- 2 **cans (16 ounces each) refried beans**
- 3 **cups (12 ounces) shredded Mexican cheese blend or cheddar cheese**
- 1⅓ **cups enchilada sauce**
- ½ **cup water**
- ⅓ **cup chopped onion**
- 2 **tablespoons chili powder**
- 1 **tablespoon garlic powder**
- 2 **teaspoons dried oregano**
- 1 **teaspoon salt**
- 16 **flour tortillas (10 inches), warmed**
  Optional toppings: shredded Mexican cheese blend, sour cream, shredded lettuce, chopped tomatoes and sliced ripe olives

1. In a Dutch oven, cook the beef over medium heat until no longer pink, breaking into crumbles; drain. Return to pan; add refried beans, cheese, enchilada sauce, water, onion and seasonings. Bring to a boil. Reduce heat; cover and simmer for 10 minutes.

2. Spoon ½ cup filling off center on each tortilla. Fold sides and end over filling and roll up.

FREEZE OPTION *Wrap individually in paper towels, then foil. Transfer to a resealable plastic bag. May be frozen for up to 2 months. To use, unwrap foil. Place the paper towel-wrapped burritos on a microwave-safe plate. Microwave on high for 3-4 minutes or until heated through. Serve with toppings of your choice.*

NOTE *This recipe was tested in a 1,100-watt microwave.*

Zucchini Pizza Casserole

My husband has a hearty appetite, our children never get tired of pizza flavors, and I grow lots of zucchini. This beefy, cheesy casserole has all of those things covered!

—**LYNN BERNSTETTER** WHITE BEAR LAKE, MN

PREP: 20 MIN. • **BAKE:** 40 MIN.
MAKES: 6-8 SERVINGS

- 4 **cups shredded unpeeled zucchini**
- ½ **teaspoon salt**
- 2 **large eggs**
- ½ **cup grated Parmesan cheese**
- 2 **cups (8 ounces) shredded part-skim mozzarella cheese, divided**
- 1 **cup (4 ounces) shredded cheddar cheese, divided**
- 1 **pound ground beef**
- ½ **cup chopped onion**
- 1 **can (15 ounces) Italian tomato sauce**
- 1 **medium green pepper, chopped**

1. Place zucchini in strainer; sprinkle with salt. Let stand for 10 minutes. Squeeze out moisture.

2. Combine the zucchini with the eggs, Parmesan and half of the mozzarella and cheddar cheeses. Press into a greased 13x9-in. baking dish.

3. Bake, uncovered, at 400° for 20 minutes. Meanwhile, cook the beef and onion over medium heat until the meat is no longer pink, breaking the meat into crumbles; drain. Add tomato sauce; spoon over zucchini mixture.

4. Sprinkle with the remaining cheeses; add green pepper. Bake 20 minutes longer or until heated through.

FREEZE OPTION *Cool the baked casserole; cover and freeze. To use, partially thaw in the refrigerator overnight. Remove from the refrigerator 30 minutes before baking. Preheat the oven to 350°. Unwrap the casserole; reheat on a lower oven rack until heated through and a thermometer inserted in the center reads 165°.*

BBQ Brisket Flatbread Pizzas

Preparing a beef brisket pizza takes a little extra time, but it's so worth it when you take that first rich, smoky, juicy bite.

—**AARON REYNOLDS** FOX RIVER GROVE, IL

PREP: 3 HOURS + MARINATING • **GRILL:** 20 MIN.
MAKES: 2 FLATBREAD PIZZAS (6 SLICES EACH)

    2   cups barbecue sauce, divided
    ½   cup cider vinegar
    ½   cup chopped green onions, divided
    ½   cup minced fresh cilantro, divided
    2   pounds fresh beef brisket
    1   teaspoon salt
    1   teaspoon pepper
    1   large red onion, cut into thick slices
    1   teaspoon olive oil
    2   cups (8 ounces) shredded smoked Gouda cheese
DOUGH
  2¾ to 3¼ cups all-purpose flour
    1   tablespoon sugar
    3   teaspoons salt
    1   package (¼ ounce) quick-rise yeast
  1¼   cups warm water (120° to 130°)
    2   tablespoons olive oil

1. In a large resealable plastic bag, combine 1 cup barbecue sauce, vinegar, ¼ cup green onions and ¼ cup cilantro. Sprinkle brisket with salt and pepper; add to bag. Seal bag and turn to coat. Refrigerate for 8 hours or overnight.
2. Drain and discard marinade. Prepare grill for indirect heat, using a drip pan. Place brisket over pan; grill, covered, over indirect low heat for 1 hour. Add 10 briquettes to coals. Cover and grill about 1¼ hours longer or until the meat is fork-tender, adding more briquettes if needed. When cool enough to handle, shred meat with two forks; set aside.
3. Meanwhile, in a large bowl, combine 2¾ cups flour, sugar, salt and yeast. Add the water and oil; beat just until smooth. Stir in enough remaining flour to form a soft dough (dough will be sticky).
4. Turn onto a floured surface; knead until smooth and elastic, about 6-8 minutes. Place in a greased bowl, turning once to grease the top. Cover and let rise in a warm place until doubled, about 1 hour. Punch dough down; divide into two portions. Roll each into a 15-in. circle.
5. Grill each circle of pizza dough, covered, over medium heat for 1-2 minutes on one side or until lightly browned. Set aside. Brush the red onion slices with olive oil; grill for 4-5 minutes or until tender, turning once. Remove from the heat; chop and set aside.
6. Spread the grilled side of each crust with the remaining barbecue sauce. Top with the shredded brisket, red onion, cheese and remaining green onions and cilantro.
7. Place a pizza on the grill; cover and cook over indirect medium heat for 8-10 minutes or until the crust is lightly browned and the cheese is melted. Rotate the pizza halfway through cooking to ensure an evenly browned crust. Repeat with remaining pizza.

Pulled Pork Taters

This slow-cooker recipe is about as hearty as it gets! It's part meat, part potatoes and completely satisfying.

—**SHANNON HARRIS** TYLER, TX

PREP: 15 MIN. • **COOK:** 6 HOURS
MAKES: 6 SERVINGS

    1   boneless pork loin roast (2 to 3 pounds)
    1   medium onion, chopped
    1   cup ketchup
    1   cup root beer
    ¼   cup cider vinegar
    2   tablespoons Worcestershire sauce
    1   tablespoon Louisiana-style hot sauce
    2   teaspoons salt
    2   teaspoons pepper
    1   teaspoon ground mustard
    6   large potatoes
    1   tablespoon cornstarch
    1   tablespoon cold water
    6   tablespoons butter
  1½   cups (6 ounces) shredded cheddar cheese
    6   tablespoons sour cream

1. Place the roast in a 5-qt. slow cooker. Top with the onion. Combine ketchup, root beer, vinegar, Worcestershire sauce, hot sauce, salt, pepper and mustard; pour over top. Cover and cook on low for 6-8 hours or until meat is tender.
2. Meanwhile, scrub and pierce potatoes. Bake at 400° for 50-55 minutes or until tender.
3. Remove the pork; shred the meat with two forks. Skim fat from cooking juices; transfer to a large saucepan. Bring the liquid to a boil. Combine cornstarch and water until smooth; gradually stir into the pan. Bring to a boil; cook and stir for 2 minutes or until thickened. Return meat to cooking juices; heat through.
4. With a sharp knife, cut an "X" in each potato; fluff with a fork. Top each with butter and pork mixture; sprinkle with cheese. Top with sour cream.

Mushroom Beef Stew

I like to ladle my mushroom-packed beef stew over a big bowlful of egg noodles, then sprinkle on crumbled blue cheese just before serving to add a burst of flavor.

—NANCY LATULIPPE SIMCOE, ON

PREP: 45 MIN. • **COOK:** 1½ HOURS
MAKES: 9 SERVINGS

 1 **carton (32 ounces) beef broth**
 1 **ounce dried mixed mushrooms**
 ¼ **cup all-purpose flour**
 1 **teaspoon salt**
 1 **teaspoon pepper**
 1 **boneless beef chuck roast (2 pounds), cubed**
 3 **tablespoons canola oil**
 1 **pound whole baby portobello mushrooms**
 5 **medium carrots, chopped**
 1 **large onion, chopped**
 3 **garlic cloves, minced**
 3 **teaspoons minced fresh rosemary or 1 teaspoon dried rosemary, crushed**

ADDITIONAL INGREDIENTS
 2 **tablespoons cornstarch**
 2 **tablespoons cold water**
    Hot cooked egg noodles, optional
 ¼ **cup crumbled blue cheese**

1. Bring the beef broth and dried mushrooms to a boil in a large saucepan. Remove from heat; let stand 15-20 minutes or until the mushrooms are softened. Drain mushrooms, reserving liquid; finely chop mushrooms. Set aside.
2. Combine the flour, salt and pepper in a large resealable plastic bag; set aside 1 tablespoon for sauce. Add the beef, a few pieces at a time, to the remaining flour mixture and shake to coat.
3. Brown the beef in oil in batches in a Dutch oven. Add the portobello mushrooms, carrots and onion; saute until the onion is tender. Add the garlic, rosemary and rehydrated mushrooms; cook 1 minute. Stir in reserved flour mixture until blended; gradually add mushroom broth.

4. Bring to a boil. Reduce the heat; cover and simmer 1½-2 hours or until beef is tender. Bring stew to a boil. Combine the cornstarch and cold water until smooth; gradually stir into the pan. Return to a boil; cook and stir 2 minutes or until thickened. Serve with noodles if desired; top with cheese.
FREEZE OPTION *Freeze the cooled stew in freezer containers for up to 6 months. To use, thaw in the refrigerator overnight. Place in a Dutch oven; reheat. Serve with noodles if desired; top with blue cheese.*

Pork with Blueberry Herb Sauce

Here's a deliciously different way to use blueberries. The tangy, sweet-savory sauce is a wonderful way to dress up pork chops and would be good with chicken, too.

—LIBBY WALP CHICAGO, IL

PREP: 15 MIN. • **COOK:** 20 MIN.
MAKES: 4 SERVINGS

 1 **garlic clove, minced**
 1 **teaspoon pepper**
 ½ **teaspoon salt**
 ⅛ **teaspoon cayenne pepper**
 4 **boneless pork loin chops (6 ounces each)**
 2 **cups fresh blueberries**
 ¼ **cup packed brown sugar**
 2 **tablespoons minced fresh parsley**
 1 **tablespoon balsamic vinegar**
 2 **teaspoons butter**
 1 **teaspoon minced fresh thyme or ¼ teaspoon dried thyme**
 1 **teaspoon fresh sage or ¼ teaspoon dried sage leaves**

1. In a small bowl, combine garlic, pepper, salt and cayenne; sprinkle over pork chops.
2. In a large ovenproof skillet coated with cooking spray, brown chops. Bake, uncovered, at 350° for 10-15 minutes or until a thermometer reads 160°. Remove chops; keep warm.
3. Add the remaining ingredients to the pan. Cook and stir over medium heat until thickened, about 8 minutes. Serve with pork.
PER SERVING *1 pork chop with ¼ cup sauce equals 343 cal., 12 g fat (5 g sat. fat), 87 mg chol., 364 mg sodium, 25 g carb., 2 g fiber, 33 g pro.* **Diabetic Exchanges:** *5 lean meat, 1 starch, ½ fruit.*

Peppered Fillets with Horseradish Cream Sauce

My quick tenderloin recipe is a family favorite. We love the creamy sauce, which has the perfect blend of horseradish and Dijon mustard.

—MARIE RIZZIO INTERLOCHEN, MI

START TO FINISH: 25 MIN.
MAKES: 4 SERVINGS

- 4 **beef tenderloin steaks (6 ounces each)**
- 1 **tablespoon plus ⅛ teaspoon coarsely ground pepper, divided**
- ¾ **teaspoon salt, divided**
- 5 **tablespoons butter, divided**
- 2 **teaspoons all-purpose flour**
- ⅔ **cup heavy whipping cream**
- 2 **tablespoons horseradish**
- 1 **teaspoon Dijon mustard**

1. Sprinkle steaks with 1 tablespoon pepper and ½ teaspoon salt. In a large skillet over medium heat, cook steaks in 1 tablespoon butter for 4-5 minutes on each side or until the meat reaches desired doneness (for medium-rare, a thermometer should read 145°; medium, 160°; well-done, 170°).

2. Meanwhile, in a small saucepan, melt remaining butter. Stir in the flour and remaining salt and pepper until smooth; gradually add cream. Bring to a boil; cook and stir for 1-2 minutes or until thickened. Stir in horseradish and mustard. Serve with steaks.

TEST FOR DONENESS

To test tenderloin steaks for doneness, insert an instant-read thermometer horizontally from the side, making sure the reading is from the center of the meat.

Company Lasagna

This is my go-to for guests. It lets me focus on visiting without stressing about dinner.

—RENEE VAUGHAN GALENA, OH

PREP: 40 MIN. + CHILLING
BAKE: 50 MIN. + STANDING
MAKES: 12 SERVINGS

- 1 **pound bulk pork sausage**
- 2 **cans (one 28 ounces, one 14½ ounces) stewed tomatoes, undrained**
- 1 **can (6 ounces) tomato paste**
- 2 **tablespoons dried oregano**
- 4 **garlic cloves, minced**
- ¼ **teaspoon salt**
- ¼ **teaspoon pepper**
- 4 **cups (16 ounces) shredded part-skim mozzarella cheese, divided**
- 3 **cups (24 ounces) 2% cottage cheese**
- 1 **cup grated Parmesan cheese**
- 2 **large eggs, lightly beaten**
- 3 **tablespoons dried parsley flakes**
- 12 **no-cook lasagna noodles**

1. In a Dutch oven, cook the pork sausage over medium heat until no longer pink, breaking into crumbles; drain. Stir in the stewed tomatoes, tomato paste, oregano, garlic, salt and pepper. Bring to a boil. Reduce the heat; simmer, uncovered, for 15-20 minutes or until thickened.

2. Meanwhile, in a large bowl, combine 2 cups mozzarella cheese, cottage cheese, Parmesan cheese, eggs and dried parsley.

3. Spread 1 cup meat mixture into a greased 13x9-in. baking dish. Layer with three no-cook lasagna noodles, 1¼ cups meat mixture and 1 cup cheese mixture. Repeat three times. Top with the remaining mozzarella cheese. Cover and refrigerate for 8 hours or overnight.

4. Remove from the refrigerator 30 minutes before baking. Cover and bake at 350° for 30 minutes. Uncover and bake 20-25 minutes longer or until bubbly and cheese is melted. Let stand for 10 minutes before cutting.

Sizzling Tex-Mex Fajitas

We're fans of garlic, so I did some experimenting and came up with a garlicky marinade for our summer fajitas. It works in eight hours, but I think the steak is even better when marinated overnight. Try substituting chicken breasts for the steak, too.

—**KARYN "KIKI" POWER** ARLINGTON, TX

PREP: 30 MIN. + MARINATING • **GRILL:** 10 MIN.
MAKES: 6 SERVINGS

- ⅓ cup beef broth
- ¼ cup lime juice
- 3 tablespoons olive oil, divided
- 4 garlic cloves, minced
- 2 teaspoons Worcestershire sauce
- 1 teaspoon salt
- 1 envelope savory herb with garlic soup mix, divided
- 1 teaspoon Dijon mustard
- ½ teaspoon pepper
- ½ teaspoon cayenne pepper
- ½ teaspoon liquid smoke, optional
- 2 pounds beef skirt steak, cut into 4- to 6-inch portions
- 2 large onions, sliced
- 1 medium green pepper, sliced
- 1 medium sweet yellow pepper, sliced
- 12 flour tortillas (8 inches)
  Salsa, shredded cheese, guacamole and sour cream, optional

1. In a large resealable plastic bag, combine the beef broth, lime juice, 1 tablespoon oil, garlic, Worcestershire sauce, salt, 1 teaspoon soup mix, mustard, pepper, cayenne and Liquid Smoke if desired. Add the steaks; seal bag and turn to coat. Refrigerate for 8 hours or overnight.
2. In a large bowl, combine the onions, green pepper, yellow pepper and remaining oil and soup mix. Place half the mixture on each of two double thicknesses of heavy-duty foil (about 12 in. square). Fold the foil around the vegetables and seal tightly.
3. Drain the beef and discard the marinade. Grill steaks

and vegetable packets, covered, over medium heat for 10-13 minutes or until meat reaches desired doneness (for medium-rare, a thermometer should read 145°; medium, 160°; well-done, 170°) and vegetables are tender, turning steaks once.
4. Open packets carefully to allow steam to escape. Thinly slice steaks; place beef and vegetables on tortillas. Serve with salsa, cheese, guacamole and sour cream if desired.

Asparagus Puff Ring

Every spring when I prepare this with the season's asparagus, I fall in love with it all over again. The savory ham and veggies are piled high in a cheesy cream puff shell.

—**SHIRLEY DE LANGE** BYRON CENTER, MI

PREP: 20 MIN. • **BAKE:** 35 MIN.
MAKES: 6 SERVINGS

- ¾ cup water
- 6 tablespoons butter
- ¾ cup all-purpose flour
- ½ teaspoon salt
- 3 large eggs
- ¼ cup grated Parmesan cheese, divided

FILLING

- 1 pound fresh asparagus, cut into 1-inch pieces
- ¼ cup diced onion
- 2 tablespoons butter
- 2 tablespoons all-purpose flour
- ½ teaspoon salt
- ¼ teaspoon pepper
- 1½ cups milk
- ½ cup shredded Swiss cheese
- 2 tablespoons grated Parmesan cheese
- 2 cups diced fully cooked ham

1. In a large saucepan over medium heat, bring the water and butter to a boil. Add flour and salt all at once; stir until a smooth ball forms. Remove from the heat; let stand for 5 minutes. Add eggs, one at a time, beating well after each; beat until smooth. Stir in 3 tablespoons Parmesan cheese.
2. Using ¼ cupfuls of dough, form a ring around the sides of a greased 10-in. quiche pan or pie plate (mounds should touch). Top with the remaining Parmesan cheese. Bake at 400° for 35 minutes.
3. Meanwhile, cook asparagus in a small amount of water for 3-4 minutes or until crisp-tender; drain.
4. In a large saucepan, saute the onion in butter until tender. Stir in the flour, salt and pepper until blended. Gradually add milk; bring to a boil over medium heat, stirring constantly. Reduce heat; add cheeses and stir until melted.
5. Stir in the diced ham and asparagus; spoon into the ring. Serve immediately.

Lentil & Chicken Sausage Stew, page 118

134

121

138

Poultry Entrees

With endless recipe options for every palate, **versatile chicken and turkey** guarantee a winning dinner for the whole family. Just page through this packed chapter and **see for yourself!**

Three-Cheese & Pepper Penne

This cheesy pasta comes together in a snap. The recipe makes two casseroles—one to eat and one to freeze or share.

—JASEY MCBURNETT ROCK SPRINGS, WY

PREP: 40 MIN. • **BAKE:** 30 MIN.
MAKES: 2 CASSEROLES (5 SERVINGS EACH)

- 1 package (16 ounces) penne pasta
- 1½ pounds boneless skinless chicken breasts, cut into ½-inch pieces
- 1¼ teaspoons salt
- ½ teaspoon pepper
- 3 teaspoons olive oil, divided
- 1 pound sliced fresh mushrooms
- 4 garlic cloves, minced
- ¼ cup butter, cubed
- ½ cup all-purpose flour
- 4 cups 2% milk
- 2 jars (7 ounces each) roasted sweet red peppers, drained and chopped
- 2 cups (8 ounces) shredded mozzarella and provolone cheese
- 2 cups grated Parmesan cheese, divided

1. Cook pasta according to package directions. Meanwhile, sprinkle the chicken with salt and pepper. In a large skillet, saute chicken in 1 teaspoon olive oil until no longer pink. Remove from the skillet. In same skillet, saute mushrooms in remaining oil until tender.

2. In a Dutch oven, saute the garlic in butter for 1 minute. Stir in the flour until blended; gradually add milk. Bring to a boil; cook and stir for 1-2 minutes or until thickened. Stir in the red peppers, mozzarella and provolone cheese, ½ cup Parmesan cheese, mushrooms and chicken.

3. Drain pasta; stir into sauce. Divide between two greased 8-in. square baking dishes. Sprinkle each with remaining Parmesan cheese. Cover and freeze one casserole for up to 3 months. Cover and bake the remaining casserole at 350° for 30-35 minutes or until bubbly.

TO USE FROZEN CASSEROLE *Thaw in the refrigerator overnight. Remove from the refrigerator 30 minutes before baking. Cover and bake at 350° for 60-70 minutes or until bubbly, stirring once.*

Stuffing Crust Turkey Potpie

Here's a wonderful stick-to-your-ribs dinner. The filling is thicker than that of traditional potpies, so it slices well for easy serving. Prebaking the crust gives it crunch.

—TAMARA FURDA NAPERVILLE, IL

PREP: 35 MIN. • **BAKE:** 20 MIN.
MAKES: 6 SERVINGS

- 2 cups cooked corn bread stuffing
- 3 to 4 tablespoons chicken broth
- ¼ cup cream cheese, softened
- ½ cup turkey gravy
- 2 cups cubed cooked turkey
- 1 cup frozen broccoli florets, thawed
- ½ cup shredded Swiss cheese
- ¼ teaspoon salt
- ¼ teaspoon pepper
- 2 cups mashed potatoes
- ¼ cup half-and-half cream
- 2 tablespoons butter, melted
- ½ cup French-fried onions, optional

1. In a small bowl, combine stuffing and enough broth to reach desired moistness; press onto the bottom and up the sides of a greased 9-in. deep-dish pie plate. Bake at 350° for 10-15 minutes or until lightly browned.

2. In a large bowl, beat the cream cheese and gravy until smooth. Stir in the turkey, broccoli, Swiss cheese, salt and pepper. Spoon over crust.

3. In a small bowl, combine potatoes and cream; spread over turkey mixture. Drizzle with butter; sprinkle with onions if desired. Bake 20-25 minutes or until heated through and lightly browned.

Roasted Chicken with Lemon Sauce

We like chicken cooked in all sorts of ways, but roasting it and adding a homemade lemon sauce is one of our favorites.

—GENEVA GARRISON JACKSONVILLE, FL

PREP: 20 MIN. • **BAKE:** 2 HOURS + STANDING
MAKES: 6 SERVINGS

- 1 roasting chicken (6 to 7 pounds)
- 1 medium lemon
- 1 garlic clove, minced
- ½ teaspoon salt
- ½ teaspoon pepper
- 6 medium carrots, cut into chunks
- 1 large onion, quartered

LEMON SAUCE

- ½ cup sugar
- 4½ teaspoons cornstarch
- 1 cup cold water
- 2 tablespoons lemon juice
- 2 tablespoons grated lemon peel
- 1 to 2 drops yellow food coloring, optional
- 1 green onion, thinly sliced

1. Preheat oven to 350°. Pat chicken dry. Cut lemon in half; squeeze the juice over chicken. Place lemon in the cavity. Rub garlic over chicken; sprinkle with salt and pepper.

2. Place chicken on a rack in a shallow roasting pan. Roast 2-2½ hours or until a thermometer inserted into thickest part of thigh reads 170°-175°, basting occasionally with pan juices and adding carrots and onion during the last hour. Cover loosely with foil if chicken browns too quickly.

3. Remove the chicken from oven; tent with foil. Let stand 15 minutes before carving.

4. Meanwhile, in a small saucepan, combine the sugar and cornstarch. Stir in cold water until smooth. Bring to a boil; cook and stir 2 minutes or until thickened. Remove from heat. Stir in lemon juice, peel and food coloring if desired.

5. Serve the sauce with chicken and vegetables. Sprinkle with green onion.

FREEZE OPTION *Cool the chicken, vegetables and sauce. Cut chicken into parts and freeze along with vegetables and sauce in freezer containers. To use, partially thaw in refrigerator overnight. Heat through slowly in a covered skillet until a thermometer inserted in chicken reads 165°, stirring occasionally and adding a little broth or water if necessary. Serve as directed.*

Tex-Mex Chicken with Black Beans & Rice

I came up with this dinner for my sister, who loves the ease and convenience of combining canned goods in a pot.

—ELIZABETH DUMONT BOULDER, CO

PREP: 15 MIN. • **COOK:** 7 HOURS
MAKES: 6 SERVINGS

- 6 chicken leg quarters, skin removed
- 1 envelope taco seasoning, divided
- 1 can (14½ ounces) Mexican diced tomatoes, undrained
- 1 can (10¾ ounces) condensed cream of chicken soup, undiluted
- 1 large onion, chopped
- 1 can (4 ounces) chopped green chilies
- 1 cup uncooked instant rice
- 1 cup canned black beans, rinsed and drained
- 1 container (8 ounces) sour cream
- 1 cup (4 ounces) shredded cheddar cheese
- 1½ cups crushed tortilla chips
  Minced fresh cilantro

1. Sprinkle the chicken with 1 tablespoon taco seasoning; transfer to a 5- or 6-qt. slow cooker. In a large bowl, combine the tomatoes, soup, onion, green chilies and remaining taco seasoning; pour over the chicken. Cover and cook on low for 7-9 hours or until chicken is tender.

2. Prepare rice according to package directions. Stir in the beans; heat through.

3. Remove chicken from cooking juices; stir sour cream into juices. Serve chicken with the rice mixture and sauce. Sprinkle servings with cheese, chips and cilantro.

Slow-Cooked Thai Peanut Chicken

Have a taste for Thai? Save the trip to an Asian restaurant and throw together a sensational entree in your kitchen.

—**BLAIR LONERGAN** ROCHELLE, VA

PREP: 25 MIN. • **COOK:** 4 HOURS
MAKES: 8 SERVINGS

- 1 **cup all-purpose flour**
- 8 **boneless skinless chicken thighs (about 2 pounds)**
- ¾ **cup creamy peanut butter**
- ½ **cup orange juice**
- ¼ **cup orange marmalade**
- 2 **tablespoons sesame oil**
- 2 **tablespoons soy sauce**
- 2 **tablespoons teriyaki sauce**
- 2 **tablespoons hoisin sauce**
- 1 **can (13.66 ounces) light coconut milk, divided**
- 1 **cup uncooked basmati rice**
- ¾ **cup water**
- ½ **cup chopped salted peanuts**

1. Place the flour in a large resealable plastic bag. Add the chicken, a few pieces at a time, and shake to coat. Transfer to a greased 4- or 5-qt. slow cooker.

2. In a small bowl, combine the peanut butter, orange juice, marmalade, oil, soy sauce, teriyaki sauce, hoisin sauce and ¾ cup coconut milk; pour over chicken. Cover and cook on low for 4-5 hours or until chicken is tender.

3. In a small saucepan, bring the rice, water and remaining coconut milk to a boil. Reduce the heat; cover and simmer for 15-20 minutes or until rice is tender. Fluff with a fork. Serve with chicken and sauce; sprinkle with peanuts.

Lentil & Chicken Sausage Stew

PREP: 15 MIN. • **COOK:** 8 HOURS
MAKES: 6 SERVINGS

- 1 **carton (32 ounces) reduced-sodium chicken broth**
- 1 **can (28 ounces) diced tomatoes, undrained**
- 3 **fully cooked spicy chicken sausage links (3 ounces each), cut into ½-inch slices**
- 1 **cup dried lentils, rinsed**
- 1 **medium onion, chopped**
- 1 **medium carrot, chopped**
- 1 **celery rib, chopped**
- 2 **garlic cloves, minced**
- ½ **teaspoon dried thyme**

In a 4- or 5-qt. slow cooker, combine all ingredients. Cover and cook on low for 8-10 hours or until lentils are tender.
PER SERVING *1½ cups equals 231 cal., 4 g fat (1 g sat. fat), 33 mg chol., 803 mg sodium, 31 g carb., 13 g fiber, 19 g pro.*
Diabetic Exchanges: *2 lean meat, 2 vegetable, 1 starch.*

> ❝Lentil & Chicken Sausage Stew will warm your family right down to their toes! Add corn bread or rolls on the side to soak up every last spoonful.❞
>
> —**JAN VALDEZ** CHICAGO, IL

Peanutty Asian Lettuce Wraps

This recipe packs an amazing amount of flavor into a fresh, healthy presentation. I usually serve it with extra hoisin.

—**MANDY RIVERS** LEXINGTON, SC

START TO FINISH: 30 MIN.
MAKES: 6 SERVINGS

- 1½ pounds lean ground turkey
- ½ cup shredded carrot
- 2 tablespoons minced fresh gingerroot
- 4 garlic cloves, minced
- 1 can (8 ounces) whole water chestnuts, drained and chopped
- 4 green onions, chopped
- ½ cup chopped fresh snow peas
- ⅓ cup reduced-sodium teriyaki sauce
- ¼ cup hoisin sauce
- 3 tablespoons creamy peanut butter
- 1 tablespoon rice vinegar
- 1 tablespoon sesame oil
- 12 Bibb lettuce leaves
  Additional hoisin sauce, optional

1. In a large skillet, cook the ground turkey and carrot over medium heat until the meat is no longer pink and the carrot is tender, breaking meat into crumbles; drain. Add ginger and garlic; cook 1 minute longer.
2. Stir in the chestnuts, onions, snow peas, teriyaki sauce, hoisin sauce, peanut butter, vinegar and oil; heat through. Divide among lettuce leaves; drizzle with additional hoisin sauce if desired. Fold lettuce over filling.
PER SERVING *2 wraps (calculated without additional hoisin sauce) equals 313 cal., 16 g fat (4 g sat. fat), 90 mg chol., 613 mg sodium, 18 g carb., 3 g fiber, 24 g pro.* **Diabetic Exchanges:** *3 lean meat, 2 vegetable, 2 fat, ½ starch.*

Mascarpone-Pesto Chicken Rolls

With spirals of rich mascarpone cheese and pesto, these golden brown roll-ups are nearly impossible to resist.

—**SHERRY LITTLE** SHERWOOD, AR

PREP: 20 MIN. • **BAKE:** 35 MIN.
MAKES: 4 SERVINGS

- 4 boneless skinless chicken breast halves (6 ounces each)
- ¾ teaspoon garlic salt
- ½ cup mascarpone cheese
- ¼ cup prepared pesto
- 1 large egg
- 2 teaspoons water
- 1 cup seasoned bread crumbs
- 8 teaspoons butter, melted, divided
- 8 ounces uncooked fettuccine
  Fresh basil leaves, optional

1. Flatten chicken to ¼-in. thickness; sprinkle with garlic salt. Combine the cheese and pesto; spread over chicken. Roll up each from a short side and secure with toothpicks.
2. In a shallow bowl, whisk the egg and water. Place bread crumbs in a separate shallow bowl. Dip the chicken in the egg mixture, then coat with crumbs. Place seam side down in a greased 11x7-in. baking dish. Drizzle with 4 teaspoons butter. Bake, uncovered, at 350° for 35-40 minutes or until a thermometer reads 170°. Discard toothpicks.
3. Meanwhile, cook the fettuccine according to package directions. Drain fettuccine; toss with remaining butter. Serve with chicken. Garnish with basil if desired.

One-Dish Moroccan Chicken

Spices work their magic on plain poultry in this change-of-pace dish. Dried fruit and couscous add to the exotic appeal.

—**KATHY MORGAN** RIDGEFIELD, WA

PREP: 20 MIN. • **COOK:** 6 HOURS
MAKES: 4 SERVINGS

- 4 medium carrots, sliced
- 2 large onions, halved and sliced
- 1 broiler/fryer chicken (3 to 4 pounds), cut up, skin removed
- ½ teaspoon salt
- ½ cup chopped dried apricots
- ½ cup raisins
- 1 can (14½ ounces) reduced-sodium chicken broth
- ¼ cup tomato paste
- 2 tablespoons all-purpose flour
- 2 tablespoons lemon juice
- 2 garlic cloves, minced
- 1½ teaspoons ground ginger
- 1½ teaspoons ground cumin
- 1 teaspoon ground cinnamon
- ¾ teaspoon pepper
  Hot cooked couscous

1. Place the carrots and onions in a greased 5-qt. slow cooker. Sprinkle the chicken with the salt; add to the slow cooker. Top with dried apricots and raisins. In a small bowl, whisk the chicken broth, tomato paste, flour, lemon juice, garlic and seasonings until blended; add to slow cooker.
2. Cook, covered, on low 6-7 hours or until the chicken is tender. Serve with couscous.

A LITTLE LEMON

I like to keep fresh-squeezed lemon juice on hand because it's such an easy way to add an extra burst of flavor to recipes. After juicing the lemons, I pour the juice into ice cube trays and pop them into the freezer. Then I defrost the cubes as needed to use in poultry recipes, desserts, iced tea and other dishes.

—**JUDY M.** SOUTH BEND, IN

Spicy Chicken and Rice

As a working mom with two kids, I don't have a lot of time for food prep during the week. My slow-cooked chicken dinner is easy to toss together in the morning and wonderful to come home to at night. Plus, my picky eaters gobble it up!

—**JESSICA COSTELLO** FITCHBURG, MA

PREP: 20 MIN. • **COOK:** 5½ HOURS
MAKES: 8 SERVINGS

- 1½ pounds boneless skinless chicken breast halves
- 2 cans (14½ ounces each) diced tomatoes with mild green chilies, undrained
- 2 medium green peppers, chopped
- 1 medium onion, chopped
- 1 garlic clove, minced
- 1 teaspoon smoked paprika
- ¾ teaspoon salt
- ½ teaspoon ground cumin
- ½ teaspoon ground chipotle pepper
- 6 cups cooked brown rice
- 1 can (15 ounces) black beans, rinsed and drained
- ½ cup shredded cheddar cheese
- ½ cup reduced-fat sour cream

1. Place chicken in a 4- or 5-qt. slow cooker. In a large bowl, combine the diced tomatoes, green peppers, onion, garlic, paprika, salt, cumin and chipotle pepper; pour over the chicken. Cover and cook on low for 5-6 hours or until chicken is tender.

2. Remove the chicken; cool slightly. Shred with two forks and return to the slow cooker. Stir in the brown rice and black beans; heat through. Garnish with shredded cheddar cheese and sour cream.

Chicken with Shallot Sauce

This flavorful main course doesn't take long to make but tastes like it simmered all day. Serve mashed potatoes and your favorite green vegetable on the side.

—**KATHY ANDERSON** ROCKFORD, IL

PREP: 10 MIN. • **COOK:** 50 MIN.
MAKES: 4 SERVINGS

- 6 bacon strips, chopped
- 1 broiler/fryer chicken (3 to 4 pounds), cut up
- ½ teaspoon salt
- ½ teaspoon pepper
- 10 shallots, thinly sliced
- 1 cup water
- 1 whole garlic bulb, cloves separated and peeled
- ½ cup balsamic vinegar

1. In a large skillet, cook the chopped bacon over medium heat until crisp. Remove to paper towels with a slotted spoon; drain, reserving 2 tablespoons of drippings.

2. Sprinkle the chicken with salt and pepper; brown in the bacon drippings. Remove and keep warm. Add shallots; cook and stir until tender. Stir in the water and garlic. Return the chicken to pan. Bring to a boil. Reduce heat; cover and simmer for 30-35 minutes or until a thermometer inserted into thigh reads 170°-175°.

3. Remove the chicken to a serving platter; keep warm. Skim fat from the cooking juices. Mash garlic; add the vinegar. Bring liquid to a boil; cook until slightly thickened. Spoon over chicken; sprinkle with reserved bacon.

Turkey Puffs with Cranberry Cabernet Sauce

Revitalize your leftover holiday turkey with caramelized onions, dried wild mushrooms and flavored cream cheese. Wrapped up in convenient puff pastry, the rich little bundles are elegant served with a tangy wine sauce for dipping.

—**SUZANNE CLARK** PHOENIX, AZ

PREP: 40 MIN. • **BAKE:** 20 MIN.
MAKES: 4 SERVINGS

- 1 **cup chicken broth**
- 1 **cup dried wild mushrooms**
- 1 **medium onion, thinly sliced**
- 2 **tablespoons butter**
- 1 **teaspoon minced fresh tarragon or ¼ teaspoon dried tarragon**
- ¼ **teaspoon salt**
- ¼ **teaspoon pepper**
- 1 **package (17.3 ounces) frozen puff pastry, thawed**
- 8 **ounces thinly sliced cooked turkey**
- ½ **cup spreadable chive and onion cream cheese**
- 1 **large egg, beaten**

SAUCE

- 1 **cup chicken broth**
- 1 **cup dry red wine or additional chicken broth**
- ½ **cup balsamic vinegar**
- ¾ **cup jellied cranberry sauce**

1. In a small saucepan, combine the chicken broth and dried wild mushrooms; bring to a boil. Remove from the heat; let stand for 15-20 minutes or until the mushrooms are softened. Using a slotted spoon, remove mushrooms; coarsely chop. Strain remaining broth through a fine mesh strainer. Set aside mushrooms and broth.

2. In a large skillet, saute the onion in butter until softened. Reduce the heat to medium-low; cook, stirring occasionally, for 10 minutes or until golden brown. Add the tarragon, salt, pepper and reserved mushrooms and broth. Bring to a boil; cook over medium heat until liquid is evaporated.

3. On a lightly floured surface, unfold the puff pastry. Roll each pastry sheet into a 12x10-in. rectangle; cut each into two pieces. Transfer to a greased baking sheet. Spoon the mushroom mixture onto each pastry; top with the turkey and cream cheese.

4. Lightly brush the pastry edges with water. Bring the long sides over the filling, pinching the seams and ends to seal. Turn pastries seam side down. Cut small slits into pastry. Brush the tops with egg. Bake at 400° for 20-25 minutes or until golden brown.

5. Meanwhile, in a small saucepan, combine the chicken broth, wine and vinegar. Bring to a boil; cook until the liquid is reduced by half. Stir in the cranberry sauce until melted. Serve with pastries.

Chicken Skewers with Marmalade

My father-in-law said these citrusy chicken skewers reminded him of growing up in Southern California. They bring a little dose of summer sunshine to chilly days.

—**LAUREL DALZELL** MANTECA, CA

PREP: 25 MIN. + MARINATING • **BROIL:** 5 MIN.
MAKES: 8 SERVINGS (1 CUP SAUCE)

- 1 **pound boneless skinless chicken breasts**
- ¼ **cup olive oil**
- ¼ **cup reduced-sodium soy sauce**
- 2 **garlic cloves, minced**
- ⅛ **teaspoon pepper**

SAUCE

- 2 **teaspoons butter**
- 2 **tablespoons chopped seeded jalapeno pepper**
- 1 **teaspoon minced fresh gingerroot**
- ¾ **cup orange marmalade**
- 1 **tablespoon lime juice**
- 1 **tablespoon thawed orange juice concentrate**
- ¼ **teaspoon salt**

1. Preheat broiler. Pound the chicken breasts with a meat mallet to ¼-in. thickness; cut lengthwise into 1-in.-wide strips. In a large resealable plastic bag, combine olive oil, soy sauce, garlic and pepper. Add the chicken; seal bag and turn to coat. Refrigerate 4 hours or overnight.

2. In a small saucepan, heat butter over medium-high heat. Add jalapeno; cook and stir until tender. Add ginger; cook 1 minute longer. Reduce heat; stir in marmalade, lime juice, orange juice concentrate and salt.

3. Drain the chicken, discarding marinade. Thread chicken strips, weaving back and forth, onto eight metal or soaked wooden skewers. Place in a greased 15x10x1-in. baking pan. Broil 6 in. from heat 2-4 minutes on each side or until the chicken is no longer pink. Serve with sauce.

NOTE *Wear disposable gloves when cutting hot peppers; the oils can burn skin. Avoid touching your face.*

GRAND PRIZE
WINNER
★★★★

Grilled Tomatillo Chicken

This top-rated dish gets its flavorful kick from a tomatillo mixture jazzed up with lime juice, cilantro and jalapeno. Spoon it all over rice and dollop on sour cream for a memorable meal.

—**AUDREY KINNE** ELKHART, IN

PREP: 25 MIN. • **GRILL:** 10 MIN.
MAKES: 4 SERVINGS

- 4 **boneless skinless chicken breast halves (6 ounces each)**
- 4 **slices provolone cheese**
- 1 **medium onion, chopped**
- 1 **tablespoon olive oil**
- 6 **tomatillos, husks removed, chopped**
- ¼ **cup lime juice**
- 6 **pickled jalapeno slices, chopped**
- 1 **garlic clove, minced**
- ¼ **cup minced fresh cilantro**
- 1 **teaspoon ground cumin**
- ½ **teaspoon salt**
- ¼ **teaspoon pepper**
  Hot cooked rice
  Sour cream, optional

1. Moisten a paper towel with cooking oil; using long-handled tongs, rub it on the grill rack to coat lightly. Grill chicken, covered, over medium heat or broil 4 in. from the heat for 4-7 minutes on each side or until a thermometer reads 170°. Top with provolone cheese; cook 1 minute longer or until cheese is melted.

2. In a large skillet, saute onion in oil until tender. Add the tomatillos, lime juice, jalapenos and garlic; cook 3 minutes longer. Stir in the cilantro, cumin, salt and pepper.

3. Serve tomatillo mixture and chicken with rice; dollop with sour cream if desired.

Italian Restaurant Chicken

Here's an Italian-style specialty you can savor any time you like. While it cooks, I boil pasta to serve alongside.

—**PATRICIA NIEH** PORTOLA VALLEY, CA

PREP: 25 MIN. • **BAKE:** 50 MIN.
MAKES: 6 SERVINGS

- 1 **broiler/fryer chicken (3 pounds), cut up and skin removed**
- ½ **teaspoon salt**
- ¼ **teaspoon pepper**
- 2 **tablespoons olive oil**
- 1 **small onion, finely chopped**
- ¼ **cup finely chopped celery**
- ¼ **cup finely chopped carrot**
- 3 **garlic cloves, minced**
- ½ **cup dry red wine or reduced-sodium chicken broth**
- 1 **can (28 ounces) crushed tomatoes**
- 1 **bay leaf**
- 1 **teaspoon minced fresh rosemary or ¼ teaspoon dried rosemary, crushed**
- ¼ **cup minced fresh basil**

1. Preheat oven to 325°. Sprinkle chicken with salt and pepper. In an ovenproof Dutch oven, brown chicken in oil in batches. Remove and keep warm.

2. In same pan, saute the onion, celery, carrot and garlic in pan drippings until tender. Add wine, stirring to loosen browned bits from pan. Stir in tomatoes, bay leaf, rosemary and chicken; bring to a boil.

3. Cover and bake 50-60 minutes or until juices run clear. Discard bay leaf; sprinkle with basil.

PER SERVING *3 ounces cooked chicken with ⅔ cup sauce equals 254 cal., 11 g fat (2 g sat. fat), 73 mg chol., 442 mg sodium, 12 g carb., 3 g fiber, 27 g pro.* **Diabetic Exchanges:** *3 lean meat, 2 vegetable, 1 fat.*

Fig & Wine-Sauced Chicken Kabobs

These aren't your average kabobs! The addition of a sweet wine and fig sauce is elegant and delicious. Garnish with mint leaves and lemon wedges for an extra-special touch.
—**BARBARA WHEELER** ROYAL OAK, MI

PREP: 1 HOUR + MARINATING • **GRILL:** 10 MIN.
MAKES: 6 SERVINGS

- 5 **small onions, divided**
- ½ **cup olive oil**
- 2 **garlic cloves, minced**
- 1½ **pounds boneless skinless chicken breasts, cut into 1-inch cubes**
- 1¼ **pounds dried figs**
- 2½ **cups sweet white wine**
- 3 **tablespoons orange marmalade**
- 2 **tablespoons fig preserves**
- 2 **tablespoons lemon juice**
- ½ **teaspoon salt**
- ¼ **teaspoon white pepper**
- ½ **pound small fresh portobello mushrooms**
  Hot cooked rice
  Fresh mint leaves and lemon wedges, optional

1. Grate two onions; place in a large resealable plastic bag. Add the oil, garlic and chicken; seal the bag and turn to coat. Refrigerate for 8 hours or overnight.
2. Meanwhile, in a large saucepan, bring figs and wine to a boil. Reduce heat; simmer, uncovered, for 50-60 minutes or until figs are plumped and tender. Remove figs; keep warm. Bring liquid to a boil; cook until reduced to ⅔ cup. Add the marmalade, preserves, lemon juice, salt and pepper. Cook and stir for 5-6 minutes or until slightly thickened.
3. Cut remaining onions into 1-in. pieces. Drain chicken; discard marinade. On six metal or soaked wooden skewers, alternately thread the chicken, onions and mushrooms.

4. Moisten a paper towel with cooking oil; using long-handled tongs, rub on the grill rack to coat. Grill the kabobs, covered, over medium heat or broil 4 in. from the heat for 10-15 minutes or until juices run clear, turning occasionally.
5. Serve the kabobs with the rice and reserved figs; drizzle with the sauce. Garnish with fresh mint leaves and lemon wedges if desired.

Homemade Chicken Alfredo Pizzas

Give these mouthwatering Alfredo pizzas a try next time you need to feed a crowd, but want something healthier than delivery pizza. Even with their from-scratch crust and sauce, you'll be surprised by how easily they come together.
—**CATHERINE NICKELSON** SCANDIA, MN

PREP: 30 MIN. + STANDING • **BAKE:** 15 MIN.
MAKES: 2 PIZZAS (6 SLICES EACH)

- 1 **package (¼ ounce) quick-rise yeast**
- 1 **cup warm water (120° to 130°)**
- 1 **teaspoon sugar**
- 1½ **teaspoons salt, divided**
- 2½ to 3 **cups all-purpose flour**
- 2 **tablespoons cornmeal**
- 1 **tablespoon olive oil**
- 2 **garlic cloves, minced**
- 2 **tablespoons butter**
- 1 **teaspoon dried parsley flakes**
- ¼ **teaspoon pepper**
- 4½ **teaspoons all-purpose flour**
- 1½ **cups 2% milk**
- 3 **cups cubed cooked chicken breasts**
- 2 **large tomatoes, chopped**
- 2 **cups chopped fresh baby spinach**
- 4 **cups (16 ounces) shredded part-skim mozzarella cheese**
- ½ **cup shredded Italian cheese blend**
- 1 **teaspoon Italian seasoning**

1. In a large bowl, dissolve yeast in warm water. Add the sugar, ½ teaspoon salt and 2½ cups flour. Beat until smooth. Stir in enough remaining flour to form a soft dough (dough will be sticky).
2. Turn onto a lightly floured surface; knead until smooth and elastic, about 6-8 minutes. Cover and let rest for 10 minutes.
3. Sprinkle cornmeal over two 12-in. pizza pans coated with cooking spray. Divide dough in half. On a floured surface, roll each portion into a 13-in. circle. Transfer to prepared pans. Build up edges slightly. Prick dough thoroughly with a fork; brush with oil. Bake at 425° for 5-8 minutes or until edges are lightly browned.
4. In a small saucepan, saute garlic in butter until tender. Stir in the parsley, pepper and remaining salt. Combine flour and milk until smooth. Stir into pan. Bring to a boil; cook and stir for 2 minutes or until slightly thickened.
5. Spread over crusts; top with chicken, tomatoes, spinach, cheeses and Italian seasoning. Bake 10-12 minutes longer or until crusts are lightly browned and cheeses are melted.

Herbed Roast Chicken

I've been using this easy recipe for years. Marinating before roasting gives the bird a mild citrus tang and irresistible look.

—**SAMUEL ONIZUK** ELKTON, MD

PREP: 15 MIN. + MARINATING
BAKE: 2¼ HOURS + STANDING
MAKES: 8 SERVINGS

- One 2-gallon resealable plastic bag
- ½ cup orange juice
- ⅓ cup olive oil
- 2 tablespoons butter, melted
- 1 tablespoon balsamic vinegar
- 1 tablespoon Worcestershire sauce
- 6 garlic cloves, minced
- 1 tablespoon minced chives
- 1 tablespoon dried parsley flakes
- 1 tablespoon dried basil
- 1 teaspoon salt
- 1 teaspoon pepper
- ½ teaspoon dried marjoram
- ½ teaspoon dried rosemary, crushed
- ¼ teaspoon dried tarragon
- 1 roasting chicken (6 to 7 pounds)

1. In the 2-gallon resealable plastic bag, combine the orange juice, olive oil, melted butter, balsamic vinegar, Worcestershire sauce, garlic, chives and seasonings. Add the chicken; seal the bag and turn to coat. Place bag in a pan. Refrigerate 8 hours or overnight, turning occasionally.
2. Preheat oven to 350°. Drain and discard the marinade. Place chicken on a rack in a shallow roasting pan. Bake, uncovered, 2¼-2¾ hours or until a thermometer inserted in the thigh reads 180°. Cover loosely with foil if chicken browns too quickly.
3. Remove the chicken from oven; tent with foil. Let stand 15 minutes before carving.

KEEN ON ZUCCHINI

Zucchini should be firm and heavy, with a moist stem end and shiny skin. Smaller zucchini are generally sweeter and more tender than larger ones. Store zucchini in a plastic bag in the refrigerator crisper for 4-5 days. Do not wash until ready to use.

Italian Sausage Marinara with Penne

Fill your house with the aroma of sausage and veggies in a rich, bold-flavored sauce. It's a zesty dinner my family loves.

—**TERESA KRIESE** EAU CLAIRE, WI

PREP: 30 MIN. • **COOK:** 1 HOUR
MAKES: 8 SERVINGS

- 1 package (19½ ounces) Italian turkey sausage links, cut into ½-inch slices
- 3 small zucchini, cut into ½-inch slices
- 1 medium sweet yellow pepper, julienned
- 1 cup sliced fresh mushrooms
- 2 tablespoons olive oil
- 2 garlic cloves, minced
- ½ cup dry red wine or reduced-sodium chicken broth
- 1 can (28 ounces) Italian crushed tomatoes
- 1 can (14½ ounces) fire-roasted diced tomatoes, undrained
- ⅓ cup grated Parmesan cheese
- 4½ teaspoons Louisiana-style hot sauce
- 3 teaspoons Italian seasoning
- 1 teaspoon sugar
- ¼ teaspoon salt
- 4 cups uncooked whole wheat penne pasta

1. In a Dutch oven, saute sausage until no longer pink; drain. Remove and set aside. In the same pan, saute zucchini, pepper and mushrooms in olive oil until tender. Add garlic; cook 1 minute longer. Add wine, stirring to loosen browned bits from pan.
2. Add the crushed tomatoes, diced tomatoes, cheese, hot sauce, Italian seasoning, sugar and salt. Stir in the sausage. Bring to a boil. Reduce heat; simmer, uncovered, for 1 hour or until slightly thickened.
3. Meanwhile, cook the penne pasta according to package directions; drain. Serve with sauce.

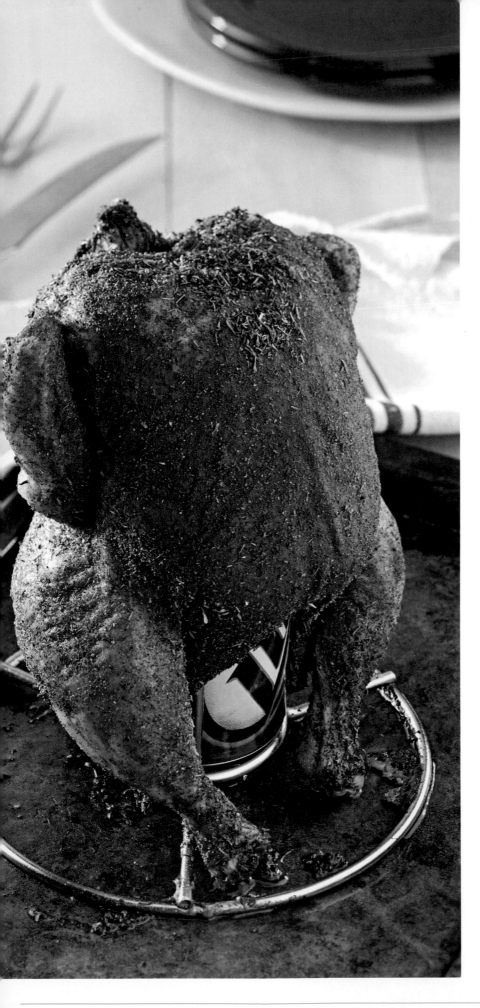

At-Attention Grilled Chicken

Once you give this cooking method a try, you'll never want to go back! The meat is so juicy and tender. I've yet to find a better way of grilling chicken.

—SHIRLEY HODGE BANGOR, PA

PREP: 15 MIN. + MARINATING
GRILL: 1¼ HOURS + STANDING
MAKES: 6 SERVINGS

- 3 **tablespoons minced fresh thyme or 1 tablespoon dried thyme**
- 1 **tablespoon grated lemon peel**
- 1 **tablespoon ground cumin**
- 1 **teaspoon salt**
- 1 **teaspoon ground allspice**
- 1 **teaspoon chili powder**
- 1 **teaspoon pepper**
- ½ **teaspoon ground nutmeg**
- 1 **broiler/fryer chicken (3 to 4 pounds)**
- 1 **tablespoon olive oil**
- 1 **can (12 ounces) beer or nonalcoholic beer**

1. Combine the first eight ingredients. Gently loosen the skin from chicken breasts; rub olive oil and 2 tablespoons spice mixture under the skin. Rub the remaining spice mixture over the skin. Place the chicken in a large resealable plastic bag; seal bag. Refrigerate for at least 1 hour or overnight.

2. Prepare grill for indirect heat, using a drip pan. Pour out a third of the beer. Carefully poke additional holes in top of the can with a can opener. Holding the chicken with legs pointed down, lower chicken over the can so it fills the body cavity.

3. Place the chicken over drip pan; grill, covered, over indirect medium heat for 1¼-1½ hours or until a thermometer reads 180°. Remove the chicken from grill; cover and let stand for 10 minutes. Remove the chicken from the can.

Slow Cooker Chicken Cacciatore

Company coming for dinner? Fill the slow cooker in the morning, switch it on, then let your guests sit down to a savory Italian feast. I like to serve the saucy cacciatore with a dry red wine and sides of couscous and green beans. Delicious!

—**MARTHA SCHIRMACHER** STERLING HEIGHTS, MI

PREP: 15 MIN. • **COOK:** 8½ HOURS
MAKES: 12 SERVINGS

- 12 **boneless skinless chicken thighs (about 3 pounds)**
- 2 **medium green peppers, chopped**
- 1 **can (14½ ounces) diced tomatoes with basil, oregano and garlic, undrained**
- 1 **can (6 ounces) tomato paste**
- 1 **medium onion, sliced**
- ½ **cup reduced-sodium chicken broth**
- ¼ **cup dry red wine or additional reduced-sodium chicken broth**
- 3 **garlic cloves, minced**
- ¾ **teaspoon salt**
- ⅛ **teaspoon pepper**
- 2 **tablespoons cornstarch**
- 2 **tablespoons cold water**

1. Place the chicken in a 4- or 5-qt. slow cooker. In a small bowl, combine the green peppers, diced tomatoes, tomato paste, onion, chicken broth, wine, garlic, salt and pepper; pour over the chicken. Cook, covered, on low 8-10 hours or until chicken is tender.

2. In a small bowl, mix cornstarch and water until smooth; gradually stir into the slow cooker. Cook, covered, on high 30 minutes or until sauce is thickened.

PER SERVING *1 chicken thigh with scant ½ cup sauce equals 207 cal., 9 g fat (2 g sat. fat), 76 mg chol., 410 mg sodium, 8 g carb., 1 g fiber, 23 g pro.* **Diabetic Exchanges:** *3 lean meat, 1 vegetable, ½ fat.*

Double Layered Souffle

The crispy cheese topping on this main-course souffle conceals a creamy turkey layer. It's a simple dish that bursts with flavor. If I don't have turkey, I just use chicken.

—**SHARON AMIDON** GUTHRIE, OK

PREP: 40 MIN. • **BAKE:** 1¼ HOURS
MAKES: 8 SERVINGS

- 6 **large eggs**
- ¼ **cup butter, cubed**
- 1 **cup chopped fresh mushrooms**
- ¼ **cup all-purpose flour**
- ½ **teaspoon salt**
- 2 **cups 2% milk**
- 3 **cups cubed cooked turkey breast**

SOUFFLE LAYER

- ⅓ **cup butter, cubed**
- 1 **shallot, finely chopped**
- ⅓ **cup all-purpose flour**
- ½ **teaspoon salt**
- 1½ **cups 2% milk**
- 1 **package (10 ounces) frozen chopped spinach, thawed and squeezed dry**
- 1½ **cups (6 ounces) shredded Swiss cheese**

1. Separate the eggs; let stand at room temperature for 30 minutes. Grease a 2½-qt. souffle dish and lightly sprinkle with flour; set aside.

2. In a large skillet over medium-high heat, melt the butter. Add the mushrooms; saute until tender. Stir in the flour and salt until blended; gradually whisk in the milk. Bring to a boil, stirring constantly; cook and stir for 2-3 minutes or until thickened. Add the turkey; heat through. Transfer to prepared dish.

3. For souffle layer, in a small saucepan over medium-high heat, melt the butter. Add the shallot; saute until tender. Stir in the flour and salt until blended; gradually whisk in milk. Bring to a boil, stirring constantly; cook and stir for 2-3 minutes or until thickened. Transfer to a large bowl; stir in spinach and cheese.

4. Stir a small amount of the hot spinach mixture into the egg yolks; return all to the bowl, stirring constantly. Allow to cool slightly.

5. In a large bowl with clean beaters, beat the egg whites until stiff peaks form. With a spatula, stir a fourth of the egg whites into spinach mixture until no white streaks remain. Fold in the remaining egg whites until combined. Pour over turkey layer.

6. Bake at 325° for 1¼-1½ hours or until the top is puffed and the center appears set. Serve immediately.

2. Meanwhile, in a 4- or 5-qt. slow cooker, combine the tomato sauce, tomatoes, zucchini, green pepper, onion, tomato paste, bay leaves, garlic and seasonings. Stir in the meatballs. Cover and cook on low for 6 hours. Cook the spaghetti according to the package directions; serve with meatballs and sauce.

Caprese Chicken with Bacon

Plain chicken breasts go from ordinary to extraordinary when you top them with smoky bacon, fresh basil, plum tomatoes and gooey mozzarella. The aroma during baking is fabulous!

—TAMMY HAYDEN QUINCY, MI

PREP: 20 MIN. • **BAKE:** 20 MIN.
MAKES: 4 SERVINGS

- 8 **bacon strips**
- 4 **boneless skinless chicken breast halves (6 ounces each)**
- 1 **tablespoon olive oil**
- ½ **teaspoon salt**
- ¼ **teaspoon pepper**
- 2 **plum tomatoes, sliced**
- 6 **fresh basil leaves, thinly sliced**
- 4 **slices part-skim mozzarella cheese**

1. Place the bacon in an ungreased 15x10x1-in. baking pan. Bake at 400° for 8-10 minutes or until partially cooked but not crisp. Remove to paper towels to drain.
2. Place the chicken in an ungreased 13x9-in. baking pan; brush with oil and sprinkle with salt and pepper. Top with plum tomatoes and basil. Wrap each in two bacon strips, arranging bacon in a crisscross.
3. Bake, uncovered, at 400° for 20-25 minutes or until a thermometer reads 170°. Top with the cheese; bake 1 minute longer or until melted.

GRAND PRIZE WINNER ★★★★

GRAND PRIZE
Turkey Meatballs and Sauce

My sweetie and I are always watching what we eat. For a lower-fat yet flavorful take on meatballs, I use lean ground turkey, salt-free seasoning and egg substitute.

—JANE WHITTAKER PENSACOLA, FL

PREP: 40 MIN. • **COOK:** 6 HOURS
MAKES: 8 SERVINGS

- ¼ **cup egg substitute**
- ½ **cup seasoned bread crumbs**
- ⅓ **cup chopped onion**
- ½ **teaspoon pepper**
- ¼ **teaspoon salt-free seasoning blend**
- 1½ **pounds lean ground turkey**

SAUCE
- 1 **can (15 ounces) tomato sauce**
- 1 **can (14½ ounces) diced tomatoes, undrained**
- 1 **small zucchini, chopped**
- 1 **medium green pepper, chopped**
- 1 **medium onion, chopped**
- 1 **can (6 ounces) tomato paste**
- 2 **bay leaves**
- 2 **garlic cloves, minced**
- 1 **teaspoon dried oregano**
- 1 **teaspoon dried basil**
- 1 **teaspoon dried parsley flakes**
- ¼ **teaspoon crushed red pepper flakes**
- ¼ **teaspoon pepper**
- 1 **package (16 ounces) whole wheat spaghetti**

1. In a large bowl, combine the egg substitute, seasoned bread crumbs, onion, pepper and seasoning blend. Crumble the ground turkey over the mixture and mix well. Shape into 1-in. balls; place on a rack coated with cooking spray in a shallow baking pan. Bake at 400° for 15 minutes or until no longer pink.

Apple-Brined Chicken Thighs

When I had a bumper crop of green beans, I wanted to try them in a main dish. This recipe with apples was the tasty result.

—KATHY RAIRIGH MILFORD, IN

PREP: 30 MIN. + CHILLING • **BAKE:** 55 MIN.
MAKES: 5 SERVINGS

- 3 **cups apple cider or juice**
- 1 **medium onion, sliced**
- 1 **medium lemon, sliced**
- 4 **fresh rosemary sprigs**
- ⅓ **cup kosher salt**
- ½ **cup packed brown sugar, divided**
- 4 **garlic cloves, minced**
- 1 **bay leaf**
- 1 **teaspoon whole peppercorns**
- 2 **cups cold water**
- 10 **bone-in chicken thighs (about 3¾ pounds)**
  One 2-gallon resealable plastic bag
- 1 **pound fresh green beans, trimmed**
- 3 **medium tart apples, cut into wedges**
- 1 **tablespoon minced fresh rosemary or 1 teaspoon dried rosemary, crushed**
- 1 **tablespoon olive oil**
- ¼ **teaspoon pepper**

1. In a Dutch oven, combine the apple cider, onion, lemon, rosemary sprigs, salt, ¼ cup brown sugar, garlic, bay leaf and peppercorns. Bring to a boil. Cook and stir until the salt and brown sugar are dissolved. Remove from the heat; stir in the cold water. Cool brine to room temperature.

2. Place the chicken in the 2-gallon resealable plastic bag. Carefully pour cooled brine into bag. Squeeze out as much air as possible; seal bag and turn to coat. Place in a roasting pan. Refrigerate for 2 hours, turning occasionally.

3. Place green beans and apples in a greased roasting pan. Drain the chicken; place in prepared pan. Bake, uncovered, at 400° for 40 minutes.

4. Combine minced rosemary, oil, pepper and remaining brown sugar; sprinkle over chicken. Bake 15-25 minutes longer or until a thermometer reads 170°-175° and green beans are tender.

Festive Stuffed Cornish Game Hens

Fill your holiday platters beautifully with these plump, golden Cornish game hens. Moistened by juicy orange sections, the crusty ciabatta bread makes a wonderful stuffing.

—MARY LISA SPEER PALM BEACH, FL

PREP: 30 MIN. • **BAKE:** 1 HOUR + STANDING
MAKES: 4 SERVINGS

- ½ **cup chopped sweet onion**
- ¼ **cup chopped celery**
- 2 **tablespoons butter**
- 3 **tablespoons olive oil, divided**
- 1 **garlic clove, minced**
- ¾ **teaspoon salt, divided**
- ¾ **teaspoon pepper, divided**
- 2 **cups cubed ciabatta bread**
- 3 **medium navel oranges, peeled and sectioned**
- ½ **cup dried cranberries**
- ½ **cup chopped pecans, toasted**
- 1 **teaspoon grated orange peel**
- 4 **Cornish game hens (20 to 24 ounces each)**
- ½ **cup orange juice**

1. Preheat oven to 350°. In a large skillet, saute the onion and celery in butter and 1 tablespoon olive oil until tender. Add the garlic, ¼ teaspoon salt and ¼ teaspoon pepper; cook 1 minute longer.

2. In a large bowl, combine the bread, oranges, cranberries, pecans and orange peel. Add onion mixture; toss to coat.

3. Loosely stuff hens with stuffing. Tuck wings under hens; tie drumsticks together. Rub with remaining oil; sprinkle with remaining salt and pepper. Place breast side up on a rack in a shallow roasting pan.

4. Roast 1-1½ hours or until a thermometer reads 165° when inserted into the center of the stuffing and the thigh reaches at least 180°, basting the hens occasionally with orange juice. Cover loosely with foil if hens brown too quickly. Cover and let stand 10 minutes before serving.

Curried Coconut Chicken

Want to dress up plain chicken breasts? Here's a simple recipe that does it with just five other ingredients. Serve it over rice or couscous with warmed apricot preserves.

—**BECKY WALCH** MANTECA, CA

PREP: 10 MIN. • **BAKE:** 30 MIN.
MAKES: 4 SERVINGS

- 3 **tablespoons butter, melted**
- 1 **cup flaked coconut**
- 2 **teaspoons curry powder**
- 4 **boneless skinless chicken breast halves (6 ounces each)**
- ¼ **teaspoon salt**
- 1 **cup apricot preserves, warmed**

1. Place butter in a shallow bowl. In another shallow bowl, combine the coconut and curry powder. Dip the chicken in butter, then coat with coconut mixture.

2. Place in a greased 13x9-in. baking dish; sprinkle with salt. Bake, uncovered, at 350° for 30-35 minutes or until a thermometer reads 170°. Serve with preserves.

FRUITFUL IDEA

I use extra pineapple juice and fruit to make an easy marinade for chicken breasts. I add oil, soy sauce and garlic, then refrigerate the chicken overnight in the marinade. The next day, it's ready to bake.

—**LENORA C.** TALLAHASSEE, FL

Chicken Cutlets with Citrus Cherry Sauce

I love the sweet dried cherries paired with tangy citrus juice in this simple but delicious dish. It's just as good when I substitute dried cranberries and use pork cutlets in place of poultry.

—**CHARLENE CHAMBERS** ORMOND BEACH, FL

START TO FINISH: 30 MIN.
MAKES: 4 SERVINGS

- 4 **boneless skinless chicken breast halves (6 ounces each)**
- ½ **teaspoon salt**
- ¼ **teaspoon pepper**
- ¼ **cup all-purpose flour**
- ½ **cup ruby red grapefruit juice**
- ½ **cup orange juice**
- ⅓ **cup dried cherries**
- 2 **teaspoons Dijon mustard**
- 1 **tablespoon butter**
- 1 **tablespoon canola oil**

1. Flatten the chicken breasts to ½-in. thickness; sprinkle with salt and pepper. Place the flour in a large resealable plastic bag. Add chicken, a few pieces at a time, and shake to coat; set aside.

2. In a small saucepan, combine the juices, dried cherries and mustard. Bring to a boil; cook until the liquid is reduced to ½ cup.

3. In a large skillet over medium heat, cook the chicken in butter and oil for 5-7 minutes on each side or until juices run clear. Serve with sauce.

PER SERVING *1 chicken breast half with 2 tablespoons sauce equals 316 cal., 10 g fat (3 g sat. fat), 102 mg chol., 458 mg sodium, 18 g carb., trace fiber, 35 g pro. **Diabetic Exchanges:** 5 lean meat, 1 starch, 1 fat.*

Lone Star Chicken Enchiladas

Start with last night's leftover meat or a deli-roasted bird to speed up the prep for my freezer-friendly casserole. Monterey Jack cheese is a milder alternative to the pepper jack.

—AVANELL HEWITT NORTH RICHLAND HILLS, TX

PREP: 30 MIN. + FREEZING • **BAKE:** 35 MIN.
MAKES: 6 SERVINGS

- 3 **cups shredded cooked chicken breast**
- 1 **can (10 ounces) diced tomatoes with mild green chilies, drained**
- ¾ **cup salsa verde**
- 1 **can (4 ounces) chopped green chilies**
- 1 **can (2¼ ounces) sliced ripe olives, drained**
- 1 **teaspoon ground cumin**
- 2½ **cups heavy whipping cream**
- ¾ **teaspoon salt**
- 12 **corn tortillas (6 inches), warmed**
- 2 **cups (8 ounces) shredded pepper jack cheese**

1. In a large bowl, combine the first six ingredients. In a shallow bowl, combine cream and salt.
2. Dip both sides of each tortilla in cream mixture; top with ¼ cup chicken mixture. Roll up and place seam side down in a greased 13x9-in. baking dish. Pour the remaining cream mixture over top; sprinkle with cheese. Cover and freeze for up to 6 months.
TO USE FROZEN CASSEROLE *Thaw in the refrigerator overnight. Remove from the refrigerator 30 minutes before baking. Cover and bake at 350° for 35-40 minutes or until heated through.*

Spicy Mustard Turkey Pizza

A different take on more traditional pies, this one is an instant family favorite thanks to the zippy sauce, mushrooms and bacon. Your pizza night may never be the same!

—KERI COTTON LAKEVILLE, MN

START TO FINISH: 30 MIN.
MAKES: 6 SLICES

- 1 **prebaked 12-inch thin pizza crust**
- 3 **tablespoons reduced-fat mayonnaise**
- 3 **tablespoons spicy brown mustard**
- 3 **tablespoons honey**
- ½ **teaspoon garlic powder**
- 2 **cups cubed cooked turkey**
- 1 **cup chopped fresh mushrooms**
- 5 **cooked bacon strips, chopped**
- 1 **cup (4 ounces) shredded Swiss cheese**

1. Place crust on an ungreased 12-in. pizza pan. In a small bowl, combine the mayonnaise, mustard, honey and garlic powder. Add turkey; toss to coat. Spread over crust.
2. Top with mushrooms, bacon and cheese. Bake at 450° for 9-11 minutes or until cheese is melted.

Sweet Potato & Caramelized Onion Shells

What a way to eat holiday dinner leftovers! Extra mashed sweet potatoes and gravy make this unusual baked pasta simple, comforting and delicious.

—ROBIN HAAS CRANSTON, RI

PREP: 40 MIN. • **BAKE:** 10 MIN.
MAKES: 7 SERVINGS

- 2 large onions, chopped
- 3 tablespoons butter
- 1 teaspoon garlic powder
- ¼ teaspoon salt
- 21 uncooked jumbo pasta shells
- ¼ cup reduced-sodium chicken broth
- 1 tablespoon sherry or apple cider
- 1 teaspoon dried thyme
- ½ teaspoon pepper
- 1½ cups mashed sweet potatoes
- 1½ cups (6 ounces) crumbled Gorgonzola cheese
- ½ cup grated Parmesan cheese
- 2 tablespoons minced fresh parsley
- 1 cup turkey gravy, warmed

1. In a large skillet, saute the chopped onions in the butter until softened. Add the garlic powder and salt. Reduce the heat to medium-low; cook, stirring occasionally, for 25-30 minutes or until deep golden brown.

2. Meanwhile, cook the pasta shells according to the package directions. Drain pasta; set aside.

3. Stir chicken broth, sherry, thyme and pepper into onions. Bring to a boil; cook until liquid is almost evaporated. Remove from the heat. Stir in sweet potatoes and Gorgonzola cheese.

4. Spoon into shells; place in a greased 11x7-in. baking dish. Sprinkle with the Parmesan cheese. Cover and bake at 375° for 10-15 minutes or until heated through. Sprinkle with parsley. Serve with gravy.

PER SERVING *3 stuffed shells equals 341 cal., 14 g fat (9 g sat. fat), 42 mg chol., 758 mg sodium, 41 g carb., 4 g fiber, 13 g pro.* **Diabetic Exchanges:** *2 starch, 1 high-fat meat.*

Fiesta Chicken Bundles

When I was on vacation and had limited ingredients to choose from, I dreamed up zesty chicken bundles. My family has enjoyed them many times since. The chili powder, salsa verde and Southwestern black beans add plenty of spice.
—**MERRY GRAHAM** NEWHALL, CA

PREP: 25 MIN. • **COOK:** 20 MIN.
MAKES: 4 SERVINGS

- 4 **boneless skinless chicken breasts (6 ounces each)**
- 4 **corn tortillas (6 inches), chopped**
- 1 **cup (4 ounces) shredded pepper jack cheese**
- 1¼ **cups salsa verde, divided**
- ½ **cup cornmeal**
- 1 **teaspoon garlic salt**
- 2 **tablespoons canola oil**
- ½ **cup water**
- 3 **tablespoons orange marmalade**
- 1 **teaspoon chili powder**
- ¼ **cup sour cream**
- ⅓ **cup minced fresh cilantro**
- 2 **cans (15 ounces each) Southwestern black beans, warmed**

1. Flatten the chicken breasts to ¼-in. thickness; set aside. In a small bowl, combine corn tortillas, pepper jack cheese and ½ cup salsa verde. Spoon the tortilla mixture down the center of each chicken breast; roll up and secure with toothpicks.

2. Combine cornmeal and garlic salt in a shallow bowl; coat chicken with cornmeal mixture.

3. In a large skillet, brown the chicken in oil. Add water, orange marmalade, chili powder and remaining salsa to the pan. Bring to a boil. Reduce heat; cover and cook for 15-20 minutes or until a thermometer reads 170°. Discard toothpicks.

4. Top chicken with sour cream and cilantro. Serve with beans.

Easy Breezy Turkey Loaf

Think preparing meat loaf takes too much time? Give this super-easy version a try. Your favorite store-bought spaghetti sauce will jazz up the ground turkey.
—**JO ANN SHAPPARD** VINCENNES, IN

PREP: 10 MIN. • **BAKE:** 1 HOUR 5 MIN.
MAKES: 6 SERVINGS

- 1 **cup seasoned bread crumbs**
- 1 **cup garden-style spaghetti sauce, divided**
- 1 **medium onion, chopped**
- 1 **large egg**
- 1 **teaspoon salt**
- 1 **teaspoon pepper**
- 1½ **pounds ground turkey**

1. In a large bowl, combine seasoned bread crumbs, ½ cup spaghetti sauce, onion, egg, salt and pepper. Crumble the ground turkey over the mixture and mix well. Pat into an ungreased 9x5-in. loaf pan.

2. Bake, uncovered, at 350° for 1 hour. Spread the remaining spaghetti sauce over loaf. Bake 5-10 minutes longer or until a thermometer reads 165° and juices run clear.

FREEZE OPTION *Securely wrap individual portions of the cooled meat loaf in plastic wrap and foil. To use, partially thaw meat loaf in refrigerator overnight. Unwrap meat loaf; reheat on a greased shallow baking pan in a preheated 350° oven until heated through and a thermometer inserted into the center reads 165°.*

Southwest Chicken Stromboli

I prefer Italian food, but my brother is a huge fan of all things Mexican. I tried combining our preferences, and the result was this from-scratch stromboli full of chicken, refried beans, salsa, shredded cheese and spices. He loved it!

—**CARLY CURTIN** ELLICOTT CITY, MD

PREP: 30 MIN. + RISING • **BAKE:** 25 MIN.
MAKES: 6 SERVINGS

- ¾ cup water (70° to 80°)
- 1 tablespoon canola oil
- 1 tablespoon nonfat dry milk powder
- 1 tablespoon sugar
- 1 teaspoon salt
- 2¼ cups bread flour
- ¼ cup yellow cornmeal
- 1 teaspoon active dry yeast

FILLING
- 1 small onion, finely chopped
- 1 small sweet yellow pepper, finely chopped
- 1 tablespoon canola oil
- 1½ cups shredded cooked chicken breast
- ¾ cup salsa
- ⅔ cup shredded Mexican cheese blend
- ½ cup refried beans
- ¾ teaspoon ground cumin
- ¼ teaspoon garlic powder
- ¼ teaspoon chili powder
- ¼ teaspoon dried oregano

EGG WASH
- 1 large egg white, beaten
- 1 tablespoon water
- Sour cream, optional

1. In bread machine pan, place the first eight ingredients in the order suggested by the manufacturer. Select the dough setting (check the dough after 5 minutes of mixing; add 1-2 tablespoons of water or flour if needed).

2. Meanwhile, for filling, in a large skillet, saute onion and pepper in oil until crisp-tender. Stir in the chicken, salsa, cheese, beans and seasonings; heat through. Remove from the heat; set aside.

3. When the cycle is completed, turn dough onto a lightly floured surface. Roll dough to a 14x12-in. rectangle. Spread the filling over half of dough to within ½ in. of the edges. Fold dough over filling; pinch seams to seal and tuck ends under. Combine egg white and water; brush over dough. Cut slits in top.

4. Place stromboli on an ungreased baking sheet. Bake at 350° for 25-30 minutes or until golden brown. Let stand for 5 minutes before cutting. Serve with sour cream if desired.

PER SERVING *1 slice (calculated without sour cream) equals 367 cal., 10 g fat (3 g sat. fat), 40 mg chol., 696 mg sodium, 48 g carb., 3 g fiber, 21 g pro.* **Diabetic Exchanges:** *3 starch, 2 lean meat, 1 fat.*

GRAND PRIZE
Terrific Turkey Enchiladas

PREP: 35 MIN. • **BAKE:** 35 MIN.
MAKES: 3 SERVINGS

- 1¼ cups frozen corn, thawed
- 1 can (4 ounces) chopped green chilies
- 1 cup fresh cilantro leaves
- ⅓ cup heavy whipping cream
- ¼ teaspoon salt
- ¼ teaspoon pepper

ENCHILADAS
- ¾ pound ground turkey
- ⅓ cup chopped onion
- 1 garlic clove, minced
- 1 tablespoon olive oil
- ¾ cup salsa
- 1 tablespoon cornmeal
- 2 teaspoons chili powder
- 1½ teaspoons ground cumin
- 1 teaspoon dried oregano
- ⅛ teaspoon salt
- ⅛ teaspoon pepper
- 6 flour tortillas (8 inches), warmed
- 1¼ cups shredded Mexican cheese blend, divided
- ¼ cup sliced ripe olives

1. Preheat oven to 350°. Place first six ingredients in a food processor; cover and pulse until blended.

2. In a large skillet, cook the turkey, onion and garlic in oil over medium heat until meat is no longer pink, breaking meat into crumbles. Remove from the heat; stir in salsa, cornmeal and seasonings.

3. Spoon ⅓ cup turkey mixture down the center of each tortilla; top with 2 tablespoons cheese. Roll up and place seam side down in a greased 11x7-in. baking dish. Spoon the corn mixture over the top; sprinkle with the ripe olives and remaining cheese.

4. Cover and bake 30 minutes. Uncover; bake 5-10 minutes or until heated through.

Terrific Turkey Enchiladas go over big with nearly everyone—especially our little girl, who calls them "laladas." The dish is a tasty take on a Southwestern classic.

—**JENNIFER TIDWELL** FAIR OAKS, CA

Mexican Skillet Rice

Leftovers are nonexistent when I take this main dish to parties. It's so good, I can't help but wish I had some to bring home!

—**MARY ANN DELL** PHOENIXVILLE, PA

START TO FINISH: 30 MIN.
MAKES: 6 SERVINGS

- 1 large egg, beaten
- 1 pound chicken tenderloins, chopped
- 1 small onion, chopped
- 1 tablespoon olive oil
- 2 garlic cloves, minced
- 2 cups cooked jasmine or long grain rice
- 1 can (15 ounces) black beans, rinsed and drained
- 1 can (11 ounces) Mexicorn, drained
- 1 jar (7 ounces) roasted sweet red peppers, drained and sliced
- 1 jar (8 ounces) taco sauce
- 2 green onions, chopped
- ¼ cup minced fresh cilantro

1. In a large skillet coated with cooking spray, cook and stir the beaten egg over medium-high heat until set. Remove and set aside.

2. In the same skillet, stir-fry chicken and onion in oil until chicken is no longer pink. Add garlic; cook 1 minute longer. Stir in the rice, beans, Mexicorn, peppers, taco sauce and green onions; heat through. Stir in reserved egg. Sprinkle rice with cilantro.

PER SERVING *1⅓ cups equals 302 cal., 4 g fat (1 g sat. fat), 80 mg chol., 793 mg sodium, 40 g carb., 5 g fiber, 25 g pro.* ***Diabetic Exchanges:*** *3 lean meat, 2 starch, ½ fat.*

Crispy Buffalo Chicken Roll-ups

Chicken rolls may appear complicated, but these are simple to prepare. Friends and family rave over the Buffalo flavor.

—**WILLIAM KEYS** KENNETT SQUARE, PA

PREP: 15 MIN. • **BAKE:** 30 MIN.
MAKES: 4 SERVINGS

- 4 boneless skinless chicken breast halves (6 ounces each)
- ¾ teaspoon salt
- ½ teaspoon pepper
- ¼ cup crumbled blue cheese
- ¼ cup hot pepper sauce
- 2 tablespoons mayonnaise
- 1 cup crushed cornflakes

1. Preheat oven to 400°. Flatten the chicken breasts to ¼-in. thickness. Season with the salt and pepper; sprinkle with the blue cheese. Roll up each from a short side and secure with toothpicks.

2. In a shallow bowl, combine the hot pepper sauce and mayonnaise. Place the crushed cornflakes in a separate shallow bowl. Dip the chicken in the pepper sauce mixture, then coat with the cornflakes. Place seam side down in a greased 11x7-in. baking dish.

3. Bake, uncovered, 30-35 minutes or until chicken is no longer pink. Discard toothpicks.

Famous BBQ Chicken

Here's a sticky, finger-lickin' sauce that everyone loves. I like to make it in big batches and give jars of it as gifts.

—STACEY NERNESS SPENCER, IA

PREP: 45 MIN. • **GRILL:** 40 MIN.
MAKES: 4 SERVINGS PLUS 3 CUPS LEFTOVER SAUCE

- 2½ cups ketchup
- ½ cup packed brown sugar
- ½ cup honey
- ¼ cup liquid smoke
- ¼ cup molasses
- 1 serrano pepper, finely chopped
- 2 tablespoons prepared mustard
- 1 tablespoon white wine vinegar
- 1 tablespoon Worcestershire sauce
- 2 teaspoons onion powder
- 2 teaspoons garlic powder
- ¼ teaspoon cayenne pepper
- 4 chicken leg quarters
- ½ teaspoon salt
- ½ teaspoon pepper

1. In a large saucepan, combine the first 12 ingredients. Bring to a boil. Reduce the heat; simmer, uncovered, for 30 minutes to allow the flavors to blend. Set aside ½ cup sauce for basting; cover and refrigerate the remaining sauce for later use.

2. Sprinkle chicken with salt and pepper. Moisten a paper towel with cooking oil; using long-handled tongs, rub on grill rack to coat lightly.

3. Prepare the grill for indirect heat, using a drip pan. Place the chicken skin side down over drip pan and grill, covered, over indirect medium heat for 20 minutes. Turn and grill 20-30 minutes longer or until a thermometer reads 170°-175°, basting occasionally with reserved sauce.

NOTE *Wear disposable gloves when cutting hot peppers; the oils can burn skin. Avoid touching your face.*

Curried Chicken Shepherd's Pie

Use extra mashed potatoes to top off a comforting casserole. This creamy meat-and-veggie mixture is mildly seasoned with curry to please almost any palate.

—LORI LOCKREY SCARBOROUGH, ON

PREP: 25 MIN. • **BAKE:** 25 MIN.
MAKES: 4 SERVINGS

- 1 large onion, chopped
- 2 celery ribs, chopped
- 3 tablespoons butter, divided
- 1 cup frozen peas and carrots
- 3 tablespoons all-purpose flour
- 1 teaspoon curry powder
- 1½ cups reduced-sodium chicken broth
- ½ cup 2% milk
- 2 cups cubed cooked chicken
- 2 tablespoons dried parsley flakes
- ½ teaspoon salt
- ½ teaspoon pepper
- 2 cups mashed potatoes (with added milk and butter)
- ¼ teaspoon paprika

1. In a large skillet, saute onion and celery in 1 tablespoon butter until tender. Add frozen vegetables and remaining butter; cook 2 minutes longer.

2. Stir in flour and curry powder until blended; gradually add the chicken broth and milk. Bring to a boil; cook and stir for 1 minute or until thickened. Add chicken, parsley, salt and pepper.

3. Transfer to a greased 2-qt. baking dish. Top with mashed potatoes; sprinkle with paprika. Bake, uncovered, at 350° for 25-30 minutes or until heated through.

Spicy Chicken Lettuce Wraps

This is one of my go-to entrees when I want a fun meal. Cool lettuce leaves balance the spicy Asian flavors, and every bite gets a nice crunch from peanuts and water chestnuts.

—**BRITTANY ALLYN** MESA, AZ

START TO FINISH: 30 MIN.
MAKES: 4 SERVINGS

- 1 **pound chicken tenderloins, cut into ½-inch pieces**
- ⅛ **teaspoon pepper**
- 2 **tablespoons canola oil, divided**
- 1 **medium onion, finely chopped**
- 1 **small green pepper, finely chopped**
- 1 **small sweet red pepper, finely chopped**
- 1 **can (8 ounces) sliced water chestnuts, drained and finely chopped**
- 1 **can (4 ounces) mushroom stems and pieces, drained and finely chopped**
- 2 **garlic cloves, minced**
- ⅓ **cup stir-fry sauce**
- 1 **teaspoon reduced-sodium soy sauce**
- 8 **Bibb or Boston lettuce leaves**
- ¼ **cup salted peanuts**
- 2 **teaspoons minced fresh cilantro**

1. Sprinkle the chicken with pepper. In a large skillet or wok, stir-fry the chicken in 1 tablespoon oil until no longer pink. Remove and set aside.
2. Stir-fry the onion and peppers in the remaining oil for 5 minutes. Add the water chestnuts, mushrooms and garlic; stir-fry 2-3 minutes longer or until the vegetables are crisp-tender. Add the stir-fry sauce and soy sauce. Stir in chicken; heat through.
3. Place ½ cup chicken mixture on each lettuce leaf; sprinkle each with 1½ teaspoons peanuts and ¼ teaspoon cilantro. Fold lettuce over filling.
NOTE *This recipe was tested with House of Tsang Saigon Sizzle Sauce.*

Country Chicken Casserole

Whenever I serve my casserole, someone asks for the recipe. I can assemble it the night before to simplify dinnertime.

—**SUE KENNEDY** GALLOWAY, OH

PREP: 45 MIN. + CHILLING
BAKE: 45 MIN. + STANDING
MAKES: 8 SERVINGS

- 1 **package (6 ounces) Stove Top chicken stuffing mix**
- ½ **pound sliced fresh mushrooms**
- 1 **small onion, chopped**
- 1 **tablespoon butter**
- 3 **garlic cloves, minced**
- 3 **cups cubed cooked chicken**
- 1 **package (16 ounces) frozen corn, thawed**
- 1 **package (16 ounces) frozen chopped broccoli, thawed**
- 1 **can (10¾ ounces) reduced-fat reduced-sodium condensed cream of mushroom soup, undiluted**
- 1 **cup 2% milk**
- 1 **cup reduced-fat sour cream**
- 1 **cup reduced-fat mayonnaise**
- ¾ **teaspoon pepper**

1. Prepare the chicken stuffing according to the package directions. Meanwhile, in a large skillet, saute the sliced mushrooms and onion in the butter until tender. Add the garlic; cook 1 minute longer.
2. In a large bowl, combine chicken, corn, broccoli, cream of mushroom soup, milk, sour cream, mayonnaise, pepper and mushroom mixture; transfer to a greased 13x9-in. baking dish. Top with the stuffing. Cover and refrigerate overnight.
3. Remove from the refrigerator 30 minutes before baking. Cover and bake at 350° for 35 minutes. Uncover and bake 10-15 minutes longer or until stuffing is lightly browned. Let stand for 10 minutes before serving.

Turkey Mushroom Sandwich Bowls

My grandmother was an amazing cook who always brought new life to leftovers. I've tried to do the same here in these creamy, mushroom-packed sandwiches.
—**ANGELA LEINENBACH** MECHANICSVLLE, VA

START TO FINISH: 30 MIN.
MAKES: 4 SERVINGS

- 4 **French rolls**
- ¼ **cup butter, melted**
- 1½ **cups sliced fresh mushrooms**
- 1 **medium onion, thinly sliced**
- 2 **tablespoons canola oil**
- ½ **cup dry vermouth or chicken broth**
- 2 **tablespoons all-purpose flour**
- ½ **teaspoon salt**
- ¼ **teaspoon pepper**
- 1¼ **cups heavy whipping cream**
- 4 **cups cubed cooked turkey**
   Minced fresh chives

1. Cut a ½-in. slice off the top of each roll; set aside the tops. Hollow out the centers, leaving ¼-in. shells (discard the removed bread or save for another use). Brush the tops and inside of rolls with butter; place on a baking sheet. Bake at 325° for 10-15 minutes or until lightly browned.

2. Meanwhile, in a large skillet, saute the mushrooms and onion in oil until tender. Add the vermouth, stirring to loosen browned bits from pan. Bring to a boil; cook until liquid is almost evaporated. Combine the flour, salt, pepper and cream; stir until smooth. Stir into skillet; bring to a boil. Reduce heat; cook and stir for 1-2 minutes or until sauce is thickened.

3. Stir in turkey; heat through. Spoon into the hollowed rolls; garnish with chives. Replace tops.

Pan-Fried Catfish with Spicy Pecan Gremolata, page 154

149

152

155

Seafood & Meatless Entrees

Skip the meat but keep all of the hearty goodness and flavor your family craves. It's a breeze with these **top-rated recipes** featuring fish, pasta, crab, veggies, shrimp and more.

1. In a large saucepan, saute the peppers and sweet onion in the olive oil until tender. Add the garlic; cook 1 minute longer. Stir in tomato sauce, tomatoes, chili powder, sugar, marjoram, basil, cumin, salt, cayenne and bay leaf. Bring to a boil. Reduce heat; simmer, uncovered, 30-35 minutes or until slightly thickened. Discard bay leaf.

2. Preheat oven to 350°. Place ⅓ cup zucchini down the center of each corn tortilla; top with 2 tablespoons cheddar cheese and 2 teaspoons ripe olives. Roll up; place seam side down in two 13x9-in. baking dishes coated with cooking spray. Pour the sauce over the top; sprinkle with remaining cheddar cheese.

3. Bake, uncovered, 30-35 minutes or until heated through. Sprinkle with the minced cilantro. Serve with sour cream if desired.

PER SERVING *2 enchiladas (calculated without sour cream) equals 326 cal., 13 g fat (6 g sat. fat), 27 mg chol., 846 mg sodium, 42 g carb., 7 g fiber, 16 g pro.* **Diabetic Exchanges:** *2 starch, 2 medium-fat meat, 2 vegetable, ½ fat.*

Ravioli Casserole

Love saucy, cheesy lasagna but not the fuss of making it? Here's a casserole with a similar taste but quicker prep. You'll need only five ingredients, and it's a cinch to make with time-saving ingredients like prepared spaghetti sauce and frozen ravioli.

—**MARY ANN ROTHERT** AUSTIN, TX

PREP: 10 MIN. • **BAKE:** 30 MIN.
MAKES: 6-8 SERVINGS

- 3½ **cups spaghetti sauce**
- 1 **package (25 ounces) frozen cheese ravioli, cooked and drained**
- 2 **cups (16 ounces) small-curd 4% cottage cheese**
- 4 **cups (16 ounces) shredded mozzarella cheese**
- ¼ **cup grated Parmesan cheese**

1. Spread 1 cup of spaghetti sauce in an ungreased 13x9-in. baking dish. Layer with half of the cooked cheese ravioli, 1¼ cups of sauce, 1 cup cottage cheese and 2 cups shredded mozzarella cheese. Repeat the layers. Sprinkle with grated Parmesan cheese.

2. Bake, uncovered, at 350° for 30-40 minutes or until bubbly. Let stand for 5-10 minutes before serving.

Zucchini Enchiladas

When my garden is bursting with zucchini, I turn to my recipe for meatless enchiladas. My family always looks forward to this garden-fresh spin on a Southwestern favorite.

—**ANGELA LEINENBACH** MECHANICSVLLE, VA

PREP: 1½ HOURS • **BAKE:** 30 MIN.
MAKES: 12 SERVINGS

- 1 **medium sweet yellow pepper, chopped**
- 1 **medium green pepper, chopped**
- 1 **large sweet onion, chopped**
- 2 **tablespoons olive oil**
- 2 **garlic cloves, minced**
- 2 **cans (15 ounces each) tomato sauce**
- 2 **cans (14½ ounces each) no-salt-added diced tomatoes, undrained**
- 2 **tablespoons chili powder**
- 2 **teaspoons sugar**
- 2 **teaspoons dried marjoram**
- 1 **teaspoon dried basil**
- 1 **teaspoon ground cumin**
- ¼ **teaspoon salt**
- ¼ **teaspoon cayenne pepper**
- 1 **bay leaf**
- 3 **pounds zucchini, shredded (about 8 cups)**
- 24 **corn tortillas (6 inches), warmed**
- 4 **cups (16 ounces) shredded reduced-fat cheddar cheese**
- 2 **cans (2¼ ounces each) sliced ripe olives, drained**
- ½ **cup minced fresh cilantro**
  Reduced-fat sour cream, optional

GRAND PRIZE
Chipotle Salmon with Strawberry Mango Salsa

I've made this sweetly spicy salmon for dinner many times and always get compliments. The savory grilled fish topped with fruity salsa goes over well with everyone—including the kids.

—NAYLET LAROCHELLE MIAMI, FL

START TO FINISH: 25 MIN.
MAKES: 4 SERVINGS

- 2 **tablespoons brown sugar**
- 3 **garlic cloves, minced**
- 2 **teaspoons finely chopped chipotle peppers in adobo sauce**
- ¼ **teaspoon salt**
- 4 **salmon fillets (6 ounces each)**

SALSA
- 2 **cups chopped fresh strawberries**
- ⅔ **cup chopped peeled mango**
- ⅓ **cup chopped red onion**
- 2 **tablespoons lime juice**
- 1 **tablespoon minced fresh cilantro**
- 1 **tablespoon minced fresh mint**
- 2 **teaspoons olive oil**

1. In a small bowl, combine brown sugar, minced garlic cloves, chopped chipotle peppers and salt; rub over the salmon fillets.
2. Moisten a paper towel with cooking oil; using long-handled tongs, lightly coat the grill rack. Place the salmon skin side down on grill rack. Grill salmon, covered, over high heat or broil 3-4 in. from the heat for 5-10 minutes or until the fish flakes easily with a fork.
3. In a small bowl, combine the salsa ingredients; serve with the salmon.

PER SERVING *1 salmon fillet with ½ cup salsa equals 368 cal., 18 g fat (4 g sat. fat), 85 mg chol., 255 mg sodium, 21 g carb., 3 g fiber, 30 g pro.* **Diabetic Exchanges:** *5 lean meat, 1½ fat, ½ starch, ½ fruit.*

Scallops with Citrus Glaze

These citrusy, garlicky scallops are especially good served over steamed rice with a tossed green salad on the side.

—PATRICIA NIEH PORTOLA VALLEY, CA

START TO FINISH: 20 MIN.
MAKES: 4 SERVINGS

- 12 **sea scallops (about 1½ pounds)**
- ½ **teaspoon pepper**
- ¼ **teaspoon salt**
- 2 **tablespoons olive oil, divided**
- 4 **garlic cloves, minced**
- ½ **cup orange juice**
- ¼ **cup lemon juice**
- 1 **tablespoon reduced-sodium soy sauce**
- ½ **teaspoon grated orange peel**

1. Sprinkle scallops with pepper and salt. In a large skillet, saute the scallops in 1 tablespoon oil until firm and opaque. Remove and keep warm.
2. In same skillet, cook the garlic in the remaining oil for 1 minute. Add the juices, soy sauce and peel. Bring to a boil; cook and stir for 5 minutes or until thickened. Serve with the scallops.
PER SERVING *3 scallops with 2 teaspoons glaze equals 235 cal., 8 g fat (1 g sat. fat), 56 mg chol., 574 mg sodium, 10 g carb., trace fiber, 29 g pro.* **Diabetic Exchanges:** *4 lean meat, 1½ fat.*

Orange-Pecan Salmon

When I was cooking for a friend's luncheon, I made this. Putting the fish in the oven just before guests arrived was so convenient.

—PAT NEAVES LEES SUMMIT, MO

PREP: 10 MIN. + MARINATING • **BAKE:** 20 MIN.
MAKES: 4 SERVINGS

- 1 **cup orange marmalade**
- ½ **cup reduced-sodium soy sauce**
- ¼ **teaspoon salt**
- ¼ **teaspoon pepper**
- 4 **salmon fillets (6 ounces each)**
- 1 **cup chopped pecans, toasted**

1. In a small bowl, combine marmalade, soy sauce, salt and pepper. Pour ⅔ cup marinade into a large resealable plastic bag. Add salmon; seal bag and turn to coat. Refrigerate for up to 30 minutes. Set aside remaining marinade.
2. Preheat oven to 350°. Drain and discard the marinade from the salmon. Place salmon in a greased 11x7-in. baking dish. Bake, uncovered, 20-25 minutes or until fish flakes easily with a fork.
3. In a small saucepan, bring reserved marinade to a boil; cook and stir until slightly thickened. Stir in the pecans; serve with salmon.

Halibut with Orange Salsa

I bake marinated halibut fillets until crispy and top them off with a homemade salsa featuring tomatoes, oranges, kalamata olives and basil. It's a colorful, company-worthy dish.

—**GLORIA BRADLEY** NAPERVILLE, IL

PREP: 25 MIN. + MARINATING • **BAKE:** 15 MIN.
MAKES: 4 SERVINGS

- 1 cup orange juice
- 1¼ teaspoons Caribbean jerk seasoning, divided
- 4 halibut fillets (6 ounces each)
- ½ cup panko (Japanese) bread crumbs
- 2 teaspoons grated orange peel
- ½ teaspoon salt

SALSA

- 2 plum tomatoes, seeded and chopped
- 1 large navel orange, peeled, sectioned and chopped
- ¼ cup pitted Greek olives, chopped
- 2 tablespoons minced fresh basil
- 1 tablespoon olive oil
- 1 garlic clove, minced
- ⅛ teaspoon salt
- ⅛ teaspoon pepper

1. In a large resealable plastic bag, combine orange juice and 1 teaspoon jerk seasoning. Add the halibut; seal the bag and turn to coat. Set aside for 15 minutes.
2. Meanwhile, in a shallow bowl, combine the panko bread crumbs, orange peel, salt and remaining jerk seasoning. Drain fish and discard the marinade. Coat halibut with bread crumb mixture. Place on a greased baking sheet.

3. Bake at 400° for 15-20 minutes or until fish flakes easily with a fork. Broil 4-6 in. from the heat for 3-4 minutes or until lightly browned.
4. In a small bowl, combine the salsa ingredients. Serve with halibut.

PER SERVING *1 fillet with ⅓ cup salsa equals 298 cal., 10 g fat (1 g sat. fat), 54 mg chol., 593 mg sodium, 13 g carb., 2 g fiber, 37 g pro.* **Diabetic Exchanges:** *5 lean meat, 1 starch, 1 fat.*

Greek Tilapia

PREP: 30 MIN. • **BAKE:** 10 MIN.
MAKES: 6 SERVINGS

- 6 tilapia fillets (4 ounces each)
- 4 teaspoons butter
- 1 large egg
- 1 cup (4 ounces) crumbled tomato and basil feta cheese
- ⅓ cup fat-free milk
- ¼ teaspoon cayenne pepper
- 1 large tomato, seeded and chopped
- ¼ cup chopped ripe olives
- ¼ cup pine nuts, toasted
- 1 tablespoon minced fresh parsley
- 1 tablespoon lemon juice
- ⅛ teaspoon pepper

1. In a large skillet, brown the tilapia fillets in the butter in batches. Transfer to a 15x10x1-in. baking pan coated with cooking spray.
2. In a small bowl, combine egg, cheese, milk and cayenne; spoon over fish. Sprinkle with tomato, olives and pine nuts. Bake, uncovered, at 425° for 10-15 minutes or until the fish flakes easily with a fork.
3. In a small bowl, combine the parsley, lemon juice and pepper; drizzle over fish.

PER SERVING *1 fillet equals 224 cal., 11 g fat (5 g sat. fat), 107 mg chol., 306 mg sodium, 4 g carb., 2 g fiber, 28 g pro.* **Diabetic Exchanges:** *3 lean meat, 2 fat.*

“While my husband and I were traveling around the Greek islands, we tasted an incredible entree. I tried to re-create it at home, and the result was Greek Tilapia.”

—**SALLY JEAN BURRELL** IDAHO FALLS, ID

Barbecued Trout

A friend gave me her recipe for trout with a simple barbecue sauce. The tangy taste goes over well with everyone—even those who usually don't care for fish.

—**VIVIAN WOLFRAM** MOUNTAIN HOME, AR

START TO FINISH: 20 MIN.
MAKES: 6 SERVINGS

- ⅔ cup reduced-sodium soy sauce
- ½ cup ketchup
- 2 tablespoons lemon juice
- 2 tablespoons canola oil
- 1 teaspoon dried rosemary, crushed
- 6 pan-dressed trout
  Lemon wedges, optional

1. Combine the soy sauce, ketchup, lemon juice, oil and rosemary; pour two-thirds of marinade into a large resealable plastic bag; add fish. Seal bag and turn to coat; refrigerate bag for 1 hour, turning once. Cover and refrigerate remaining marinade for basting.

2. Drain and discard marinade. Place fish in a single layer in a well-greased hinged wire grill basket. Grill, covered, over medium heat for 8-10 minutes or until the fish is browned on the bottom. Turn and baste with the reserved marinade; grill 5-7 minutes longer or until fish flakes easily with a fork. Serve with lemon if desired.

GINGERROOT 101

Look for fresh gingerroot in your grocery store's produce department. Choose a root that has a smooth, wrinkle-free skin and a spicy fragrance. Wrap the fresh, unpeeled root in a paper towel, place it in a plastic bag and refrigerate it for up to 3 weeks. Or place the unpeeled root in a heavy-duty resealable plastic bag and freeze it for up to 1 year. When needed, simply peel the root, then mince or grate.

Tangerine Cashew Snapper

With sweetness from the tangerines and a nice crunch from the cashews, these snapper fillets make a winning dinner. Eating lighter? You'll appreciate them even more!

—**CRYSTAL JO BRUNS** ILIFF, CO

START TO FINISH: 30 MIN.
MAKES: 4 SERVINGS

- 4 tangerines
- 2 tablespoons lime juice
- 2 tablespoons reduced-sodium soy sauce
- 1 tablespoon brown sugar
- 2 teaspoons minced fresh gingerroot
- 1 teaspoon sesame oil
- ⅛ teaspoon crushed red pepper flakes
- 4 red snapper fillets (4 ounces each)
- ⅓ cup chopped unsalted cashews
- 2 green onions, thinly sliced

1. Peel, slice and remove the seeds from two tangerines; chop the fruit and place in a small bowl. Squeeze the juice from the remaining tangerines; add to bowl. Stir in the lime juice, soy sauce, brown sugar, ginger, sesame oil and pepper flakes.

2. Place the fillets in a 13x9-in. baking dish coated with cooking spray. Pour tangerine mixture over fillets; sprinkle with cashews and green onions. Bake, uncovered, at 425° for 15-20 minutes or until fish flakes easily with a fork.

PER SERVING *1 fish fillet with about 2 tablespoons sauce equals 260 cal., 8 g fat (2 g sat. fat), 40 mg chol., 358 mg sodium, 22 g carb., 2 g fiber, 26 g pro.* **Diabetic Exchanges:** *3 lean meat, 1 fruit, 1 fat.*

Eggplant Parmesan

This healthier version of a classic dish calls for baking the eggplant instead of frying it. The prep may a take a few minutes more, but you'll be rewarded with an Italian feast of rustic elegance and wonderful flavor.

—**LACI HOOTEN** MCKINNEY, TX

PREP: 40 MIN. • **COOK:** 25 MIN.
MAKES: 8 SERVINGS

- 3 **large eggs, beaten**
- 2½ **cups panko (Japanese) bread crumbs**
- 3 **medium eggplants, cut into ¼-inch slices**
- 2 **jars (4½ ounces each) sliced mushrooms, drained**
- ½ **teaspoon dried basil**
- ⅛ **teaspoon dried oregano**
- 2 **cups (8 ounces) shredded part-skim mozzarella cheese**
- ½ **cup grated Parmesan cheese**
- 1 **jar (28 ounces) spaghetti sauce**

1. Preheat oven to 350°. Place eggs and panko bread crumbs in separate shallow bowls. Dip the eggplant slices in the eggs, then coat in the crumbs. Place on baking sheets coated with cooking spray. Bake 15-20 minutes or until tender and golden brown, turning once.

2. In a small bowl, combine the mushrooms, basil and oregano. In another small bowl, combine mozzarella and Parmesan cheeses.

3. Spread ½ cup sauce into a 13x9-in. baking dish coated with cooking spray. Layer with a third of the mushroom mixture, a third of the eggplant, ¾ cup sauce and a third of the cheese mixture. Repeat layers twice.

4. Bake casserole, uncovered, at 350° 25-30 minutes or until heated through and cheese is melted.

Crab & Shrimp Stuffed Sole

Even your most casual backyard cookout will be extra special when you serve delicate sole stuffed with a rich seafood filling. Add a salad and baguette on the side for a memorable meal.

—**BRYN NAMAVARI** CHICAGO, IL

PREP: 25 MIN. • **GRILL:** 15 MIN.
MAKES: 4 SERVINGS

- 1 can (6 ounces) crabmeat, drained, flaked and cartilage removed
- ½ cup chopped cooked peeled shrimp
- ¼ cup soft bread crumbs
- ¼ cup butter, melted, divided
- 2 tablespoons whipped cream cheese
- 2 teaspoons minced chives
- 1 garlic clove, minced
- 1 teaspoon grated lemon peel
- 1 teaspoon minced fresh parsley
- 4 sole fillets (6 ounces each)
- 1½ cups cherry tomatoes
- 2 tablespoons dry white wine or chicken broth
- 2 tablespoons lemon juice
- ½ teaspoon salt
- ½ teaspoon pepper

1. In a small bowl, combine the crab, shrimp, soft bread crumbs, 2 tablespoons butter, cream cheese, chives, garlic, lemon peel and parsley. Spoon about ¼ cup stuffing onto each fillet; roll up and secure with toothpicks.
2. Place each fillet on a double thickness of heavy-duty foil (about 18x12 in.). Combine the tomatoes, wine, lemon juice, salt, pepper and remaining butter; spoon over fillets. Fold foil around fish and seal tightly.
3. Grill, covered, over medium heat for 12-15 minutes or until the fish flakes easily with a fork. Open foil carefully to allow steam to escape.

Fiery Stuffed Poblanos

I love Southwestern cooking, but many of the dishes can be high in fat, calories and sodium. As a dietitian, I try to come up with nutritious twists...which is how my poblanos were born.

—**AMBER MASSEY** ARGYLE, TX

PREP: 50 MIN. + STANDING • **BAKE:** 20 MIN.
MAKES: 8 SERVINGS

- 8 poblano peppers
- 1 can (15 ounces) black beans, rinsed and drained
- 1 medium zucchini, chopped
- 1 small red onion, chopped
- 4 garlic cloves, minced
- 1 can (15¼ ounces) whole kernel corn, drained
- 1 can (14½ ounces) fire-roasted diced tomatoes, undrained
- 1 cup cooked brown rice
- 1 tablespoon ground cumin
- 1 to 1½ teaspoons ground ancho chili pepper
- ¼ teaspoon salt
- ¼ teaspoon pepper
- 1 cup (4 ounces) shredded reduced-fat Mexican cheese blend, divided
- 3 green onions, chopped
- ½ cup reduced-fat sour cream

1. Broil the peppers 3 in. from the heat until skins blister, about 5 minutes. With tongs, rotate peppers a quarter turn. Broil and rotate until all sides are blistered and blackened. Immediately place peppers in a large bowl; cover and let stand for 20 minutes.
2. Meanwhile, in a small bowl, coarsely mash black beans; set aside. In a large nonstick skillet coated with cooking spray, cook and stir the zucchini and onion until tender. Add garlic; cook 1 minute longer. Add corn, tomatoes, rice, seasonings and beans. Remove from the heat; stir in ½ cup cheese. Set aside.
3. Peel off and discard the charred skins from poblanos. Cut a lengthwise slit down each pepper, leaving the stem intact; remove the membranes and seeds. Fill each pepper with ⅔ cup filling.
4. Place the peppers in a 13x9-in. baking dish coated with cooking spray. Bake, uncovered, at 375° for 18-22 minutes or until heated through, sprinkling with the green onions and remaining cheese during the last 5 minutes of baking. Garnish with sour cream.

PER SERVING *1 stuffed poblano pepper with 1 tablespoon sour cream equals 223 cal., 5 g fat (2 g sat. fat), 15 mg chol., 579 mg sodium, 32 g carb., 7 g fiber, 11 g pro.* **Diabetic Exchanges:** *2 vegetable, 1 starch, 1 lean meat, 1 fat.*

Heavenly Greek Tacos

When my fiance and I tried these, we couldn't believe how good they were. I don't think I've ever said "*mmm*" so many times!

—**MEAGAN JENSEN** RENO, NV

PREP: 30 MIN. + MARINATING • **GRILL:** 10 MIN.
MAKES: 6 SERVINGS

- ⅓ cup lemon juice
- 2 tablespoons olive oil
- 4 teaspoons grated lemon peel
- 3 garlic cloves, minced, divided
- 1 teaspoon dried oregano
- ¼ teaspoon salt
- ¼ teaspoon pepper
- 2 pounds mahi mahi
- 1½ cups shredded red cabbage
- ½ medium red onion, thinly sliced
- ½ medium sweet red pepper, julienned
- ½ cup crumbled feta cheese
- 6 tablespoons chopped pitted Greek olives, divided
- ¼ cup minced fresh parsley
- 1½ cups plain Greek yogurt
- ½ medium English cucumber, cut into 1-inch pieces
- 1 teaspoon dill weed
- ½ teaspoon ground coriander
- 12 whole wheat tortillas (8 inches), warmed

1. In a large resealable plastic bag, combine the lemon juice, oil, lemon peel, 2 garlic cloves, oregano, salt and pepper. Add the mahi mahi; seal bag and turn to coat. Refrigerate for up to 30 minutes.
2. In a large bowl, combine the cabbage, onion, red pepper, cheese, 3 tablespoons olives and parsley; set aside.

3. Place the plain yogurt, cucumber, dill, coriander and remaining garlic and olives in a food processor; cover and process until blended.
4. Drain fish and discard marinade. Moisten a paper towel with cooking oil; using long-handled tongs, lightly coat the grill rack. Grill the mahi mahi, covered, over medium heat or broil 4 in. from the heat for 3-4 minutes on each side or until fish flakes easily with a fork.
5. Place a portion of fish on each tortilla; top with cabbage mixture and sauce.

Firecracker Grilled Salmon

Light up the dinner table tonight with an amazing salmon entree from the grill. Used for the marinade and glaze, the tangy sauce has hints of maple syrup, red pepper flakes and ginger.

—**MELISSA ROGERS** TUSCALOOSA, AL

PREP: 20 MIN. + MARINATING • **GRILL:** 5 MIN.
MAKES: 4 SERVINGS

- 2 tablespoons balsamic vinegar
- 2 tablespoons reduced-sodium soy sauce
- 1 green onion, thinly sliced
- 1 tablespoon olive oil
- 1 tablespoon maple syrup
- 2 garlic cloves, minced
- 1 teaspoon ground ginger
- 1 teaspoon crushed red pepper flakes
- ½ teaspoon sesame oil
- ¼ teaspoon salt
- 4 salmon fillets (6 ounces each)

1. In a small bowl, combine the first 10 ingredients. Pour ¼ cup marinade into a large resealable plastic bag. Add the salmon fillets; seal bag and turn to coat. Refrigerate for up to 30 minutes. Cover and refrigerate remaining marinade.
2. Drain salmon, discarding marinade. Using long-handled tongs, moisten a paper towel with cooking oil and lightly coat the grill rack. Place salmon skin side down on grill rack. Grill, covered, over high heat or broil 3-4 in. from the heat for 5-10 minutes or until the fish flakes easily with a fork, basting occasionally with remaining marinade.
PER SERVING *1 fillet equals 306 cal., 18 g fat (4 g sat. fat), 85 mg chol., 367 mg sodium, 4 g carb., trace fiber, 29 g pro.* **Diabetic Exchanges:** *5 lean meat, 1 fat.*

DRESSING IT UP

Short on time? Bottled Italian salad dressing makes an easy marinade for salmon. Just marinate the fish in the dressing in the fridge overnight, then drain and discard the marinade and cook the fish as desired.

—**KATHRYN M.** WARRENSBURG, MO

Fruity Halibut Steaks

My family loves this dish so much I think they'd eat it every day! I like it because it's wholesome, low in calories and delicious. I refrigerate the salsa four hours ahead so the flavors can blend.
—**PATRICIA NIEH** PORTOLA VALLEY, CA

START TO FINISH: 30 MIN.
MAKES: 6 SERVINGS

- 1 cup chopped fresh pineapple
- 1 cup chopped peeled mango
- ⅔ cup chopped sweet red pepper
- 1 medium tomato, seeded and chopped
- ⅓ cup chopped seeded peeled cucumber
- ¼ cup minced fresh cilantro
- 2 tablespoons chopped seeded jalapeno pepper
- 2 tablespoons lime juice
- 6 halibut steaks (8 ounces each)
- 2 tablespoons olive oil
- ½ teaspoon salt
- ½ teaspoon pepper

1. In a small bowl, combine the first eight ingredients; chill until serving.
2. Brush the halibut with oil; sprinkle with salt and pepper. Moisten a paper towel with cooking oil; using long-handled tongs, lightly coat the grill rack. Grill the halibut, covered, over high heat or broil 3-4 in. from the heat for 3-5 minutes on each side or until the fish flakes easily with a fork. Serve with the salsa.
NOTE *Wear disposable gloves when cutting hot peppers; the oils can burn skin. Avoid touching your face.*

Feta Shrimp Tacos

An unusual combination of taco seasoning and feta cheese works remarkably well in these refreshing favorites. You won't want to stop at just one! A little avocado makes them even yummier.
—**ATHENA RUSSELL** FLORENCE, SC

START TO FINISH: 30 MIN.
MAKES: 4 SERVINGS

- 2 cups shredded red cabbage
- ¼ cup finely chopped sweet onion
- 1 banana pepper, finely chopped
- ¼ cup Miracle Whip Light or reduced-fat mayonnaise
- 1 tablespoon cider vinegar
- 1 tablespoon stone-ground mustard
- ¼ teaspoon pepper
- 1 pound uncooked medium shrimp, peeled and deveined
- 1 tablespoon reduced-sodium taco seasoning
- 1 tablespoon olive oil
- 8 whole wheat tortillas (8 inches), warmed
- ¾ cup crumbled feta cheese
  Sliced avocado, optional

1. In a small bowl, combine cabbage, onion and banana pepper. In another bowl, mix the Miracle Whip, vinegar, mustard and pepper; add to the cabbage mixture and toss to coat. Refrigerate until serving.
2. Toss the shrimp with the taco seasoning. In a large nonstick skillet, heat oil over medium-high heat. Add the shrimp; cook and stir 3-4 minutes or until the shrimp turn pink. Serve in whole wheat tortillas with slaw, feta cheese and, if desired, avocado.

Pan-Fried Catfish with Spicy Pecan Gremolata

Gremolata, a citrusy minced herb mix, makes a flavorful garnish. This recipe's well-seasoned version featuring pecans gives fried catfish fillets an unexpected but deliciously nutty twist.

—**LAUREEN PITTMAN** RIVERSIDE, CA

PREP: 25 MIN. • **COOK:** 10 MIN./BATCH
MAKES: 4 SERVINGS

- ½ cup packed fresh parsley sprigs
- ½ cup glazed pecans
- 2 tablespoons grated lemon peel
- 1 tablespoon grated orange peel
- 1 garlic clove, halved
- 1 teaspoon brown sugar
- ¼ teaspoon cayenne pepper
- 1 cup buttermilk
- 1 cup all-purpose flour
- 1 cup cornmeal
- 2 teaspoons Cajun seasoning
- 4 catfish fillets (6 ounces each)
- ½ cup canola oil

1. Place the first seven ingredients in a food processor. Cover and process until chunky; set aside.

2. Place buttermilk in a shallow bowl. In another shallow bowl, combine the flour, cornmeal and Cajun seasoning. Dip fish in buttermilk, then coat with cornmeal mixture.

3. In a large skillet, cook the fillets in the oil in batches over medium heat for 4-5 minutes on each side or until the fish flakes easily with a fork. Serve with gremolata.

MAKE IT CAJUN

Spicy Cajun seasoning brings heat and bold flavor to recipes. Look for Cajun seasoning in the spice section of your grocery store. Or experiment in the kitchen to make your own Cajun seasoning using common items. Although there are numerous different blends of this zippy ingredient, a typical mix includes salt, onion powder, celery seed, garlic powder, cayenne pepper, ground mustard and pepper.

Pesto Veggie Pizza

When it comes to the foods we love most, pizza is tops. Here's a great one!

—DANA DIRKS SAN DIEGO, CA

PREP: 30 MIN. + STANDING • **BAKE:** 10 MIN.
MAKES: 6 SERVINGS

- 1 package (¼ ounce) active dry yeast
- 1 cup warm water (110° to 115°)
- ⅓ cup grated Parmesan cheese
- 2 tablespoons canola oil
- 1 tablespoon sugar
- 1 tablespoon dried basil
- ½ teaspoon salt
- ¾ cup all-purpose flour
- 1 to 1½ cups whole wheat flour
- 3½ cups fresh baby spinach
- ¼ cup prepared pesto
- 1¾ cups coarsely chopped fresh broccoli
- ¾ cup chopped green pepper
- 2 green onions, chopped
- 4 garlic cloves, minced
- 2 cups (8 ounces) shredded part-skim mozzarella cheese

1. In a small bowl, dissolve the yeast in the warm water. Add the grated Parmesan cheese, oil, sugar, basil, salt, all-purpose flour and ¾ cup whole wheat flour. Beat until smooth. Stir in enough remaining whole wheat flour to form a soft dough (the dough will be sticky).

2. Turn the dough onto a lightly floured surface; knead until smooth and elastic, about 6-8 minutes. Cover and let rest for 10 minutes.

3. Roll the dough into a 16x12-in. rectangle. Transfer to a baking sheet coated with cooking spray; build up edges slightly. Prick dough with a fork. Bake at 375° for 8-10 minutes or until lightly browned.

4. Meanwhile, in a large saucepan, bring ½ in. of water to a boil. Add the spinach; cover and boil for 3-5 minutes or until wilted. Drain and place in a food processor. Add pesto; cover and process until blended.

5. Spread over pizza crust. Top with broccoli, green pepper, green onions, garlic and mozzarella cheese. Bake 10-12 minutes longer or until the cheese is melted.

PER SERVING *⅙ of pizza equals 364 cal., 17 g fat (6 g sat. fat), 29 mg chol., 543 mg sodium, 35 g carb., 5 g fiber, 19 g pro.* **Diabetic Exchanges:** *2 starch, 2 medium-fat meat, 2 fat, 1 vegetable.*

> ❝This is our all-time favorite way to fix salmon. For the best flavor, wait until the wood chips are really smoking before adding the fish to the grill.❞
>
> **—JERI KILPATRICK** HOODSPORT, WA

Mesquite Salmon

START TO FINISH: 30 MIN.
MAKES: 4 SERVINGS

- ½ cup mayonnaise
- 2 tablespoons brown sugar
- 2 tablespoons minced fresh parsley
- 1 tablespoon minced fresh dill
- 1 tablespoon lemon juice
- ½ teaspoon grated lemon peel
- ¼ teaspoon salt
- ⅛ teaspoon pepper
- 2 cups soaked mesquite wood chips
- 1 salmon fillet (1½ pounds)

1. In a small bowl, combine the first eight ingredients; set aside.

2. Add wood chips to grill according to manufacturer's directions. Using long-handled tongs, moisten a paper towel with cooking oil and lightly coat the grill rack. Place salmon skin side down on the rack. Grill, covered, over medium heat for 7 minutes.

3. Spoon mayonnaise mixture over the salmon. Grill 7-10 minutes longer or until fish flakes easily with a fork.

GRAND PRIZE **WINNER** ★★★

Martha's Fish Tacos

We can't get enough barbecued fish at our house. This recipe can be eaten hot off the grill or made ahead and served cold.

—MARTHA BENOIT PROCTORSVILLE, VERMONT

PREP: 25 MIN. • **GRILL:** 10 MIN.
MAKES: 6 SERVINGS

- 2 large ears sweet corn
- 1 teaspoon butter, softened
- ⅛ teaspoon salt
- ⅛ teaspoon pepper
- 1 haddock fillet (8 ounces)
- 2 teaspoons chili powder, divided
- 2 cups shredded lettuce
- 2 medium tomatoes, seeded and chopped
- 1 medium sweet red pepper, chopped
- 1 medium ripe avocado, peeled and chopped
- 3 tablespoons taco sauce
- 2 tablespoons lime juice, divided
- 1 tablespoon minced fresh cilantro
- 1½ teaspoons grated lime peel
- 12 flour tortillas (8 inches)

1. Spread the corn with butter and sprinkle with salt and pepper. Grill, covered, over medium heat for 10-12 minutes or until tender, turning occasionally.

2. Meanwhile, sprinkle the haddock with 1 teaspoon chili powder. Using long-handled tongs, moisten a paper towel with cooking oil and lightly coat the grill rack. Grill the fish, covered, over medium heat for 7-9 minutes or until the fish flakes easily with a fork.

3. Cool the corn slightly; remove the kernels from the cobs. Place in a large bowl. Add the lettuce, tomatoes, red pepper, avocado, taco sauce, 1 tablespoon lime juice, cilantro, lime peel and remaining chili powder.

4. Drizzle the remaining lime juice over the fish; cut into ½-in. cubes. Add to corn mixture. Spoon ½ cup mixture over each tortilla. Serve immediately.

Inspired by a fabulous dish I had at a local restaurant, I came up with Porcini Mac & Cheese. When I added a splash of pumpkin ale for a little fall flavor, I liked it even better!
—LAURA DAVIS CHINCOTEAGUE ISLAND, VA

Porcini Mac & Cheese

PREP: 30 MIN. + STANDING • **BAKE:** 35 MIN.
MAKES: 6 SERVINGS

- 1 package (1 ounce) dried porcini mushrooms
- 1 cup boiling water
- 1 package (16 ounces) small pasta shells
- 6 tablespoons butter, cubed
- 1 cup chopped baby portobello mushrooms
- 1 shallot, finely chopped
- 1 garlic clove, minced
- 3 tablespoons all-purpose flour
- 2½ cups 2% milk
- ½ cup pumpkin or amber ale
- 2 cups (8 ounces) shredded sharp white cheddar cheese
- 1 cup (4 ounces) shredded fontina cheese
- 1 teaspoon salt
- 1 cup soft bread crumbs

1. Preheat oven to 350°. In a small bowl, combine dried mushrooms and boiling water; let stand 15-20 minutes or until mushrooms are softened. Remove with a slotted spoon; rinse and finely chop. Discard liquid. Cook pasta shells according to package directions for al dente.

2. Meanwhile, in a Dutch oven, heat the butter over medium-high heat. Add the portobello mushrooms and shallot; cook and stir 2-3 minutes or until tender. Add the garlic; cook 1 minute longer. Stir in the flour until blended; gradually stir in the milk and beer. Bring to a boil, stirring constantly; cook and stir 3-4 minutes or until slightly thickened. Stir in cheeses, salt and reserved mushrooms.

3. Drain the pasta shells; add to the mushroom mixture and toss to combine. Transfer to a greased 13x9-in. baking dish. Top with the soft bread crumbs. Bake, uncovered, 35-40 minutes or until golden brown.

NOTE *To make soft bread crumbs, tear the bread into pieces and place in a food processor or blender. Cover; pulse until crumbs form. One slice of bread yields ½ -¾ cup crumbs.*

Grilled Tilapia with Raspberry Chipotle Chutney

I eat fish frequently and am always looking for tasty yet healthy ways to enjoy it. Making the chutney ahead of time really makes this a quick dinner option.

—**MEGAN DICOU** BERKELEY, CA

PREP: 40 MIN. • **GRILL:** 5 MIN.
MAKES: 4 SERVINGS

- 1 medium red onion, chopped
- 1 medium sweet red pepper, chopped
- 2 teaspoons olive oil
- 3 garlic cloves, minced
- 2 teaspoons minced fresh gingerroot
- 1½ cups fresh raspberries
- ¾ cup reduced-sodium chicken broth
- ¼ cup honey
- 2 tablespoons cider vinegar
- 1 tablespoon minced chipotle peppers in adobo sauce
- ½ teaspoon salt, divided
- ½ teaspoon pepper, divided
- 4 tilapia fillets (6 ounces each)

1. In a large saucepan, saute the onion and pepper in oil until tender. Add garlic and ginger; cook 1 minute longer. Stir in the raspberries, chicken broth, honey, cider vinegar, chipotle peppers, ¼ teaspoon salt and ¼ teaspoon pepper. Bring to a boil. Reduce the heat; simmer, uncovered, for 25-30 minutes or until thickened.

2. Meanwhile, sprinkle the tilapia fillets with remaining salt and pepper. Using long-handled tongs, moisten a paper towel with cooking oil and lightly coat the grill rack. Grill fish, covered, over high heat or broil 3-4 in. from the heat for 3-5 minutes or until fish flakes easily with a fork. Serve with chutney.

PER SERVING *1 tilapia fillet with ¼ cup chutney equals 277 cal., 4 g fat (1 g sat. fat), 83 mg chol., 491 mg sodium, 29 g carb., 5 g fiber, 33 g pro.* ***Diabetic Exchanges:*** *5 lean meat, 2 starch, ½ fat.*

GRAND PRIZE WINNER

GRAND PRIZE

Pineapple Pico Tuna Steaks

Here's an entree that gets a one-two punch of flavor—first from a sensational marinade, then from pico de gallo made with pineapple, tomatoes, lime juice and jalapeno.

—**SALLY SIBTHORPE** SHELBY TOWNSHIP, MI

PREP: 10 MIN. + MARINATING • **GRILL:** 10 MIN.
MAKES: 4 SERVINGS

- ½ cup tequila
- 3 tablespoons brown sugar
- 2 tablespoons lime juice
- 1 tablespoon chili powder
- 1 tablespoon olive oil
- 1 teaspoon salt
- 4 tuna steaks (6 ounces each)

PICO DE GALLO

- 1 cup chopped fresh pineapple
- 1 plum tomato, finely chopped
- ⅓ cup finely chopped onion
- ¼ cup minced fresh cilantro
- 2 tablespoons minced seeded jalapeno pepper
- 2 tablespoons lime juice
- 1 tablespoon olive oil
- 2 teaspoons grated lime peel
- ½ teaspoon salt

1. In a large resealable plastic bag, combine the first six ingredients. Add the tuna; seal the bag and turn to coat. Refrigerate for 30 minutes. Meanwhile, in a small bowl, combine pico de gallo ingredients. Cover and refrigerate until serving.

2. Drain and discard marinade. Using long-handled tongs, moisten a paper towel with cooking oil and lightly coat the grill rack. For medium-rare, grill the tuna, covered, over high heat or broil 3-4 inches from the heat for 3-4 minutes on each side or until slightly pink in the center. Serve with pico de gallo.

NOTE *Wear disposable gloves when cutting hot peppers; the oils can burn skin. Avoid touching your face.*

PER SERVING *1 tuna steak with ½ cup pico de gallo equals 385 cal., 9 g fat (1 g sat. fat), 77 mg chol., 974 mg sodium, 20 g carb., 2 g fiber, 41 g pro.* ***Diabetic Exchanges:*** *5 lean meat, ½ starch, ½ fat.*

Four-Cheese Baked Penne

You'll never miss the meat in this protein-packed, rich and cheesy pasta bake. Red pepper flakes bring a little heat.
—SCARLETT ELROD NEWNAN, GA

PREP: 30 MIN. + COOLING • **BAKE:** 20 MIN.
MAKES: 6 SERVINGS

- 4 **cups uncooked whole wheat penne pasta**
- 1 **medium onion, chopped**
- 2 **teaspoons olive oil**
- 4 **garlic cloves, minced**
- 1 **can (15 ounces) crushed tomatoes**
- 1 **can (8 ounces) tomato sauce**
- 3 **tablespoons minced fresh parsley or 1 tablespoon dried parsley flakes**
- 1 **teaspoon dried oregano**
- 1 **teaspoon dried rosemary, crushed**
- ½ **teaspoon crushed red pepper flakes**
- ¼ **teaspoon pepper**
- 1½ **cups (12 ounces) 2% cottage cheese**
- 1¼ **cups (5 ounces) shredded part-skim mozzarella cheese, divided**
- 1 **cup part-skim ricotta cheese**
- ¼ **cup grated Parmesan cheese**

1. Cook the penne pasta according to package directions.
2. Meanwhile, in a large skillet, saute the onion in oil until tender. Add garlic; cook 1 minute longer. Stir in tomatoes, tomato sauce, parsley, oregano, rosemary, red pepper flakes and pepper. Bring to a boil. Remove from the heat; cool for 15 minutes.
3. Preheat oven to 400°. Drain the penne pasta; add to the sauce. Stir in the cottage cheese, ½ cup mozzarella cheese and all of the ricotta cheese. Transfer to a 13x9-in. baking dish coated with cooking spray. Top with Parmesan cheese and remaining mozzarella cheese.
4. Bake, uncovered, 20-25 minutes or until bubbly.

BBQ Shrimp Quesadillas

My husband loves corn, shrimp and anything with barbecue sauce. One night when I was short on ingredients, ideas and time, I headed for the garden. My quesadillas were born!
—CHRISTINE PARSONS BOUNTIFUL, UT

PREP: 30 MIN. + MARINATING • **COOK:** 5 MIN.
MAKES: 4 SERVINGS

- 2 **tablespoons lime juice**
- 2 **teaspoons olive oil**
- 1½ **teaspoons grated lime peel**
- ¼ **teaspoon salt**
- ¼ **teaspoon pepper**
- ¾ **pound uncooked medium shrimp, peeled and deveined**
- 2 **medium ears sweet corn, husks removed**
- 2 **medium zucchini, chopped**
- 4 **green onions, thinly sliced**
- 2 **tablespoons barbecue sauce**
- 2 **cups (8 ounces) shredded Monterey Jack cheese**
- 8 **flour tortillas (8 inches)**
  Salsa and additional barbecue sauce

1. In a large resealable plastic bag, combine the lime juice, oil, lime peel, salt and pepper. Add the shrimp; seal bag and turn to coat. Refrigerate for 15 minutes.
2. Meanwhile, remove the corn from the cobs. Drain and discard the marinade from the shrimp. Chop shrimp and set aside. In a large nonstick skillet coated with cooking spray, saute zucchini, corn and onions until crisp-tender. Add shrimp; saute 2-3 minutes longer or until shrimp turn pink. Remove from the heat; stir in barbecue sauce.
3. Sprinkle the cheese over half of the flour tortillas. Spoon shrimp mixture over cheese. Top with remaining tortillas. Cook on a griddle coated with cooking spray over low heat for 1-2 minutes on each side or until the cheese is melted. Serve with salsa and additional barbecue sauce.

Durango Potato Casserole, page 174

164

170

181

Sides & Breads

Round out your spread with these **most-requested side dishes,** loaves and more! With a flavorful variety of dinner additions like colorful vegetables, bubbling casseroles, **golden rolls** and savory rice specialties, it'll be a snap to serve a **memorable menu** any day of the week.

Pecan-Stuffed Butternut Squash

I love autumn because it's when butternut squash is at its peak. The squash in this side dish is tender, and the creamy pecan filling is fabulous.

—**SHERRY LITTLE** SHERWOOD, AR

PREP: 10 MIN. • **BAKE:** 1¼ HOURS
MAKES: 8 SERVINGS

  2 **medium butternut squash (about 3 pounds each)**
  ¾ **teaspoon salt**
      Pepper, optional
  4 **ounces cream cheese, softened**
  ¼ **cup butter, softened**
  3 **tablespoons brown sugar**
  ½ **cup chopped pecans**

1. Cut each squash in half lengthwise; discard seeds. Place squash cut side down in two 13x9-in. baking dishes; add ½ in. water. Bake, uncovered, at 350° for 1 hour.
2. Turn squash over; sprinkle with salt and, if desired, pepper. In a small bowl, beat the cream cheese, butter and brown sugar until light and fluffy; stir in pecans. Spoon into squash cavities.
3. Bake 15-20 minutes longer or until filling is lightly browned and squash is tender.

❝We love Mexican food and corn on the cob, so I combined the two into something fresh and spicy. For Italian flair, I make this corn with basil, oregano butter and Parmesan cheese.❞

—**MACKENZIE SEVERSON** GERMANTOWN, MD

Fiesta Grilled Corn

PREP: 25 MIN. + SOAKING • **GRILL:** 25 MIN.
MAKES: 6 SERVINGS

  ½ **cup butter, softened**
  ¼ **cup minced fresh cilantro**
  2 **teaspoons grated lime peel**
  ½ **teaspoon garlic powder**
  6 **large ears sweet corn in husks**
  ½ **cup mayonnaise**
  1 **tablespoon chili powder**
  ½ **teaspoon paprika**
  ½ **cup crumbled queso fresco or fresh goat cheese**

1. In a small bowl, combine the butter, cilantro, lime peel and garlic powder. Shape into a log; wrap in plastic wrap. Refrigerate for 30 minutes or until firm.
2. Carefully peel back corn husks to within 1 in. of bottoms; remove silk. Place in a Dutch oven; cover with cold water. Soak for 20 minutes; drain. In a small bowl, combine the mayonnaise, chili powder and paprika. Spread over corn. Rewrap corn in husks and secure with kitchen string.
3. Grill corn, covered, over medium heat for 25-30 minutes or until tender, turning often. Serve with butter slices and sprinkle with cheese.

Roasted Vegetables with Gremolata

Traditional gremolata, an herb condiment, is made with parsley, lemon peel and garlic. In this recipe, Parmesan and walnuts add richness and crunch that enhance the potatoes and parsnips.

—FRAN FEHLING STATEN ISLAND, NY

PREP: 20 MIN. • **BAKE:** 45 MIN.
MAKES: 9 SERVINGS

- 3 **pounds sweet potatoes (about 4 large), peeled and cut into 1-inch cubes**
- 1 **pound parsnips, peeled and cut into 1-inch lengths**
- 6 **shallots, quartered**
- 5 **tablespoons olive oil, divided**
- 1 **teaspoon salt**
- ½ **teaspoon pepper**
- 1 **tablespoon lemon juice**

GREMOLATA
- ¾ **cup chopped walnuts, toasted**
- ⅓ **cup grated Parmesan cheese**
- 3 **tablespoons minced fresh parsley**
- 1 **tablespoon grated lemon peel**
- 1 **tablespoon lemon juice**
- 1 **tablespoon olive oil**
- 1 **garlic clove, minced**
- ¼ **teaspoon ground nutmeg**

1. Place the sweet potatoes, parsnips and shallots in a greased shallow roasting pan. Drizzle with 4 tablespoons olive oil; sprinkle with salt and pepper. Bake at 425° for 45-50 minutes or until tender, stirring occasionally. Drizzle with lemon juice and remaining oil.

2. For gremolata, place walnuts in a food processor; cover and process until coarsely ground. Transfer to a small bowl; stir in the cheese, parsley, lemon peel and juice, oil, garlic and nutmeg. Sprinkle over vegetables. Serve warm.

Summer Risotto

My mom always made this hearty dish to use up summer garden vegetables. I'll often add sauteed mushrooms and serve it as an entree with crusty bread and a salad.

—SHIRLEY HODGE BANGOR, PA

PREP: 25 MIN. • **COOK:** 30 MIN.
MAKES: 12 SERVINGS

- 5½ **to 6 cups reduced-sodium chicken broth**
- 1 **small onion, finely chopped**
- 2 **tablespoons olive oil**
- 1 **tablespoon butter**
- 2 **cups uncooked arborio rice**
- 3 **large tomatoes, chopped**
- 2 **cups fresh or frozen corn, thawed**
- ½ **cup crumbled feta cheese**
- 2 **tablespoons minced fresh thyme or 2 teaspoons dried thyme**
- 2 **tablespoons minced fresh rosemary or 2 teaspoons dried rosemary, crushed**
- 2 **tablespoons minced fresh basil or 2 teaspoons dried basil**
- ¼ **teaspoon salt**
- ¼ **teaspoon pepper**
  Shredded Parmesan cheese

1. In a large saucepan, heat the broth and keep warm. In a large skillet, saute onion in oil and butter until tender. Add rice; cook and stir for 2-3 minutes or until lightly browned. Stir in 1 cup warm broth. Cook and stir until all of the liquid is absorbed.

2. Add remaining broth, ½ cup at a time, stirring constantly. Allow the liquid to be absorbed between additions. Cook until risotto is creamy and rice is almost tender (total cooking time will be about 20 minutes).

3. Add the tomatoes, corn, feta cheese, herbs, salt and pepper; heat through. Sprinkle with Parmesan cheese. Serve immediately.

Roasted Brussels Sprouts & Cauliflower

My grandkids aren't huge fans of cauliflower, but the bacon transformed this dish into one they love! They like it even more with golden cauliflower instead of white.

—**PATRICIA HUDSON** RIVERVIEW, FL

PREP: 25 MIN. • **COOK:** 20 MIN.
MAKES: 12 SERVINGS (½ CUP EACH)

- 8 bacon strips, chopped
- 6 garlic cloves, minced
- 1 tablespoon olive oil
- 1 tablespoon butter, melted
- ¼ teaspoon kosher salt
- ¼ teaspoon coarsely ground pepper
- 4 cups Brussels sprouts, halved
- 4 cups fresh cauliflowerets
- ¼ cup grated Parmesan cheese
  Additional grated Parmesan cheese, optional

1. In a large skillet, cook bacon over medium heat until crisp, stirring occasionally. Remove with a slotted spoon; drain on paper towels. Discard drippings, reserving 1 tablespoon.

2. In a large bowl, mix the garlic, oil, butter, salt, pepper and reserved drippings. Add the Brussels sprouts and cauliflowerets; toss to coat. Transfer to two greased 15x10x1-in. baking pans.

3. Bake at 350° for 15 minutes. Sprinkle each pan with 2 tablespoons cheese. Bake 3-5 minutes longer or until vegetables are tender. Sprinkle with bacon and, if desired, additional cheese.

International Potato Cake

I used to prepare food for an embassy function in Turkey, where diplomats from European and Middle Eastern countries were present. This potato cake was devoured by everyone!

—**JUDY BATSON** TAMPA, FL

PREP: 40 MIN. • **BAKE:** 35 MIN. + COOLING
MAKES: 12 SERVINGS

- ¼ cup seasoned bread crumbs
- 3 pounds potatoes (about 9 medium), peeled and cubed
- ½ cup heavy whipping cream
- ¼ cup butter, cubed
- 3 large eggs, beaten
- 1 teaspoon Greek seasoning
- ¼ teaspoon garlic salt
- ¼ teaspoon lemon-pepper seasoning
- ¼ pound thinly sliced fontina cheese
- ¼ pound thinly sliced hard salami, coarsely chopped

TOPPING
- ⅓ cup grated Parmesan cheese
- 1 tablespoon seasoned bread crumbs
- 1 tablespoon butter, melted

1. Sprinkle bread crumbs onto the bottom of a greased 9-in. springform pan; set aside.

2. Place the cubed potatoes in a large saucepan and cover with water. Bring to a boil. Reduce the heat; cover and simmer potatoes for 10-15 minutes or until tender. Drain; transfer to a large bowl. Mash potatoes with cream, butter, eggs and seasonings.

3. Preheat oven to 350°. Spoon half the potatoes into prepared pan. Layer with cheese and salami; top with remaining potatoes. Combine topping ingredients; spoon over potatoes.

4. Cover and bake 30 minutes. Uncover; bake 5-10 minutes longer or until topping is golden brown and a thermometer reads 160°. Cool on a wire rack 10 minutes. Carefully run a knife around edge of pan to loosen; remove sides of pan. Serve warm.

Rosemary Cheddar Muffins

My 96-year-old stepmother gave me this recipe many years ago. We have enjoyed these luscious biscuitlike muffins ever since. You might not even need butter!

—**BONNIE STALLINGS** MARTINSBURG, WV

START TO FINISH: 25 MIN.
MAKES: 1 DOZEN

  2 **cups self-rising flour**
  ½ **cup shredded sharp cheddar cheese**
  1 **tablespoon minced fresh rosemary or 1 teaspoon dried rosemary, crushed**
1¼ **cups 2% milk**
  3 **tablespoons mayonnaise**

1. Preheat oven to 400°. In a large bowl, combine flour, cheese and rosemary. In another bowl, combine milk and mayonnaise; stir into dry ingredients just until moistened. Spoon into 12 greased muffin cups.
2. Bake 8-10 minutes or until lightly browned and toothpick inserted in muffin comes out clean. Cool 5 minutes before removing from pan to a wire rack. Serve warm.

Cilantro-Pepita Pesto

I created this full-flavored recipe to use the fresh cilantro in my garden. I serve it with pasta, but you can use it with tortilla chips for dipping or in any dish that needs a little perking up.

—**AMI OKASINSKI** MEMPHIS, TN

START TO FINISH: 20 MIN.
MAKES: 1½ CUPS

1 **package (6 ounces) fresh baby spinach**
2 **cups fresh cilantro leaves**
⅓ **cup grated Romano cheese**
⅓ **cup salted pumpkin seeds or pepitas, toasted**
3 **to 4 garlic cloves, peeled**
2 **tablespoons lime juice**
1 **tablespoon lemon juice**
⅛ **teaspoon salt**
3 **tablespoons olive oil**

Place the first five ingredients in a food processor; cover and pulse just until chopped. Add the lime and lemon juices and salt; cover and process until blended. While processing, gradually add oil in a steady stream. Store in an airtight container in the refrigerator.

Spicy Sweet Potato Fries

PREP: 25 MIN. • **BAKE:** 30 MIN.
MAKES: 5 SERVINGS

- 1 teaspoon coriander seeds
- ½ teaspoon fennel seed
- ½ teaspoon dried oregano
- ½ teaspoon crushed red pepper flakes
- ½ teaspoon salt
- 2 pounds sweet potatoes (about 4 medium), peeled and cut into wedges
- 2 tablespoons canola oil

SPICY MAYONNAISE DIP

- 1¼ cups mayonnaise
- 2 tablespoons lime juice
- 2 tablespoons minced fresh cilantro
- 2 garlic cloves, minced
- 1 teaspoon ground mustard
- ¼ teaspoon cayenne pepper
- ⅛ teaspoon salt

1. In a spice grinder or with a mortar and pestle, combine the coriander, fennel, oregano and pepper flakes; grind until mixture becomes a fine powder. Stir in salt.

2. In a large bowl, combine the sweet potatoes, oil and ground spices; toss to coat. Transfer potatoes to a greased 15x10x1-in. baking pan.

3. Bake, uncovered, at 400° for 30-35 minutes or until crisp and golden brown, turning occasionally.

4. In a small bowl, combine the dip ingredients; chill until serving. Serve with fries.

Better pile these sweet and spicy fries high on the plate! Served with a thick dipping sauce, they instill a craving for more. Try them with burgers or as a snack!
—**MARY JANE JONES** ATHENS, OH

Beernana Bread

It's simple arithmetic: Beer is good. Banana bread is good. Beernana bread is great! This recipe is a guaranteed crowd-pleaser. Even novices who don't know their way around the kitchen can pull this one off.

—STEVE CAYFORD DUBUQUE, IA

PREP: 15 MIN. • **BAKE:** 55 MIN. + COOLING
MAKES: 1 LOAF (16 SLICES)

- 3 cups self-rising flour
- ¾ cup quick-cooking oats
- ½ cup packed brown sugar
- 1½ cups mashed ripe bananas (about 3 medium)
- 1 bottle (12 ounces) wheat beer
- ¼ cup maple syrup
- 2 tablespoons olive oil
- 1 tablespoon sesame seeds
- ¼ teaspoon kosher salt

1. Preheat oven to 375°. In a large bowl, mix the flour, oats and brown sugar. In another bowl, mix bananas, beer and maple syrup until blended. Add to the flour mixture; stir just until moistened.
2. Transfer to a greased 9x5-in. loaf pan. Drizzle with olive oil; sprinkle with sesame seeds and salt. Bake 55-60 minutes or until a toothpick inserted in center comes out clean. Cool in pan 10 minutes before removing to wire rack to cool.
FREEZE OPTION *Securely wrap cooled loaf in plastic wrap and foil, then freeze. To use, thaw at room temperature.*
PER SERVING *1 slice equals 173 cal., 2 g fat (trace sat. fat), 0 chol., 304 mg sodium, 35 g carb., 1 g fiber, 3 g pro.* **Diabetic Exchanges:** *2 starch, ½ fat.*

Zucchini in Dill Cream Sauce

My husband and I were dairy farmers until we retired in 1967, so I always use fresh, real dairy products in my recipes. This creamy sauce combines all of our favorite foods, and folks just love it!

—JOSEPHINE VANDEN HEUVEL HART, MI

START TO FINISH: 30 MIN.
MAKES: 8 SERVINGS

- 7 cups unpeeled zucchini, cut in 1½x¼-inch strips
- ¼ cup finely chopped onion
- ½ cup water
- 1 teaspoon salt
- 1 teaspoon chicken bouillon granules or 1 chicken bouillon cube
- ½ teaspoon dill weed
- 2 tablespoons butter, melted
- 2 teaspoons sugar
- 1 teaspoon lemon juice
- 2 tablespoons all-purpose flour
- ¼ cup sour cream

1. In large saucepan, combine the zucchini, onion, water, salt, bouillon and dill; bring to a boil. Add the butter, sugar and lemon juice; mix. Remove from heat; do not drain.
2. Combine flour and sour cream; stir half of the mixture into hot zucchini. Return to heat; add remaining cream mixture and cook until thickened.
PER SERVING *1 serving equals 73 cal., 419 mg sodium, 11 mg chol., 8 g carb., 2 g pro., 4 g fat.* **Diabetic Exchanges:** *1 vegetable, 1 fat.*

FLOUR POWER

Keep a plastic knife, skewer or chopstick in your flour-storage container. Then, when you need to level a measuring cup, you have a tool at the ready and don't need to wash off another utensil. Another idea is to keep a small container of flour handy. If you need just a few tablespoons of flour for a sauce or another recipe, you don't need to haul out your larger flour canister.

Ranch Potato Casserole

I make this side dish casserole often, and it's especially good in place of baked potatoes when you're having barbecued pork or chicken. I appreciate that I can put it together a day ahead.

—LYDIA SCHNITZLER KINGSBURG, CA

PREP: 30 MIN. • **BAKE:** 40 MIN.
MAKES: 8 SERVINGS

- 6 to 8 medium red potatoes (about 2 to 2½ pounds)
- ½ cup sour cream
- ½ cup prepared ranch-style dressing
- ¼ cup bacon bits or crumbled cooked bacon
- 2 tablespoons minced fresh parsley
- 1 cup (4 ounces) shredded cheddar cheese

TOPPING
- ½ cup (2 ounces) shredded cheddar cheese
- 2 cups coarsely crushed cornflakes
- ¼ cup butter, melted

1. Cook the potatoes until tender; quarter (leaving skins on if desired) and set aside.
2. Combine the sour cream, dressing, bacon, parsley and 1 cup cheese. Place potatoes in a greased 13x9-in. baking dish. Pour sour cream mixture over potatoes and gently toss. Top with ½ cup of cheese. Combine cornflakes and butter; sprinkle over top. Bake at 350° for 40-45 minutes.

Marvelous Mediterranean Vegetables

With so many barbecues in the summer, I created this simple, tasty dish to complement any entree. I like to prepare it earlier in the day and let it marinate, then I just throw it on the grill.

—CATHY GODBERSON OAKVILLE, ON

PREP: 25 MIN. + MARINATING • **GRILL:** 10 MIN.
MAKES: 9 SERVINGS

- 3 large portobello mushrooms, sliced
- 1 each medium sweet red, orange and yellow peppers, sliced
- 1 medium zucchini, sliced
- 10 fresh asparagus spears, cut into 2-inch lengths
- 1 small onion, sliced and separated into rings
- ¾ cup grape tomatoes
- ½ cup fresh sugar snap peas
- ½ cup fresh broccoli florets
- ½ cup pitted Greek olives
- 1 bottle (14 ounces) Greek vinaigrette
- ½ cup crumbled feta cheese

1. In a large resealable plastic bag, combine the mushrooms, peppers and zucchini. Add the asparagus, onion, tomatoes, peas, broccoli and olives. Pour vinaigrette into bag; seal bag and turn to coat. Refrigerate for at least 30 minutes.
2. Discard marinade. Transfer vegetables to a grill wok or basket. Grill vegetables, uncovered, over medium heat for 8-12 minutes or until tender, stirring frequently. Place on a serving plate; sprinkle with cheese.

EASY FIX

If you do not have a grill wok or basket, use a disposable foil pan when preparing Marvelous Mediterranean Vegetables. Simply poke holes in the bottom of the pan with a meat fork to allow liquid to drain. Toss away the pan when done to make cleanup a snap.

You can also avoid the grill altogether by setting the marinated veggies on a baking sheet and cooking them up in the oven. Finish off the vegetables by setting them under the broiler for a moment.

Maple-Glazed Green Beans

After picking green beans for the first time, I decided to create a robust side dish to highlight them. I couldn't stop eating the yummy beans, so the next day I went back to pick more so I could make this recipe again!

—**MERRY GRAHAM** NEWHALL, CA

START TO FINISH: 25 MIN.
MAKES: 4 SERVINGS

- 3 **cups cut fresh green beans**
- 1 **large onion, chopped**
- 4 **bacon strips, cut into 1-inch pieces**
- ½ **cup dried cranberries**
- ¼ **cup maple syrup**
- ¼ **teaspoon salt**
- ¼ **teaspoon pepper**
- 1 **tablespoon bourbon, optional**

1. In a large saucepan, place steamer basket over 1 in. of water. Place beans in basket. Bring water to a boil. Reduce heat to maintain a low boil; steam, covered, 4-5 minutes or until crisp-tender.
2. Meanwhile, in a large skillet, cook onion and bacon over medium heat until bacon is crisp; drain. Stir cranberries, syrup, salt, pepper and, if desired, bourbon into onion mixture. Add beans; heat through, tossing to combine.

Boston Baked Beans

Simmered in molasses, these beans are perfect to take to your next potluck. The sauce is sweet, dark and rich. The beans complement anything served with them.

—**DARLENE DUNCAN** LANGHORNE, PA

PREP: 20 MIN. + SOAKING • **COOK:** 10 HOURS
MAKES: 10 SERVINGS

- 1 **pound dried navy beans**
- 6 **cups water, divided**
- ¼ **pound diced salt pork or 6 bacon strips, cooked and crumbled**
- 1 **large onion, chopped**
- ½ **cup packed brown sugar**
- ½ **cup molasses**
- ¼ **cup sugar**
- 1 **teaspoon ground mustard**
- 1 **teaspoon salt**
- ½ **teaspoon ground cloves**
- ½ **teaspoon pepper**

1. Sort the beans and rinse in cold water. Place beans in a 3- or 4-qt. slow cooker; add 4 cups water. Cover and let stand overnight.
2. Drain and rinse beans, discarding liquid. Return beans to slow cooker; add salt pork.
3. In a small bowl, combine the chopped onion, brown sugar, molasses, sugar, mustard, salt, cloves, pepper and remaining water. Pour mixture over beans; stir to combine.
4. Cover and cook on low for 10-12 hours or until the beans are tender.

Tangerine Tabbouleh

Citrus really comes through in this great mix of fruit, nuts and chickpeas. It makes a hearty and flavorful side dish that's perfect with grilled chicken, pork or beef.
—**VIVIAN LEVINE** SUMMERFIELD, FL

PREP: 35 MIN. + CHILLING
MAKES: 8 SERVINGS

- 1 **cup bulgur**
- 1 **cup boiling water**
- 1 **can (15 ounces) garbanzo beans or chickpeas, rinsed and drained**
- 2 **tangerines, peeled, sectioned and chopped**
- ⅔ **cup chopped dates**
- ½ **cup pistachios, coarsely chopped**
- ⅓ **cup dried cranberries**
- ½ **cup tangerine juice**
- 2 **tablespoons olive oil**
- 1 **teaspoon grated tangerine peel**
- ¼ **teaspoon ground ginger**
- ⅛ **teaspoon salt**

1. Place bulgur in a large bowl. Stir in water. Cover and let stand for 30 minutes or until most of the liquid is absorbed. Drain well.
2. Stir in the garbanzo beans, tangerines, dates, pistachios and cranberries. In a small bowl, combine the tangerine juice, oil, tangerine peel, ginger and salt. Pour over bulgur mixture and toss to coat. Cover and refrigerate for at least 1 hour. Stir before serving.

Asian Corn Succotash

Since I'm not a fan of lima beans, I use edamame in this colorful succotash instead. The Asian-inspired dressing alone is addictive.
—**DIERDRE CALLAWAY** PARKVILLE, MO

START TO FINISH: 25 MIN.
MAKES: 3 SERVINGS

- 1 **cup frozen shelled edamame**
- 2 **cups fresh corn**
- ¼ **cup chopped red onion**
- ¼ **cup chopped sweet red pepper**
VINAIGRETTE
- ¼ **cup rice vinegar**
- ¼ **cup olive oil**
- 1 **tablespoon sugar**
- ½ **teaspoon sesame oil**
- ¼ **teaspoon reduced-sodium soy sauce**
- ⅛ **teaspoon salt**
- ⅛ **teaspoon pepper**
  Dash hot pepper sauce

1. Place edamame in a saucepan and cover with 3 cups water. Bring to a boil. Cover and cook for 4-5 minutes or until tender, adding the corn during the last 2 minutes of cooking. Drain and rinse under cold water. Transfer to a large bowl; add onion and pepper.
2. In a small bowl, combine the vinaigrette ingredients. Pour over corn mixture and toss to coat. Chill until serving.
PER SERVING *⅔ cup equals 261 cal., 17 g fat (2 g sat. fat), 0 chol., 104 mg sodium, 25 g carb., 4 g fiber, 6 g pro.* **Diabetic Exchanges:** *2 starch, 1 fat.*

Sausage Sourdough Stuffing

Sourdough's tangy chewiness gives this stuffing texture, while sausage makes it hearty and mushrooms and cranberries lend an earthy sweetness. Consider the other two versions as well.
—**JENNIFER BRAZELL** LEWISTON, ID

PREP: 30 MIN. • **BAKE:** 30 MIN.
MAKES: 18 SERVINGS (¾ CUP EACH)

- 1 **pound bulk pork sausage**
- 1 **pound sliced baby portobello mushrooms**
- 1 **large sweet onion, chopped**
- 2 **celery ribs, chopped**
- 2 **tablespoons canola oil**
- 3 **garlic cloves, minced**
- 1 **loaf (1 pound) day-old sourdough bread, cubed**
- 2 **jars (7½ ounces each) marinated quartered artichoke hearts, drained and chopped**
- 1 **cup grated Parmesan cheese**
- ½ **cup dried cranberries**
- 1½ **teaspoons poultry seasoning**
- 1 **teaspoon dried rosemary, crushed**
- ½ **teaspoon salt**
- ½ **teaspoon pepper**
- 1 **large egg**
- 1½ **cups reduced-sodium chicken broth**

1. Preheat oven to 350°. In a Dutch oven, cook sausage over medium heat until no longer pink; drain. Transfer to a large bowl. In the same pan, saute mushrooms, onion and celery in oil until tender. Add garlic; cook 1 minute.

2. Add bread, artichokes, cheese, cranberries, poultry seasoning, rosemary, salt, pepper and mushroom mixture to the sausage. Whisk egg and broth; pour over bread mixture and toss to coat. Transfer to a greased 13x9-in. baking dish (dish will be full).

3. Bake, uncovered, 30-35 minutes until top is lightly browned and a thermometer reads at least 160°.

SOURDOUGH ALMOND STUFFING: *Omit sausage, oil, Parmesan, cranberries and poultry seasoning. Increase mushrooms to 2 cups. Saute vegetables in ¾ cup butter. To stuffing mixture, stir in ¾ cup slivered almonds, ⅔ cup chopped oil-packed sun-dried tomatoes and ½ cup minced fresh basil. Mix broth with 2 large eggs. Bake as directed. Cover with foil if stuffing browns too quickly.*

TURKEY PECAN STUFFING: *Omit the sausage, artichoke hearts, Parmesan cheese, dried cranberries and rosemary. Use bread cubes of your choice. Cook 1 pound lean ground turkey, mushrooms, onion, celery, 1 teaspoon fennel seed, ¼ teaspoon cayenne and ⅛ teaspoon ground nutmeg over medium heat until turkey is no longer pink. Add garlic; cook 1 minute. Drain. Transfer to a large bowl. Add bread cubes, 1 chopped large tart apple, 2 teaspoons rubbed sage, poultry seasoning, salt and pepper. Whisk 2 large eggs and broth; pour over bread mixture and toss to coat. Bake as directed.*

Maple & Bacon Glazed Brussels Sprouts

For special meals, here's a fantastic side dish that even children will love. The sweet maple syrup and smoky bacon complement the Brussels sprouts perfectly.

—**JAN VALDEZ** CHICAGO, IL

PREP: 15 MIN. • **COOK:** 20 MIN.
MAKES: 4 SERVINGS

- 5 bacon strips, chopped
- 1 pound fresh Brussels sprouts, trimmed
- 3 tablespoons butter
- ½ cup chicken broth
- ¼ cup chopped pecans
- ¼ cup maple syrup
- ¼ teaspoon salt
- ¼ teaspoon pepper

1. In a small skillet, cook bacon over medium heat until crisp. Remove to paper towels with a slotted spoon; drain.
2. Meanwhile, cut an "X" in the core of each Brussels sprout. In a large skillet, saute Brussels sprouts in butter for 4-5 minutes or until lightly browned.
3. Stir in the chicken broth, pecans, maple syrup, salt and pepper. Bring to a boil. Reduce heat; cover and simmer for 5 minutes. Uncover; cook and stir 8-10 minutes longer or until Brussels sprouts are tender. Sprinkle with bacon.

Garlic, Bacon & Stilton Mashed Potatoes

Creamy and savory, these mashed potatoes are a perfect partner for nearly any entree. They're a snap to put together in advance.

—**JAMIE BROWN-MILLER** NAPA, CA

PREP: 30 MIN. • **COOK:** 20 MIN.
MAKES: 8 SERVINGS

- 6 garlic cloves, peeled
- 1 teaspoon olive oil
- 2½ pounds small red potatoes, scrubbed
- 4 ounces cream cheese, softened
- ½ cup butter, cubed
- ½ cup 2% milk
- ½ teaspoon salt
- ½ teaspoon pepper
- ⅓ pound Stilton cheese, crumbled
- 6 bacon strips, cooked and crumbled
- 3 tablespoons minced fresh parsley, divided

1. Place garlic on a double thickness of heavy-duty foil. Drizzle with oil. Wrap foil around garlic. Bake at 425° for 15-20 minutes or until softened. Cool for 10-15 minutes.
2. Meanwhile, place the potatoes in a large saucepan and cover with water. Bring to a boil. Reduce heat; cover and cook for 15-20 minutes or until tender. Drain; transfer to a large bowl.
3. Squeeze softened garlic into potatoes. Add the cream cheese, butter, milk, salt and pepper. Mash potatoes until combined. Stir in the Stilton cheese, crumbled bacon and 2 tablespoons parsley. Sprinkle with remaining parsley before serving.

Hush Puppies

Some years ago, I was a cook on a large cattle ranch. One day, I thought back to the hush puppies I'd had as a child on a Southern trip, and I ended up creating my own version of them. They go well as part of an old-fashioned fried chicken dinner with mashed potatoes and gravy, buttermilk biscuits, corn on the cob and watermelon pickles!

—**KARYL GOODHART** GERALDINE, MT

PREP: 15 MIN. • **COOK:** 20 MIN.
MAKES: 12-15 SERVINGS

- 2 **cups yellow cornmeal**
- ½ **cup all-purpose flour**
- 2 **tablespoons sugar**
- 2 **teaspoons baking powder**
- 1 **teaspoon salt**
- ½ **teaspoon baking soda**
- 1 **large egg, beaten**
- ¾ **cup milk**
- ¾ **cup cream-style corn**
  Oil for deep-fat frying
  Confectioners' sugar, optional

1. In a bowl, combine cornmeal, flour, sugar, baking powder, salt and baking soda. Add egg, milk and corn; stir just until mixed.
2. In a deep-fat fryer, heat oil to 375°. Drop batter by teaspoonfuls into oil. Fry until golden brown.
3. Allow to cool slightly and, if desired, roll in confectioners' sugar.

CHANGE-OF-PACE MEAL SPECIALTY

Sometimes called Corn Bread Balls or Corn Dodgers, Hush Puppies make a great side dish for chicken, pork and fish. The crunchy coating and tender corn bread interior make the tasty bites popular with diners of all ages. Many family cooks add a bit of garlic or onion powder to the cornmeal mixture. Some enjoy adding very finely chopped jalapeno pepper.

GRAND PRIZE WINNER ★★★★

GRAND PRIZE

Durango Potato Casserole

For those who like spicy food, it's easy to turn up the heat on my potatoes by adding a little more chili powder or jalapenos for extra kick.

—**PATRICIA HARMON** BADEN, PA

PREP: 35 MIN. • **BAKE:** 25 MIN.
MAKES: 12 SERVINGS (⅔ CUP EACH)

- 2½ **pounds potatoes (about 8 medium), peeled and cut into 1-inch cubes**
- 8 **thick-sliced bacon strips**
- 1 **can (14½ ounces) diced tomatoes and green chilies, drained**
- 3 **cups (12 ounces) shredded Mexican cheese blend**
- 4 **green onions, chopped**
- ⅓ **cup chopped green pepper**
- ⅓ **cup chopped sweet red pepper**
- 1½ **cups reduced-fat mayonnaise**
- 2 **tablespoons lime juice**
- 1 **teaspoon seasoned salt**
- ¼ **teaspoon pepper**
- 1½ **teaspoons chili powder**
- 2 **tablespoons minced fresh cilantro**

1. Place potatoes in a large saucepan and cover with water. Bring to a boil. Reduce heat; cover and simmer for 10-15 minutes or until tender.
2. In a large skillet, cook bacon over medium heat until partially cooked but not crisp. Remove to paper towels to drain; set aside.
3. Drain potatoes and transfer to a large bowl; add the tomatoes, cheese, onions and peppers.
4. In a small bowl, whisk mayonnaise, lime juice, seasoned salt and pepper; add to potatoes and gently stir to coat. Transfer to a greased 13x9-in. baking dish. Coarsely chop bacon; sprinkle over the top. Sprinkle casserole with chili powder.
5. Bake, uncovered, at 350° for 25-30 minutes or until heated through. Sprinkle with cilantro. Let stand for 5 minutes before serving.

Irish Soda Bread

My husband's family is Irish. Wanting to impress my future mother-in-law, I baked this bread and took it along with me when I met her the first time. Lucky for me, she gave it a thumbs-up!

—PADMINI ROY-DIXON COLUMBUS, OH

PREP: 20 MIN. • **BAKE:** 50 MIN. + COOLING
MAKES: 1 LOAF (16 SLICES)

- ¾ **cup raisins**
- 1 **cup boiling water**
- 2 **cups all-purpose flour**
- 1 **cup whole wheat flour**
- ⅓ **cup sugar**
- 3 **teaspoons baking powder**
- 1 **teaspoon baking soda**
- 1 **teaspoon salt**
- 1 **large egg**
- 2 **cups buttermilk**
- ¼ **cup butter, melted**

1. Place the raisins in a small bowl. Cover with boiling water; let stand for 5 minutes. Drain and pat dry.
2. In a large bowl, combine the flours, sugar, baking powder, baking soda and salt. In a small bowl, whisk the egg, buttermilk and butter. Stir into dry ingredients just until moistened. Fold in raisins.
3. Transfer to a 9x5-in. loaf pan coated with cooking spray. Bake at 350° for 50-60 minutes or until a toothpick inserted near the center of the bread comes out clean. Cool for 10 minutes before removing from pan to a wire rack.
PER SERVING *1 slice equals 161 cal., 4 g fat (2 g sat. fat), 22 mg chol., 359 mg sodium, 28 g carb., 2 g fiber, 4 g pro.* **Diabetic Exchanges:** *2 starch, 1 fat.*

Spanakopita Mashed Potatoes

I learned to cook by watching my mom in the kitchen. This was the first recipe I created by myself, and it's turned out to be my favorite! By not peeling the potatoes, you can save on prep time.

—ASHLEY LEVY CLARKSVILLE, MD

PREP: 10 MIN. • **COOK:** 25 MIN.
MAKES: 6 SERVINGS

- 6 medium red potatoes, quartered
- 1 package (6 ounces) fresh baby spinach
- ¼ cup 2% milk
- 1 tablespoon butter
- ½ teaspoon salt
- ½ teaspoon pepper
- ¾ cup crumbled feta cheese

1. Place potatoes in a large saucepan and cover with water. Bring to a boil. Reduce heat; cover and cook for 15-20 minutes or until tender.
2. Meanwhile, in another large saucepan, bring ½ in. of water to a boil. Add spinach; cover and boil for 3-5 minutes or until wilted. Drain and coarsely chop; keep warm.
3. Drain potatoes and return to the saucepan. Add milk, butter, salt and pepper; mash until smooth. Fold in cheese and spinach.

PER SERVING ¾ cup equals 145 cal., 5 g fat (3 g sat. fat), 13 mg chol., 379 mg sodium, 20 g carb., 3 g fiber, 6 g pro. *Diabetic Exchanges: 1 starch, 1 fat.*

Zesty Lemon Broccoli

I invented this recipe when I began changing my eating habits to incorporate more vegetables into my diet. This broccoli tastes so decadent, you won't know it's healthy.

—BROOKE SZCZEPANSKI GLOUCESTER, VA

START TO FINISH: 15 MIN.
MAKES: 4 SERVINGS

- 4 cups fresh broccoli florets
- 1 tablespoon butter, melted
- 1 tablespoon grated lemon peel
- 1 tablespoon lemon juice
- 1 garlic clove, minced
- ½ teaspoon Dijon mustard
- ¼ teaspoon salt
- ⅛ teaspoon pepper
- ¼ cup pine nuts, toasted

1. Place the broccoli in a steamer basket; place in a large saucepan over 1 in. of water. Bring to a boil; cover and steam for 3-4 minutes or until crisp-tender.
2. Meanwhile, in a large bowl, combine the butter, lemon peel, juice, garlic, mustard, salt and pepper. Add broccoli and pine nuts; toss to coat.

PER SERVING ¾ cup equals 97 cal., 7 g fat (3 g sat. fat), 8 mg chol., 202 mg sodium, 6 g carb., 3 g fiber, 4 g pro. *Diabetic Exchanges: 1½ fat, 1 vegetable.*

Garlic Knotted Rolls

Using frozen yeast dough is an easy way to make homemade rolls. These cute knots add a special touch to any menu.

—KATHY HARDING RICHMOND, MO

PREP: 15 MIN. + RISING • **BAKE:** 15 MIN.
MAKES: 10 ROLLS

- 1 loaf (1 pound) frozen bread dough, thawed
- 1½ teaspoons dried minced onion
- 3 tablespoons butter
- 4 garlic cloves, minced
- ⅛ teaspoon salt
- 1 large egg, beaten
- 1 teaspoon poppy seeds, optional

1. Pat out dough on a work surface; sprinkle with minced onion and knead until combined. Divide dough in half. Shape each half into five balls. To form knots, roll each ball into a 10-in. rope; tie into a knot. Tuck ends under. Place rolls 2 in. apart on a greased baking sheet.
2. In a small skillet over medium heat, melt butter. Add garlic and salt; cook and stir 1-2 minutes. Brush over rolls. Cover and let rise until doubled, about 30 minutes.
3. Preheat oven to 375°. Brush tops with egg; if desired, sprinkle with poppy seeds. Bake 15-20 minutes or until golden brown.

PER SERVING 1 roll equals 168 cal., 6 g fat (2 g sat. fat), 30 mg chol., 315 mg sodium, 22 g carb., 2 g fiber, 5 g pro. *Diabetic Exchanges: 1½ starch, 1 fat.*

Homemade Pierogies

Pierogies are dumplings or tiny pies stuffed with a filling—often potatoes and cheese—and boiled, then cooked in butter. Our friends always ask us to bring them to potlucks.

—DIANE GAWRYS MANCHESTER, TN

PREP: 1 HOUR • **COOK:** 5 MIN./BATCH
MAKES: 1 SERVING

- 5 **cups all-purpose flour**
- 1 **teaspoon salt**
- 1 **cup water**
- 3 **large eggs**
- ½ **cup butter, softened**
- **FILLING**
- 4 **medium potatoes, peeled and cubed**
- 2 **medium onions, chopped**
- 2 **tablespoons butter**
- 5 **ounces cream cheese, softened**
- ½ **teaspoon salt**
- ½ **teaspoon pepper**
- **ADDITIONAL INGREDIENTS (FOR EACH SERVING)**
- ¼ **cup chopped onion**
- 1 **tablespoon butter**
   Minced fresh parsley

1. In a food processor, combine flour and salt; cover and pulse to blend. Add water, eggs and butter; cover and pulse until dough forms a ball, adding an additional 1 to 2 tablespoons of water or flour if needed. Let rest, covered, 15 to 30 minutes.

2. Place potatoes in a large saucepan and cover with water. Bring to a boil. Reduce heat; cover and simmer 10-15 minutes or until tender. Meanwhile, in a large skillet, saute onions in butter until tender; set aside.

3. Drain potatoes. Over very low heat, stir potatoes for 1-2 minutes or until steam has evaporated. Press through a potato ricer or strainer into a large bowl. Stir in cream cheese, salt, pepper and onion mixture; set aside.

4. Divide dough into four parts. On a lightly floured surface, roll one portion of dough to ⅛-in. thickness; cut with a floured 3-in. biscuit cutter. Place 2 teaspoons of filling in center of each circle. Moisten edges with water; fold in half and press edges to seal. Repeat with remaining dough and filling.

5. Bring a Dutch oven of water to a boil; add pierogies in batches. Reduce heat to a gentle simmer; cook for 1-2 minutes or until pierogies float to the top and are tender. Remove with a slotted spoon. In a large skillet, saute four pierogies and onion in butter until pierogies are lightly browned and heated through; sprinkle with parsley.

FREEZE OPTION *Place cooled pierogies on waxed paper-lined 15x10x1-in. baking pans; freeze until firm. Transfer to resealable plastic freezer bags; freeze up to 3 months. To use, for each serving, in a large skillet, saute four pierogies and ¼ cup chopped onion in 1 tablespoon butter until pierogies are lightly browned and heated through; sprinkle with minced fresh parsley.*

Italian Parmesan Bread

When my grown children come home for visits, they always ask me to make this bread along with their favorite spaghetti dinner. In between times, the easy-to-prepare loaf is a hit at church socials and potluck suppers.

—FRANCES POSTE WALL, SD

PREP: 20 MIN. + RISING • **BAKE:** 35 MIN.
MAKES: 1 LOAF

- 1 **cup warm water (110° to 115°)**
- 1 **package (¼ ounce) active dry yeast**
- 3 **cups all-purpose flour, divided**
- ¼ **cup butter, softened**
- 1 **large egg, beaten**
- 2 **tablespoons sugar**
- 1 **teaspoon salt**
- 1½ **teaspoons dried minced onion**
- ½ **teaspoon Italian seasoning**
- ½ **teaspoon garlic salt**
- ½ **cup grated Parmesan cheese, divided**
   Butter, melted

1. In a large bowl, dissolve yeast in warm water. Add 2 cups flour, ¼ cup butter, egg, sugar, salt and seasonings. Beat at low speed until mixed, about 30 seconds; increase speed to medium and continue beating for 2 minutes. Stir in remaining flour and ⅓ cup cheese; beat until smooth.

2. Cover bowl and let rise in a warm place until doubled, about 1 hour. Stir batter 25 strokes. Spread batter into a greased 1½-qt. casserole; brush with melted butter and sprinkle with the remaining cheese. Cover and let rise until doubled, about 30 minutes.

3. Bake at 350° about 35 minutes or until golden brown. Cool on a wire rack for 10 minutes before removing from the casserole.

PER SERVING *One serving (1 slice) equals 97 cal., 216 mg sodium, 21 mg chol., 13 g carb., 3 g pro., 3 g fat.* **Diabetic Exchanges:** *1 starch, ½ fat.*

Russian Potatoes

A standout at potlucks, these creamy potatoes always get "vacuumed" out of the dish and leave guests asking for more. Try them with prime rib or a beef roast.

—**JUDY WILSON** SUN CITY WEST, AZ

PREP: 1¼ HOURS • **BAKE:** 30 MIN.
MAKES: 12 SERVINGS

- 6 **cups chopped sweet onions**
- ¼ **cup olive oil**
- ⅓ **cup plus ½ cup butter, cubed, divided**
- 1 **tablespoon sugar**
- 4 **pounds potatoes, peeled and cubed**
- 4 **cans (14½ ounces each) chicken broth or 8 cups water plus 8 teaspoons chicken bouillon granules**
- 3 **cups sour cream, divided**
- 1 **cup heavy whipping cream**
- 4 **large eggs, beaten**
- 1 **teaspoon dill weed**

1. In a large skillet, saute onions in oil and ⅓ cup butter until softened. Stir in sugar. Reduce heat to medium-low; cook, stirring occasionally, for 40 minutes or until deep golden brown.

2. Meanwhile, place potatoes in a large saucepan and cover with broth. Bring to a boil. Reduce heat; cover and cook for 15-20 minutes or until tender. Drain potatoes; transfer to a large bowl. Add 1 cup sour cream, the cream, eggs, dill and remaining butter. Beat until mashed.

3. Spread half of potatoes into a greased 13x9-in. baking dish; layer with onions and remaining potatoes. Gently spread remaining sour cream over the top. Bake, uncovered, at 350° for 30-35 minutes or until a thermometer reads 160°.

Gourmet Potatoes au Gratin

Here's a different take on a classic potato dish. Bursting with sun-kissed tomato flavor, it's special enough for entertaining and goes together easily.

—**KATHERINE BARRETT** BELLEVUE, WA

PREP: 55 MIN. • **BAKE:** 70 MIN.
MAKES: 12 SERVINGS (⅔ CUP EACH)

- ½ **cup sun-dried tomatoes (not packed in oil), chopped**
- 1 **cup boiling water**
- 1 **large onion, sliced**
- 3 **tablespoons butter**
- 1 **tablespoon minced fresh oregano**
- ½ **teaspoon salt**
- ¼ **teaspoon pepper**
- ¼ **cup all-purpose flour**
- 2¼ **cups fat-free milk**
- 1 **cup grated Parmesan cheese**
- 3 **pounds potatoes (about 9 medium), peeled and thinly sliced**

1. Place tomatoes in a small bowl. Cover with boiling water; let stand for 5 minutes. Drain and set aside.

2. In a large skillet over medium heat, cook onion in butter until tender. Add the oregano, salt, pepper and reserved tomatoes; cook 2 minutes longer. Sprinkle with flour; stir until blended. Gradually add milk. Bring to a boil; cook and stir for 2 minutes or until thickened. Remove from the heat; stir in cheese.

3. Place potatoes in a greased 13x9-in. baking dish; top with sauce. Cover and bake at 350° for 1 hour. Uncover; bake 10-15 minutes longer or until potatoes are tender.

PER SERVING ⅔ cup equals 156 cal., 5 g fat (3 g sat. fat), 14 mg chol., 290 mg sodium, 22 g carb., 2 g fiber, 6 g pro. *Diabetic Exchanges:* 1½ starch, 1 fat.

Polenta Fries with Blue Cheese Dip

These fries are a great alternative to traditional ones made with potatoes. They bake up crispy and golden in the oven, too.

—REBEKAH BEYER SABETHA, KS

PREP: 35 MIN. + CHILLING • **COOK:** 10 MIN./BATCH
MAKES: 15 SERVINGS (1¾ CUPS DIP)

- 7 cups 2% milk
- 2 cups water
- 2 tablespoons butter
- ¾ teaspoon salt
- ½ teaspoon pepper
- 2¼ cups yellow cornmeal
- 1 cup (4 ounces) shredded smoked Gouda cheese
- 2 tablespoons minced fresh basil or 2 teaspoons dried basil
- 2 tablespoons minced fresh thyme or 2 teaspoons dried thyme
- 1 cup mayonnaise
- ½ cup crumbled blue cheese
- 2 ounces cream cheese, softened
- 1 cup all-purpose flour
- 1 cup canola oil

1. In a Dutch oven, bring the milk, water, butter, salt and pepper to a boil. Reduce heat to a gentle boil; slowly whisk in the cornmeal. Cook and stir with a wooden spoon for 15-20 minutes or until polenta is thickened and pulls away cleanly from the sides of the pan.

2. Stir in the Gouda cheese, basil and thyme. Spread into a greased 15x10x1-in. baking pan. Refrigerate for 1 hour.
3. Meanwhile, in a small bowl, combine the mayonnaise, blue cheese and cream cheese; chill until serving.
4. Cut polenta into 3¼x½-in. strips. Place flour in a shallow bowl. Dip polenta in flour; shake off excess.
5. In a large skillet, cook polenta in oil in batches for 3-4 minutes on each side or until golden brown. Serve with dip.

Razorback Corn Bread

This dish is almost a meal in itself! It's great alongside grilled foods such as chicken or ribs. I recently took it to our senior citizens club and received plenty of compliments and requests for the recipe.

—LOUISE FORD JUNCTION CITY, AR

PREP: 15 MIN. • **BAKE:** 20 MIN.
MAKES: 12 SERVINGS

- 8 ounces bulk pork sausage
- 2 cups cornmeal
- ½ cup all-purpose flour
- 3 teaspoons baking powder
- 1 teaspoon baking soda
- 1 teaspoon salt
- 2 large eggs, beaten
- 3 canned green chilies, chopped
- 1 large onion, chopped
- 1 can (11 ounces) Mexican-style or whole-kernel corn, drained
- 2 cups buttermilk
- ½ cup shredded cheddar cheese

1. In a deep 10-in. cast-iron skillet, fry sausage until done. Reserve 2-3 tablespoons drippings. Crumble the sausage.
2. Combine cornmeal, flour, baking powder, baking soda and salt. In separate bowl, combine eggs, chilies, onion, corn, buttermilk and cheese.
3. Add egg mixture to cornmeal mixture. Stir in sausage and reserved drippings. Pour into the greased skillet and bake at 450° for 20-25 minutes or until done. Serve warm from skillet.

NO TEARS

Looking for a speedy way to chop onions? Consider your blender! Quarter the onions, place them in the blender and cover with water. Put the top back on the blender, and process on high speed for a second or two or until chopped. Pour into a colander to drain, and you're all done. The chopped onions don't lose their flavor and they freeze beautifully.

—SHIRLEY M. ALVIN, TEXAS

Chipotle Lime Corn Cobs

In Mexico, grilled corn sometimes comes slathered in mayonnaise, rolled in grated cheese and served with lime and chili powder. This is my family's take on the dish, with our own flavor enhancements.

—**CAROLYN KUMPE** EL DORADO, CA

PREP: 25 MIN. • **GRILL:** 25 MIN.
MAKES: 6 SERVINGS

- 6 large ears sweet corn in husks
- ½ cup mayonnaise
- 1 chipotle pepper in adobo sauce, finely chopped
- 2 tablespoons minced fresh cilantro
- 2 tablespoons lime juice
- 1½ teaspoons grated lime peel
- 1 garlic clove, minced
- ½ cup grated Asiago cheese

1. Carefully peel back corn husks to within 1 in. of bottoms; remove silk. Rewrap corn in husks and secure with kitchen string. Place in a stockpot; cover with cold water. Soak for 20 minutes; drain.
2. Grill corn, covered, over medium heat for 25-30 minutes or until tender, turning often.
3. In a small bowl, combine the mayonnaise, chipotle, cilantro, lime juice, lime peel and minced garlic; spread one heaping tablespoon over each ear of corn. Sprinkle with Asiago cheese.

Cranberry Muffins

Our town is the hub of all the area's large cranberry bogs, which are beautiful year-round. The fresh cranberries make the perfect addition to these tasty treats! These muffins are my husband's favorite, and my friends like them, too.

—**DOROTHY BATEMAN** CARVER, MA

START TO FINISH: 30 MIN.
MAKES: 12 STANDARD-SIZE OR 6 JUMBO MUFFINS

- 1 cup fresh cranberries, quartered
- 8 tablespoons sugar, divided
- 1¾ cups all-purpose flour
- 2½ teaspoons baking powder
- ¼ teaspoon salt
- 1 large egg
- ¾ cup milk
- ⅓ cup vegetable oil
- 1 teaspoon grated lemon peel, optional
  Cinnamon sugar

1. Sprinkle cranberries with 2 tablespoons sugar; set aside. Sift remaining sugar, flour, baking powder and salt into large bowl.
2. In another bowl, beat egg, milk and oil. Make a hole in center of dry ingredients; pour in liquid ingredients. Stir just until moistened. Add berries and, if desired, lemon peel. Fill 12 greased standard or 6 greased jumbo muffin cups. Sprinkle with cinnamon sugar.
3. Bake at 400° for 18 minutes for standard-size muffins or for 22 minutes for jumbo muffins.

Salted Peanut Bars, page 194

185

194

192

Cookies, Bars & Candies

There's always **time for a snack,** and with the award-winning bites in this chapter, you're sure to **satisfy your sweet tooth!** Whether you want cookies to enjoy during a coffee break, brownies to top off your dinner or a batch of goodies for a bake sale, turn here for **special nibbles** that are guaranteed to please.

Coconut Citrus Bars

PREP: 30 MIN. • **BAKE:** 20 MIN. + COOLING
MAKES: 2 DOZEN

¾ cup butter, softened
⅓ cup confectioners' sugar
1½ cups all-purpose flour
½ cup crisp rice cereal

FILLING

4 eggs
1½ cups sugar
1 cup flaked coconut
⅓ cup orange juice
¼ cup lemon juice
2 tablespoons lime juice
2 tablespoons all-purpose flour
3 teaspoons grated orange peel
2 teaspoons grated lemon peel
1½ teaspoons grated lime peel
Confectioners' sugar

1. Preheat oven to 350°. In a small bowl, cream butter and confectioners' sugar until light and fluffy; gradually beat in flour until crumbly. Stir in cereal. Press into a greased 13x9-in. baking pan. Bake 18-22 minutes or until lightly browned.

2. Meanwhile, in a large bowl, beat eggs, sugar, coconut, juices, flour and peels until frothy. Pour over hot crust. Bake 18-22 minutes longer or until lightly browned. Cool on a wire rack. Dust with confectioners' sugar; cut into bars. Store in the refrigerator.

A "GRATE" IDEA

These delightful bars rely on grated orange, lemon and lime peel to give the sweets a burst of unbeatable citrus flavor. Citrus peel, also called zest, can be grated into fine shreds with a microplane grater. For slightly thicker and longer shreds, use a zester. Remove only the colored portion of the peel, not the bitter white pith.

Sweet oranges are the key to my amazing bars with loads of orange flavor in every bite. The unique crust and vibrant orange zing make them unlike regular lemon bars.
—**HEATHER ROTUNDA** ST. CLOUD, MN

German Chocolate Thumbprint Cookies

I love anything with the combination of chocolate, pecans and coconut. That popular flavor combo has usually been associated with cake...until now!

—**KATHY MORROW** HUBBARD, OH

PREP: 45 MIN. + CHILLING
BAKE: 10 MIN./BATCH
MAKES: 5 DOZEN

- 1 cup sugar
- 1 cup evaporated milk
- ½ cup butter, cubed
- 3 large egg yolks
- 1½ cups flaked coconut
- 1½ cups chopped pecans
- 1 teaspoon vanilla extract
- 1 package German chocolate cake mix (regular size)
- ½ cup all-purpose flour
- ⅓ cup butter, melted

1. In a large heavy saucepan, combine the sugar, milk, butter and egg yolks. Cook and stir over medium-low heat until mixture is thickened and coats the back of a spoon. Remove from the heat. Stir in the coconut, pecans and vanilla. Set aside 1¼ cups for topping.

2. In a large bowl, combine the cake mix, flour, melted butter and the remaining coconut mixture. Cover and refrigerate for at least 1 hour.

3. Shape dough into 1-in. balls. Place 2 in. apart on greased baking sheets. Using the end of a wooden spoon handle, make an indentation in the center of each cookie. Fill each cookie with a teaspoonful of the reserved topping.

4. Bake at 350° for 10-12 minutes or until set. Let stand for 2 minutes before removing to wire racks to cool. Store in an airtight container.

Aunt Rose's Fantastic Butter Toffee

This toffee regularly wins at my local county fair. It's an old-fashioned favorite!

—**KATHY DORMAN** SNOVER, MI

START TO FINISH: 30 MIN.
MAKES: ABOUT 2 LBS.

- 2 cups unblanched whole almonds
- 11 ounces milk chocolate
- 1 cup butter, cubed
- 1 cup sugar
- 3 tablespoons cold water

1. Preheat oven to 350°. In a shallow baking pan, toast almonds 5-10 minutes or until golden brown, stirring occasionally. Cool. Place chocolate in a food processor; pulse until fine (do not overprocess). Remove and set aside. Place cooled almonds in food processor; process until coarsely chopped. Sprinkle 1 cup almonds over bottom of a greased 15x10x1-in. baking pan. Sprinkle 1 cup chocolate over nuts; set aside.

2. In heavy saucepan, combine butter, sugar and water. Cook over medium heat until a candy thermometer reads 290° (soft-crack stage), stirring occasionally.

3. Immediately pour mixture over the almonds and chocolate in pan. Sprinkle with remaining chocolate; top with the remaining almonds. Refrigerate until set; break into pieces.

NOTE *We recommend that you test your candy thermometer before each use by bringing water to a boil; the thermometer should read 212°. Adjust your recipe temperature up or down based on your test.*

Cappuccino Brownies

There's something about coffee that seems to intensify chocolate. These three-layer wonders freeze well, but most of them disappear before they reach my freezer.

—SUSIE JONES BUHL, ID

PREP: 30 MIN. + CHILLING • **BAKE:** 25 MIN. + COOLING
MAKES: 2 DOZEN

- 8 **ounces bittersweet chocolate, chopped**
- ¾ **cup butter, cut up**
- 2 **tablespoons instant coffee granules**
- 1 **tablespoon hot water**
- 4 **large eggs**
- 1½ **cups sugar**
- 2 **teaspoons vanilla extract**
- 1 **cup all-purpose flour**
- ½ **teaspoon salt**
- 1 **cup chopped walnuts**

TOPPING
- 1 **package (8 ounces) cream cheese, softened**
- 6 **tablespoons butter, softened**
- 1½ **cups confectioners' sugar**
- 1 **teaspoon ground cinnamon**
- 1 **teaspoon vanilla extract**

GLAZE
- 4 **teaspoons instant coffee granules**
- 1 **tablespoon hot water**
- 5 **ounces bittersweet chocolate, chopped**
- 2 **tablespoons butter**
- ½ **cup heavy whipping cream**

1. Preheat oven to 350°. In a microwave, melt chocolate and butter; stir until smooth. Cool slightly. Dissolve coffee granules in hot water. In a large bowl, beat eggs and sugar. Stir in vanilla, chocolate mixture and coffee mixture. Combine flour and salt; gradually add to chocolate mixture until blended. Fold in walnuts.

2. Transfer to a greased and floured 13x9-in. baking pan. Bake 25-30 minutes or until a toothpick inserted near the center comes out clean. Cool completely on a wire rack.

3. For topping, in a large bowl, beat cream cheese and butter until blended. Add confectioners' sugar, cinnamon and vanilla; beat on low speed until combined. Spread over bars. Refrigerate until firm, about 1 hour.

4. For glaze, dissolve coffee granules in hot water. In a microwave, melt chocolate and butter; cool slightly. Stir in cream and coffee mixture. Spread over cream cheese layer. Let stand until set. Cut into bars. Refrigerate leftovers.

FREEZE OPTION *Cover and freeze for up to 1 month. To use, thaw at room temperature. Cut into bars. Refrigerate leftovers.*

Cherry Whoopie Pies

Red velvet cake is so good that I decided to create whoopie pies out of packaged cake mix. The individual pies are filled with velvety cream cheese frosting. Your family will love them!

—LESLEY MARIE BOYLAN CENTERVILLE, IA

PREP: 30 MIN. • **BAKE:** 10 MIN./BATCH + COOLING
MAKES: 3 DOZEN

- 1 **package red velvet cake mix (regular size)**
- 3 **large eggs**
- ½ **cup canola oil**
- 1 **teaspoon almond extract**
- 36 **maraschino cherries, halved**

FILLING
- ¾ **cup canned cream cheese frosting**
- ⅔ **cup whipped topping**
- ½ **cup chopped maraschino cherries**

1. In a large bowl, combine the cake mix, eggs, oil and extract; beat on low speed for 30 seconds. Beat on medium for 2 minutes.

2. Drop by heaping teaspoonfuls 2 in. apart onto greased baking sheets. Top each with a cherry half. Bake at 350° for 8-10 minutes or until edges are set. Cool for 2 minutes before removing to wire racks to cool completely.

3. For filling, beat frosting and whipped topping until blended; fold in chopped cherries. Spread filling on the bottoms of half of the cookies; top with remaining cookies. Refrigerate until serving.

TO MAKE AHEAD *Cookies can be baked the day before assembly. Store in an airtight container.*

Caramel-Pecan Dream Bars

These ooey-gooey cake bars that pull ever so gently from the pan and hold a firm cut are a baker's dream come true.
—CAY KEPPERS NISSWA, MN

PREP: 15 MIN. • **BAKE:** 20 MIN. + COOLING
MAKES: 2 DOZEN

- 1 **package yellow cake mix (regular size)**
- ½ **cup butter, softened**
- 1 **large egg**

FILLING

- 1 **can (14 ounces) sweetened condensed milk**
- 1 **large egg**
- 1 **teaspoon vanilla extract**
- 1 **cup chopped pecans**
- ½ **cup brickle toffee bits**

1. Preheat oven to 350°. In a large bowl, beat cake mix, butter and egg until crumbly. Press onto the bottom of a greased 13x9-in. baking pan.
2. In a small bowl, beat the milk, egg and vanilla until combined. Stir in pecans and toffee bits. Pour over crust.
3. Bake 20-25 minutes or until golden brown. Cool on a wire rack. Cut into bars.

Italian Pignoli Cookies

Cookies are the crown jewels of Italian confections. I can't let a holiday go by without baking these traditional almond cookies rolled in mild pine nuts.
—MARIA REGAKIS SAUGUS, MA

PREP: 30 MIN. • **BAKE:** 15 MIN./BATCH
MAKES: 2½ DOZEN

- 1¼ **cups (12 ounces) almond paste**
- ½ **cup sugar**
- 4 **egg whites, divided**
- 1 **cup confectioners' sugar**
- 1½ **cups pine nuts**

1. In a small bowl, beat almond paste and sugar until crumbly. Beat in 2 egg whites. Gradually add confectioners' sugar; mix well.
2. Whisk remaining egg whites in a shallow bowl. Place pine nuts in another shallow bowl. Shape dough into 1-in. balls. Roll in egg whites and coat with pine nuts. Place 2 in. apart on parchment paper-lined baking sheets. Flatten slightly.
3. Bake at 325° for 15-18 minutes or until lightly browned. Cool for 1 minute before removing from pans to wire racks. Store in an airtight container.

Chocolate-Peanut Cheesecake Bars

You won't hear any complaints about these rich bars layered with a can't-miss combination of flavors.

—DIANE NEMITZ LUDINGTON, MI

PREP: 25 MIN. • **BAKE:** 15 MIN. + CHILLING
MAKES: 2 DOZEN

- 1 package (17½ ounces) peanut butter cookie mix
- ¼ cup butter, melted
- 1 cup chopped salted peanuts
- 2 packages (8 ounces each) cream cheese, softened
- 1 cup sugar
- 2 large eggs, beaten
- 1 teaspoon vanilla extract

GANACHE
- 4 ounces semisweet chocolate, chopped
- ½ cup heavy whipping cream

1. In a large bowl combine the cookie mix and butter; stir in peanuts. Press onto the bottom of a greased 13x9-in. baking pan. Bake at 350° for 10-12 minutes or until edges are lightly browned.
2. Meanwhile, in a large bowl, beat cream cheese and sugar until smooth. Add eggs and vanilla; beat on low speed just until combined. Pour over crust.
3. Bake for 15-20 minutes or until center is almost set. Cool on a wire rack for 1 hour. Refrigerate for at least 2 hours.
4. Place chocolate in a small bowl. In a small saucepan, bring cream just to a boil. Pour over chocolate; whisk until smooth. Cool, stirring occasionally, to room temperature or until ganache reaches a spreading consistency, about 40 minutes. Spread over top. Refrigerate until firm. Cut into bars. Refrigerate leftovers.

Orange Cashew Bars

Two of my favorite ingredients, oranges and cashews, elevate this fantastic bar, especially when you use fresh orange juice in the glaze.

—ANNA WOOD CULLOWHEE, NC

PREP: 25 MIN. • **BAKE:** 15 MIN. + COOLING
MAKES: 2½ DOZEN

- 4 ounces reduced-fat cream cheese
- ½ cup confectioners' sugar
- ¼ cup packed brown sugar
- 1 large egg yolk
- 2 teaspoons vanilla extract
- 1½ cups all-purpose flour

FILLING
- 1 cup packed brown sugar
- 3 large egg whites
- 1 large egg
- 3 tablespoons all-purpose flour
- 2 teaspoons vanilla extract
- ½ teaspoon orange extract
- ¼ teaspoon salt
- 1½ cups salted cashews, coarsely chopped

ICING
- ¾ cup confectioners' sugar
- 4 teaspoons orange juice
- 1 teaspoon grated orange peel

1. Preheat oven to 350°. In a large bowl, beat cream cheese and sugars until smooth. Beat in egg yolk and vanilla. Gradually beat in flour.
2. Press dough onto bottom and ¼ in. up sides of a 13x9-in. baking pan coated with cooking spray. Bake 15-20 minutes or until edges are light brown. Cool for 10 minutes on a wire rack.
3. For filling, in a large bowl, beat brown sugar, egg whites, egg, flour, extracts and salt until smooth. Stir in cashews. Pour into crust. Bake 15-20 minutes longer or until set.
4. Cool completely in pan on a wire rack. In a small bowl, mix icing ingredients; drizzle over top. Cut into bars.

SHOP SMART

Orange Cashew Bars make a great gift. To make things extra special, pick up an inexpensive serving platter at a discount store or even at a rummage sale. The hostess receives a new platter and you don't have to worry about getting your plate back.

Maple Pecan Bars

Baking these bars fills me with warm memories of my Grandma Marie, who made a similar recipe. The pecan treats are popular at our office cookie exchange.

—AMANDA SPEARING NEWTON, IA

PREP: 30 MIN. • **BAKE:** 20 MIN. + COOLING
MAKES: 5 DOZEN

- 3 cups all-purpose flour
- ¾ cup confectioners' sugar
- 1½ cups cold butter

TOPPING

- 1½ cups packed brown sugar
- 1 cup butter, cubed
- ½ cup maple syrup
- 2 teaspoons ground cinnamon
- ¼ teaspoon salt
- 4 cups coarsely chopped pecans
- 2 tablespoons plus 1 teaspoon heavy whipping cream
- ¾ teaspoon vanilla extract

1. In a large bowl, combine flour and confectioners' sugar. Cut in the butter until crumbly. Press into a greased 15x10x1-in. baking pan. Bake at 350° for 12-15 minutes or until edges are lightly browned.

2. Meanwhile, in a large heavy saucepan, combine the brown sugar, butter, syrup, cinnamon and salt. Bring to a boil. Cook and stir over low heat until butter is melted. Stir in the pecans, cream and vanilla. Remove from the heat; spread over crust.

3. Bake 20-25 minutes longer or until bubbly. Cool on a wire rack. Cut into bars.

Key Lime Bites

Key limes don't provide much peel, so sometimes I cheat and use regular limes—for the peel only—in these bites. If you can wait, these are even better the next day.

—JONI LARSEN WELLINGTON, UT

PREP: 20 MIN. • **BAKE:** 10 MIN./BATCH + STANDING
MAKES: 2½ DOZEN

- 1 cup butter, softened
- ¼ cup confectioners' sugar
- 2 teaspoons Key lime juice
- 2 teaspoons grated Key lime peel
- 2 cups all-purpose flour
- ¼ teaspoon salt
- ½ cup chopped macadamia nuts

ICING

- 2 cups confectioners' sugar
- ¼ cup Key lime juice
- 1 teaspoon grated Key lime peel

1. Preheat oven to 400°. In a large bowl, cream butter and confectioners' sugar until light and fluffy. Beat in lime juice and peel. Combine flour and salt; gradually add to creamed mixture and mix well. Stir in nuts.

2. Shape into 1-in. balls. Place 2 in. apart on ungreased baking sheets; flatten slightly.

3. Bake 8-10 minutes or until bottoms are lightly browned. Remove to wire racks to cool completely.

4. In a small bowl, combine icing ingredients. Dip cookies in icing; allow excess to drip off. Place on a wire rack; let stand until set. Store in an airtight container.

Delectable Maple Nut Chocolates

This recipe goes back about 40 years. My father loved anything with maple flavoring, so my mother tweaked a brownie recipe to suit his tastes. She would be so happy to know her recipe is still being made after all these years.

—**BETSY KING** DULUTH, MN

PREP: 1 HOUR + CHILLING
MAKES: ABOUT 13 DOZEN

- 1 **can (14 ounces) sweetened condensed milk**
- ½ **cup butter, cubed**
- 7½ **cups confectioners' sugar**
- 2 **cups chopped walnuts**
- 2 **teaspoons maple flavoring**
- 1 **teaspoon vanilla extract**
- 4 **cups (24 ounces) semisweet chocolate chips**
- 2 **ounces bittersweet chocolate, chopped**
- 2 **teaspoons shortening**

1. In a small saucepan, combine milk and butter. Cook and stir over low heat until butter is melted. Place the confectioners' sugar in a large bowl; add milk mixture and beat until smooth. Stir in the walnuts, maple flavoring and vanilla. Roll into ¾-in. balls; place on waxed paper-lined baking sheets. Refrigerate until firm, about 1 hour.
2. In a microwave, melt the chips, bittersweet chocolate and shortening; stir until smooth. Dip balls into chocolate; allow excess to drip off. Place on waxed paper; let stand until set. Store in an airtight container.
FREEZE OPTION *Shape and freeze the balls of maple candy for up to 2 months if desired. Thaw candy before dipping into melted chocolate mixture.*

Apple Danish Bars

Here's a perfect addition to breakfast or brunch. A friend gave me this delightful recipe that makes good use of our bountiful apple harvest.

—**SANDY LYNCH** DECATUR, IL

PREP: 25 MIN. • **BAKE:** 40 MIN. + COOLING
MAKES: 20-24 SERVINGS

PASTRY
- 3 **cups all-purpose flour**
- ½ **teaspoon salt**
- 1 **cup shortening**
- 1 **egg yolk**
- ½ **cup milk**

FILLING
- 6 **cups sliced peeled apples**
- 1½ **cups sugar**
- ¼ **cup butter, melted**
- 2 **tablespoons all-purpose flour**
- 1 **teaspoon ground cinnamon**

GLAZE
- 1 **egg white, lightly beaten**
- ½ **cup confectioners' sugar**
- 2 **to 3 teaspoons water**

1. In a bowl, combine flour and salt; cut in shortening until mixture resembles coarse crumbs. Combine egg yolk and milk; add to flour mixture. Stir just until the dough clings together. Divide dough in half.
2. On a lightly floured surface, roll half of dough into a 15x10-in. rectangle; transfer to a greased 15x10x1-in. baking pan. Set aside.
3. In a bowl, toss together filling ingredients; spoon over pastry in pan. Roll out the remaining dough into another 15x10-in. rectangle. Place over filling. Brush with egg white. Bake at 375° for 40 minutes or until golden brown. Cool on a wire rack.
4. For glaze, combine the confectioners' sugar and enough water to achieve a drizzling consistency. Drizzle over warm pastry. Cut into squares. Serve warm or cold.

Cranberry Nut Swirls

My sister-in-law came up with this recipe. We use it a lot over the holidays when we want to pull a fast one on the guys in our family—they claim they don't like cranberries in any shape or form, but everyone enjoys these.

—**CARLA HODENFIELD** RAY, ND

PREP: 15 MIN. + CHILLING
BAKE: 15 MIN./BATCH
MAKES: ABOUT 3½ DOZEN

- ½ cup butter, softened
- ¾ cup sugar
- 1 egg
- 1 teaspoon vanilla extract
- 1½ cups all-purpose flour
- ¼ teaspoon baking powder
- ¼ teaspoon salt
- ½ cup finely ground cranberries
- ½ cup finely chopped walnuts
- 1 tablespoon grated orange peel
- 3 tablespoons brown sugar
- 2 teaspoons milk

1. In a large bowl, combine first four ingredients. Beat until light and fluffy, scraping the bowl occasionally. Combine dry ingredients; add to the creamed mixture. Refrigerate at least 1 hour.

2. In a small bowl, combine the cranberries, walnuts and orange peel; set aside. On a lightly floured surface, roll out the dough into a 10-in. square. Combine the brown sugar and milk; spread over dough. Sprinkle with the cranberry mixture, leaving about a ½-in. edge at both ends of dough; roll up tightly, jelly-roll style. Wrap with waxed paper; chill several hours or overnight.

3. Cut roll into ¼-in. slices and place on well-greased baking sheets. Bake at 375° for 14-15 minutes or until edges are light brown.

PLAN AHEAD

One of the great things about these cookies is that you can roll the dough, wrap it and freeze it up to 2 months. When ready to bake, simply thaw the dough, slice and bake as directed.

Caramel Toffee Brownies

I love to make up recipes for foods that I am craving, such as chocolate, toffee and caramel. The three came together in this brownie recipe for one sensational treat. I often bake these to add to care packages for family and friends.

—**BRENDA L. CAUGHELL** DURHAM, NC

PREP: 30 MIN. • **BAKE:** 40 MIN. + COOLING
MAKES: 2 DOZEN

CARAMEL LAYER
- ½ cup butter, softened
- ⅓ cup sugar
- ⅓ cup packed brown sugar
- 1 large egg
- ½ teaspoon vanilla extract
- 1 cup all-purpose flour
- ½ teaspoon baking soda
- ¼ teaspoon salt
- ½ cup caramel ice cream topping
- 2 tablespoons 2% milk
- 1 cup toffee bits

BROWNIE LAYER
- 1 cup butter, cubed
- 4 ounces unsweetened chocolate
- 4 large eggs, lightly beaten
- 2 cups sugar
- 2 teaspoons vanilla extract
- 2 cups all-purpose flour

1. Preheat oven to 350°. In a large bowl, cream butter and sugars until light and fluffy; beat in egg and vanilla. Combine flour, baking soda and salt; gradually add to creamed mixture and mix well. In a small bowl, combine caramel topping and milk; add to the batter and mix well. Fold in toffee bits; set aside.

2. In a microwave, melt butter and chocolate. Beat in eggs, sugar and vanilla; gradually beat in flour.

3. Spread half of brownie batter into a greased 13x9-in. baking pan. Drop caramel batter by spoonfuls onto brownie batter; swirl to combine. Drop remaining brownie batter on top.

4. Bake 40-45 minutes or until a toothpick inserted in center comes out clean. Cool on a wire rack.

Lime Coconut Biscotti

Dunk this delicious biscotti into your morning cup of coffee or enjoy as an afternoon snack or after-dinner dessert.

—**DIANA BURRINK** CRETE, IL

PREP: 25 MIN. • **BAKE:** 30 MIN. + COOLING
MAKES: 32 COOKIES

- ¾ cup sugar
- ¼ cup canola oil
- 2 large eggs
- ¼ cup lime juice
- 1 teaspoon vanilla extract
- ¼ teaspoon coconut extract
- 1¾ cups all-purpose flour
- ⅔ cup cornmeal
- 1½ teaspoons baking powder
- ¼ teaspoon salt
- 1 cup flaked coconut
- 1 teaspoon grated lime peel

1. In a small bowl, beat sugar and oil until blended. Beat in the eggs, lime juice and extracts. Combine the flour, cornmeal, baking powder and salt; gradually add to sugar mixture and mix well (dough will be sticky). Stir in coconut and lime peel.

2. Divide dough in half. With lightly floured hands, shape each half into a 12x2-in. rectangle on a parchment paper-lined baking sheet. Bake at 350° for 20-25 minutes or until set.

3. Place pan on a wire rack. When cool enough to handle, transfer loaves to a cutting board; cut diagonally with a serrated knife into ¾-in. slices. Place cut side down on ungreased baking sheets. Bake for 5-6 minutes on each side or until golden brown. Remove to wire racks to cool. Store in an airtight container.

PER SERVING *1 cookie equals 89 cal., 3 g fat (1 g sat. fat), 13 mg chol., 49 mg sodium, 14 g carb., 1 g fiber, 1 g pro.* **Diabetic Exchanges:** *1 starch, ½ fat.*

Salted Peanut Bars

You'll never look at Rice Krispies treats the same way again after trying these nutty three-tiered cookie, marshmallow and cereal bars. They travel well, too!

—DENISE KIRSCH MCLEANSBORO, IL

PREP: 20 MIN. • **BAKE:** 15 MIN. + CHILLING
MAKES: 2 DOZEN

- 1 package (17½ ounces) peanut butter cookie mix
- 3 tablespoons canola oil
- 1 tablespoon water
- 1 large egg
- 1 package (10 ounces) peanut butter chips
- ⅔ cup corn syrup
- ¼ cup butter, cubed
- 2 cups Rice Krispies
- 2 cups salted peanuts
- 2 teaspoons vanilla extract
- 3 cups miniature marshmallows

1. In a large bowl, combine the cookie mix, oil, water and egg. Press onto the bottom of a greased 13x9-in. pan.
2. Bake at 350° for 12-15 minutes or until set. Meanwhile, in a large saucepan, combine the chips, corn syrup and butter. Cook and stir over medium-low heat until smooth. Remove from the heat. Stir in the Rice Krispies, peanuts and vanilla.
3. Sprinkle marshmallows over crust. Bake 1-2 minutes longer or until marshmallows begin to puff. Spread the cereal mixture over top. Cool completely on a wire rack. Refrigerate until firm. Cut into bars.

Crunchy Chocolate Mint Balls

My mom made these for us every year when we were growing up. We'd always have an ice cream container full of them in the freezer that never lasted until Christmas. I now make them every year for my family. For a special touch, I like to place my truffles in mini cupcake holders.

—AMANDA TRIFF DARTMOUTH, NS

PREP: 50 MIN. + FREEZING
MAKES: 4½ DOZEN

- 1 package (10 ounces) mint chocolate chips
- ¼ cup butter, softened
- 1 can (14 ounces) sweetened condensed milk
- 1¼ cups chocolate wafer crumbs (about 22 wafers)
  White jimmies

1. In a double boiler or metal bowl over hot water, melt chips and butter; stir until smooth. Stir in milk. Add wafer crumbs; mix to coat. Refrigerate for 1 hour or until easy to handle.
2. Roll into 1-in. balls; roll in jimmies. Place on a waxed paper-lined 15x10x1-in. baking pan; freeze until firm. Transfer to a resealable plastic freezer bag. May be frozen for up to 1 month.
TO USE FROZEN BALLS *Thaw at room temperature.*

Holly Wreaths

PREP: 20 MIN. • **BAKE:** 10 MIN./BATCH + COOLING
MAKES: ABOUT 3 DOZEN

- 1 **cup butter, softened**
- 1 **package (3 ounces) cream cheese, softened**
- ½ **cup sugar**
- 1 **teaspoon vanilla extract**
- 2 **cups all-purpose flour**
  Green cherries, cut into thin slices
  Red Hots candies
  Frosting and decorator gel

1. In a bowl, cream butter and cream cheese. Add sugar; blend well. Stir in vanilla. Gradually beat in flour.
2. Using a cookie press fitted with star tip, form dough into 2½-in. wreaths on ungreased baking sheets. Bake at 375° for 10-12 minutes or until set but not brown. Cool on wire racks. Decorate wreaths with green cherry pieces to make leaves and Red Hots for berries, attaching with a drop of frosting. Add bows with decorator gel.

> ❝I've never come across another spritz cookie like this one calling for cream cheese as an ingredient. That helps to keep these wreaths moist a long time, while also adding a delicious flavor.❞

—**DEE LEIN** LONGMONT, CO

Pumpkin Walnut Squares

My mother-in-law handed this recipe down to me as a surefire way to keep my husband happy during the holidays. It's his favorite childhood dessert.

—**MELISSA CONCHIERI** JEFFERSON, MA

PREP: 15 MIN. • **BAKE:** 45 MIN. + COOLING
MAKES: 12 SERVINGS

- 1 **package yellow cake mix (regular size), divided**
- ¼ **cup canola oil**
- 4 **large eggs**
- 1 **cup chopped walnuts, divided**
- 1 **can (15 ounces) solid-pack pumpkin**
- 1 **can (14 ounces) sweetened condensed milk**
- 1 **teaspoon vanilla extract**
- ½ **teaspoon salt**
- ½ **teaspoon ground cinnamon**

1. Set aside ½ cup cake mix for filling. In a small bowl, combine the oil, 1 egg and remaining cake mix. Press into a greased 13x9-in. baking pan. Sprinkle with ½ cup walnuts.
2. In a large bowl, combine the pumpkin, milk, vanilla, salt, cinnamon, reserved cake mix and remaining eggs. Pour over crust; sprinkle with remaining walnuts.
3. Bake at 350° for 45-50 minutes or until a knife inserted near the center comes out clean. Cool on a wire rack. Cut into squares. Store leftovers in the refrigerator.

Peach Blueberry Pie, page 206

204

208

211

Cakes & Pies

Cakes and pies have long been **blue-ribbon staples** at county fairs, bake-offs and the like. Now you can serve these contest-winning specialties and indulge in their **comforting goodness** right in your very own home! From piled-high cakes and impressive tortes to cute cupcakes and **finger-licking** berry pies, turn here for all of your dessert solutions!

Triple-Chocolate Cake with Raspberry Sauce

Chocolate lovers, brace yourselves. This cocoa creation and its saucy accompaniment make a heavenly combination.

—JENNY STANIEC OAK GROVE, MN

PREP: 20 MIN. • **BAKE:** 1 HOUR + COOLING
MAKES: 12 SERVINGS (2⅔ CUPS SAUCE)

- 1 package chocolate cake mix (regular size)
- 1 package (3.4 ounces) instant vanilla pudding mix
- 1 package (3.4 ounces) instant chocolate pudding mix
- 4 large eggs
- 1½ cups water
- ½ cup canola oil
- 1 cup (6 ounces) semisweet chocolate chips

RASPBERRY SAUCE

- 1 cup water
- 2 packages (10 ounces each) frozen sweetened raspberries, thawed
- 1 tablespoon sugar
- 3 tablespoons cornstarch
- 2 tablespoons lemon juice
  Confectioners' sugar

1. Preheat oven to 325°. In a large bowl, combine cake mix, pudding mixes, eggs, water and oil; beat on low speed for 30 seconds. Beat on medium 2 minutes. Fold in the chocolate chips.

2. Pour into a well-greased 10-in. fluted tube pan. Bake 60-65 minutes or until a toothpick inserted near center comes out clean. Cool 10 minutes before removing from pan to a wire rack to cool completely.

3. Meanwhile, place water, raspberries and sugar in a blender; cover and process until well blended. In a small saucepan, combine cornstarch and lemon juice; stir in raspberry puree. Bring to a boil. Cook and stir 2 minutes or until thickened. Refrigerate until serving.

4. Dust cake with confectioners' sugar. Serve with sauce.

Sweet Potato Praline Pie

I wanted to create a recipe that was similar to pumpkin pie but with a new twist. The macadamia nuts are a family favorite, and the praline topping is what makes this pie special and enjoyable.

—MARIE RIZZIO INTERLOCHEN, MI

PREP: 30 MIN. • **BAKE:** 50 MIN. + COOLING
MAKES: 8 SERVINGS

-   Pastry for single-crust pie (9 inches)
- 2 large eggs
- 2 cups mashed sweet potatoes
- 1 can (12 ounces) evaporated milk
- ¾ cup sugar
- 1 teaspoon ground cinnamon
- 1 teaspoon vanilla extract
- ½ teaspoon ground ginger
- ½ teaspoon ground nutmeg
- ¼ teaspoon salt

TOPPING

- 3 tablespoons brown sugar
- 3 tablespoons light corn syrup
- 1 tablespoon butter
- ½ teaspoon vanilla extract
- 1 jar (3 ounces) macadamia nuts, coarsely chopped
- ½ cup heavy whipping cream, whipped

1. Line a 9-in. pie plate with pastry. Trim pastry to ½ in. beyond edge of plate; flute edges.

2. In a large bowl, combine the eggs, sweet potatoes, milk, sugar, cinnamon, vanilla, ginger, nutmeg and salt. Pour into pastry. Bake at 425° for 15 minutes. Reduce heat to 350°; bake 25 minutes longer.

3. Meanwhile, in a small saucepan, bring the brown sugar, corn syrup and butter to a boil. Reduce heat; simmer, uncovered, for 2 minutes. Remove pan from the heat; stir in vanilla.

4. Sprinkle nuts over pie; drizzle with caramel. Place a foil-lined baking sheet on a rack below the pie to catch any spills. Bake the pie 10-15 minutes longer or until caramel starts to bubble. Cover pie edges with foil to prevent overbrowning if necessary. Cool on a wire rack.

5. Garnish pie with whipped cream. Refrigerate leftovers.

Fudgy Peppermint Stick Torte

I created this recipe from a chocolate cake my friend made for me several years ago. I love the fact that it has brown sugar instead of granulated sugar. It's a favorite around Christmas, not only because of the great flavors, but because it makes a spectacular presentation.

—MARY SHIVERS ADA, OK

PREP: 25 MIN. • **BAKE:** 20 MIN. + CHILLING
MAKES: 16 SERVINGS

- 1½ **cups butter, softened**
- 3¼ **cups packed brown sugar**
- 4 **large eggs**
- 2 **teaspoons vanilla extract**
- 4 **cups all-purpose flour**
- 1¼ **cups baking cocoa**
- 2 **teaspoons baking powder**
- 1 **teaspoon salt**
- 1 **teaspoon baking soda**
- 2½ **cups cold water**

FROSTING

- 4½ **cups heavy whipping cream**
- 1½ **cups confectioners' sugar, divided**
- ¾ **teaspoon peppermint extract**
- 3 **packages (8 ounces each) cream cheese, softened**
- 1 **cup crushed peppermint candies, divided**

1. In a large bowl, cream butter and brown sugar until light and fluffy. Add eggs, one at a time, beating well after each addition. Beat in vanilla. Combine the flour, cocoa, baking powder, salt and baking soda; add to the creamed mixture alternately with water, beating well after each addition.
2. Transfer to four greased and floured 9-in. round baking pans. Bake at 350° for 18-22 minutes or until a toothpick inserted near the center comes out clean. Cool cake for 10 minutes before removing from pans to wire racks to cool completely.
3. In a small bowl, beat cream until it begins to thicken. Add ¾ cup confectioners' sugar and extract; beat until soft peaks form. In another bowl, beat the cream cheese and remaining confectioners' sugar until smooth. Fold in whipped cream, then ¾ cup crushed candies.
4. Spread frosting between layers and over top and sides of cake. Refrigerate for at least 1 hour. Just before serving, sprinkle remaining candies over the top.

Holiday Ambrosia Cake

This is from an old recipe that came to me as a typical fruitcake, but I added pineapple, coconut and pineapple juice, which made it really moist and gave it a bit of a tropical taste.

—DOTTY STODULSKI NORTH PORT, FL

PREP: 40 MIN. • **BAKE:** 50 MIN. + COOLING
MAKES: 12 SERVINGS

- ½ **cup butter, softened**
- 1 **cup sugar**
- 4 **large eggs**
- 1 **teaspoon coconut extract**
- 2½ **cups all-purpose flour**
- 1 **teaspoon baking powder**
- ½ **teaspoon salt**
- ½ **cup unsweetened pineapple juice**
- 2¼ **cups flaked coconut**
- 1½ **cups chopped candied pineapple**
- 1 **cup chopped macadamia nuts**
- 1 **cup golden raisins**
- ½ **cup chopped dried mangoes**
- ½ **cup chopped green candied cherries**
- ½ **cup chopped red candied cherries**

COCONUT GLAZE

- 1 **cup confectioners' sugar**
- 2 **tablespoons coconut milk or milk**
- ¼ **teaspoon coconut extract**
- ¼ **teaspoon vanilla extract**

1. In a large bowl, cream butter and sugar until light and fluffy. Add the eggs, one at a time, beating well after each addition. Beat in extract. Combine the flour, baking powder and salt; add to the creamed mixture alternately with pineapple juice, beating well after each addition. Fold in the coconut, pineapple, macadamia nuts, raisins, mangoes and candied cherries.
2. Transfer to a greased and floured 10-in. fluted tube pan. Bake at 350° for 50-60 minutes or until a toothpick inserted near the center comes out clean. Cool cake for 10 minutes before removing from pan to a wire rack to cool completely.
3. In a small bowl, combine the confectioners' sugar, coconut milk and extracts. Drizzle over cake.

Peppermint Cream Pound Cake

I came up with this recipe because I was looking for a new twist on a tried-and-true pound cake, and I really like the look and flavor of peppermint, especially around Christmas. Everyone at work loved the results, and my family did, too.

—CAROLYN WEBSTER WINSTON-SALEM, NC

PREP: 35 MIN. • **BAKE:** 1 HOUR + COOLING
MAKES: 12 SERVINGS

- 1 cup unsalted butter, softened
- ½ cup butter-flavored shortening
- 2 cups sugar
- 6 large eggs
- 1 teaspoon vanilla extract
- ½ teaspoon peppermint extract
- 3 cups all-purpose flour
- 1 teaspoon baking powder
- 1 cup heavy whipping cream
- ½ cup finely crushed peppermint candies

GLAZE

- 1½ cups confectioners' sugar
- 1 teaspoon unsalted butter, melted
- ¼ teaspoon vanilla extract
- ⅛ teaspoon salt
- 4 to 5 tablespoons heavy whipping cream
  Additional crushed peppermint candies

1. In a large bowl, cream the butter, shortening and sugar until light and fluffy. Add eggs, one at a time, beating well after each addition. Beat in extracts. Combine flour and baking powder; add to creamed mixture alternately with whipping cream. Fold in candies.

2. Transfer to a well-greased and floured 10-in. fluted tube pan. Bake at 325° for 1-1¼ hours or until a toothpick inserted near the center comes out clean. Cool cake for 10 minutes before removing from pan to a wire rack to cool completely.

3. In a small bowl, combine the confectioners' sugar, butter, vanilla and salt. Stir in enough cream to achieve a drizzling consistency. Drizzle over cake. Sprinkle with additional candies. Refrigerate leftovers.

Blueberry Cream Pie

PREP: 50 MIN. + CHILLING 10 MIN. + COOLING
MAKES: 6-8 SERVINGS

- 1⅓ cups vanilla wafer crumbs (about 40 wafers)
- 2 tablespoons sugar
- 5 tablespoons butter, melted
- ½ teaspoon vanilla extract

FILLING

- ¼ cup sugar
- 3 tablespoons all-purpose flour
  Pinch salt
- 1 cup half-and-half cream
- 3 large egg yolks, beaten
- 3 tablespoons butter
- 1 teaspoon vanilla extract
- 1 tablespoon confectioners' sugar

TOPPING

- 5 cups fresh blueberries, divided
- ⅔ cup sugar
- 1 tablespoon cornstarch

1. Combine the first four ingredients; press onto the bottom and up the sides of an ungreased 9-in. pie plate. Bake at 350° for 8-10 minutes or until crust just begins to brown. Cool.

2. In a saucepan, combine sugar, flour and salt. Gradually whisk in the cream; cook and stir over medium heat until thickened and bubbly. Cook and stir for 2 minutes more. Gradually whisk half into egg yolks; return all to pan. Bring to a gentle boil; cook and stir 2 minutes. Remove from heat; stir in butter and vanilla until butter is melted. Cook for 5 minutes, stirring occasionally. Pour into crust; sprinkle with confectioners' sugar. Chill 30 minutes or until set.

3. Meanwhile, crush 2 cups of blueberries in a medium saucepan; bring to a boil. Boil 2 minutes, stirring constantly. Press berries through sieve; set aside 1 cup juice (add water if necessary). Discard pulp.

4. In a saucepan, combine sugar and cornstarch. Gradually stir in the blueberry juice; bring to a boil. Boil 2 minutes, stirring constantly. Remove from heat; cool 15 minutes. Gently stir in the remaining berries; carefully spoon over the filling. Chill for 3 hours or until set. Store pie in the refrigerator.

Best Lime Tart

This treat is the perfect balance between tart and sweet, and the almonds in the crust are just wonderful. This is one of my husband's favorite desserts.

—CHARIS O'CONNELL MOHNTON, PA

PREP: 35 MIN. • **BAKE:** 15 MIN. + CHILLING
MAKES: 12 SERVINGS

- 1¼ cups graham cracker crumbs
- 5 tablespoons butter, melted
- ¼ cup ground almonds
- 3 tablespoons sugar

FILLING
- 4 large egg yolks
- 1 can (14 ounces) sweetened condensed milk
- ½ cup lime juice
- 2 teaspoons grated lime peel

TOPPING
- ½ cup heavy whipping cream
- 1 tablespoon sugar
- ½ cup sour cream
- 1 teaspoon grated lime peel
  Fresh raspberries and lime wedges

1. Preheat oven to 325°. In a small bowl, combine cracker crumbs, butter, almonds and sugar. Press onto the bottom and up the sides of a greased 9-in. tart pan. Bake for 15-18 minutes or until edges are lightly browned.
2. In a large bowl, whisk egg yolks, milk, lime juice and peel. Pour over the crust. Bake 12-14 minutes or until center is almost set. Cool on a wire rack. Refrigerate at least 2 hours.
3. In a large bowl, beat cream until it begins to thicken. Add sugar; beat until stiff peaks form. Fold in sour cream and grated lime peel. Spread over tart. Garnish with raspberries and lime wedges.

Chocolate Frosted Peanut Butter Cupcakes

My dad and brothers love peanut butter cups, so I used them as the inspiration for these special treats.

—ALISA CHRISTENSEN RANCHO SANTA MARGARITA, CA

PREP: 30 MIN. • **BAKE:** 20 MIN. + COOLING
MAKES: 2 DOZEN

- 1 package yellow cake mix (regular size)
- ¾ cup creamy peanut butter
- 3 large eggs
- 1¼ cups water
- ¼ cup canola oil

FROSTING
- 1⅔ cups semisweet chocolate chips
- ½ cup heavy whipping cream
- ½ cup butter, softened
- 1 cup confectioners' sugar

1. In a large bowl, combine the cake mix, peanut butter, eggs, water and oil; beat on low speed for 30 seconds. Beat on medium for 2 minutes.
2. Fill paper-lined muffin cups two-thirds full. Bake at 350° for 18-22 minutes or until a toothpick inserted near the center comes out clean. Cool for 10 minutes before removing from pans to wire racks to cool completely.
3. Place the chocolate chips in a large bowl. In a small saucepan, bring cream just to a boil. Pour over chocolate; whisk until smooth. Cool, stirring occasionally, to room temperature. Add butter and confectioners' sugar; beat until smooth. Frost cupcakes.
NOTE *Reduced-fat peanut butter is not recommended for this recipe.*

Cinnamon & Sugar Cake

This simple but elegant cake makes everything nice. You can even enjoy the frosting on other desserts such as cupcakes. Your guests will never know it started with a white cake mix unless you happen to let the secret slip. I'll never tell.

—**MAIAH MILLER** MONTEREY, CA

PREP: 25 MIN. • **BAKE:** 20 MIN. + COOLING
MAKES: 12 SERVINGS

- 1 **package white cake mix (regular size)**
- 1 **cup 2% milk**
- ½ **cup sour cream**
- 6 **tablespoons butter, melted**
- 3 **large eggs**
- 2½ **teaspoons ground cinnamon**
- 1½ **teaspoons vanilla extract**

FROSTING

- 1 **cup butter, softened**
- 5 **cups confectioners' sugar**
- 2 **tablespoons 2% milk**
- 1 **teaspoon ground cinnamon**
- 1 **teaspoon vanilla extract**
- 1 **tablespoon cinnamon-sugar**

1. In a large bowl, combine the first seven ingredients; beat on low speed for 30 seconds. Beat on medium for 2 minutes. Transfer to two greased and floured 9-in. round baking pans.
2. Bake at 350° for 20-25 minutes or until a toothpick inserted near the middle comes out clean. Cool cake for 10 minutes before removing from pans to wire racks to cool completely.
3. In a large bowl, beat butter until fluffy. Add the confectioners' sugar, milk, cinnamon and vanilla; beat until smooth.
4. Spread frosting between layers and over top and sides of cake. Sprinkle with cinnamon-sugar. Store in the refrigerator.

GRAND PRIZE
WINNER
★ ★ ★ ★

Candy Apple Pie

This is the only apple pie my husband will eat, but that's all right since he makes it as often as I do. Like a combination of apple and pecan pie, it's a sweet treat that usually tops off our holiday meals from New Year's all the way through to Christmas! Give it a try this season.

—CINDY KLEWENO BURLINGTON, CO

PREP: 20 MIN. • **BAKE:** 45 MIN.
MAKES: 8 SERVINGS

- 6 cups sliced peeled tart apples
- 2 tablespoons lime juice
- ¾ cup sugar
- ¼ cup all-purpose flour
- ½ teaspoon ground cinnamon
- ¼ teaspoon salt
  Pastry for double-crust pie (9 inches)
- 2 tablespoons butter

TOPPING

- 2 tablespoons butter
- ¼ cup packed brown sugar
- 1 tablespoon heavy whipping cream
- ¼ cup chopped pecans

1. In a large bowl, toss apples with lime juice. Combine the sugar, flour, cinnamon and salt; add to apples and toss lightly.

2. Line a 9-in. pie plate with bottom crust and trim even with edge; fill with apple mixture. Dot with butter. Roll out remaining pastry to fit top of pie. Place over filling. Trim, seal and flute edges; cut slits in pastry.

3. Bake at 400° for 40-45 minutes or until golden brown and the apples are tender.

4. For topping, melt butter in a small saucepan. Stir in the brown sugar and cream; bring to a boil, stirring constantly. Remove from the heat and stir in pecans.

5. Pour over top crust. Bake for 3-4 minutes longer or until bubbly. Place on a wire rack. Serve warm.

Mom's Cheese Pie

My mother brought this traditional recipe with her from the Ukraine. A sprinkling of cinnamon enhances the pie's subtly sweet flavor. It's simplicity at its tastiest!

—ANNE KULICK PHILLIPSBURG, NJ

PREP: 20 MIN. • **BAKE:** 45 MIN. + COOLING
MAKES: 4 SERVINGS

- 2 large eggs
- 1 sheet refrigerated pie pastry
- 1 teaspoon ground cinnamon, divided
- 1¾ cups ricotta cheese
- 4 ounces cream cheese, softened
- 3 tablespoons confectioners' sugar
- 1½ teaspoons cornstarch
- ½ teaspoon vanilla extract
- ⅛ teaspoon salt

1. Separate one egg. In a small bowl, lightly beat egg white; set aside. In another small bowl, combine egg and egg yolk; set aside.

2. On a lightly floured surface, unroll pastry; cut in half. Roll out one half of pastry into an 8-in. circle. Transfer to a 7-in. pie plate; trim pastry even with edge. Brush with egg white; sprinkle with ½ teaspoon cinnamon.

3. In a large bowl, combine the ricotta and cream cheeses, confectioners' sugar, cornstarch, vanilla, salt and egg mixture. Pour into prepared pastry.

4. Roll out remaining pastry to fit top of pie. Place over filling. Trim, seal and flute edges. Cut slits in pastry. Brush the remaining egg white over pastry; sprinkle with remaining cinnamon.

5. Bake at 350° for 45-50 minutes or until a knife inserted near the center comes out clean. Cool completely on wire rack. Refrigerate leftovers.

Chocolate Cannoli Cake Roll

PREP: 20 MIN. + CHILLING • **BAKE:** 15 MIN. + COOLING
MAKES: 12 SERVINGS

- 1 package (8 ounces) cream cheese, softened
- 2 cups ricotta cheese
- 1 cup confectioners' sugar
- 1 teaspoon vanilla extract
- ½ teaspoon ground cinnamon
- ½ cup miniature semisweet chocolate chips

CAKE

- 1¾ cups chocolate cake mix
- ⅓ cup water
- 2 tablespoons canola oil
- 3 large eggs

1. In a small bowl, beat cream cheese until fluffy. Add the ricotta cheese, confectioners' sugar, vanilla and cinnamon. beat until smooth. Stir in chips; refrigerate for 1 hour.

2. Preheat oven to 350°. Line a greased 15x10x1-in. baking pan with waxed paper and grease the paper; set aside. In a large bowl, combine the cake mix, water, oil and eggs; beat on low speed for 30 seconds. Beat on medium for 2 minutes. Pour into prepared pan. Bake 12-14 minutes or until cake springs back when lightly touched. Cool for 5 minutes.

3. Invert onto a kitchen towel dusted with confectioners' sugar. Gently peel off waxed paper. Roll up cake in the towel jelly-roll style, starting with a short side. Cool completely on a wire rack.

4. Unroll cake; spread filling over cake to within ½ in. of edges. Roll up again. Place seam side down on a serving platter. Refrigerate for 2 hours before serving.

Ozark Mountain Berry Pie

I think the best berries in the world are grown in the Ozarks. We own a small berry farm, and this is one of my favorite recipes. It's delicious served warm.

—**ELAINE MOODY** CLEVER, MO

PREP: 15 MIN. • **BAKE:** 55 MIN. + COOLING
MAKES: 8 SERVINGS

- 1 cup sugar
- ¼ cup cornstarch
- ½ teaspoon ground cinnamon, optional
  Dash salt
- ⅓ cup water
- 1 cup fresh blueberries
  Pastry for a double-crust pie (9 inches)
- 1 cup halved fresh strawberries
- 1 cup fresh raspberries
- ¾ cup fresh blackberries
- 1 tablespoon lemon juice
- 2 tablespoons butter

1. In a large saucepan, combine the sugar, cornstarch, cinnamon if desired, salt and water until smooth; add the blueberries. Bring to a boil; cook and stir for 2 minutes or until thickened. Set aside to cool slightly.

2. Line a 9-in. pie plate with bottom crust; trim pastry even with edge. Gently fold the strawberries, raspberries, blackberries and lemon juice into the blueberry mixture. Pour into pastry; dot with butter. Roll out remaining pastry; make a lattice crust. Trim, seal and flute edges.

3. Bake at 400° for 10 minutes. Reduce heat to 350°; bake for 45-50 minutes or until the crust is golden brown and the filling is bubbly. Cool on a wire rack. Store in the refrigerator.

TIMELY TOOL

When I'm preparing a pie, I get out my pizza cutter! It's the perfect tool for cutting strips of dough for a lattice crust.

—**LAURIE T.** COLUMBUS, MS

Chocolate Espresso-Nut Torte

I love chocolate and nuts, and they come together deliciously in this torte. Serve it with sweetened whipped cream or your favorite ice cream.

—**THOMAS FAGLON** SOMERSET, NJ

PREP: 40 MIN. • **BAKE:** 35 MIN. + CHILLING
MAKES: 14 SERVINGS

- 5 **large eggs, separated**
- 1 **teaspoon baking cocoa**
- 1 **cup hazelnuts, toasted and skins removed**
- 3 **tablespoons dark brown sugar**
- ½ **cup butter, softened**
- ⅔ **cup sugar**
- 6 **ounces bittersweet chocolate, melted and cooled**
- 1 **teaspoon instant espresso powder**
- 1 **teaspoon almond extract**
- ¼ **teaspoon salt**

GANACHE
- 6 **ounces bittersweet chocolate, chopped**
- ½ **cup heavy whipping cream**
- ½ **cup finely chopped almonds, toasted**

1. Place the egg whites in a large bowl; let stand at room temperature for 30 minutes. Line the bottom of a greased 9-in springform pan with waxed paper; grease the paper and dust with cocoa. Set aside.

2. Place hazelnuts and brown sugar in a food processor; cover and process until ground. In a large bowl, cream butter and sugar until light and fluffy, about 5 minutes. Add egg yolks, one at a time, beating well after each addition. Beat in the melted chocolate, espresso powder, extract and salt. Gradually add hazelnut mixture.

3. In a large bowl with clean beaters, beat egg whites until stiff peaks form. Fold into batter. Spread into prepared pan. Place pan on a baking sheet.

4. Bake at 375° for 35-40 minutes or until a toothpick inserted near center comes out with a few moist crumbs. Cool on a wire rack to room temperature. Remove sides of pan and invert onto a serving plate.

5. Place chocolate in a small bowl. In a small saucepan, bring cream just to a boil. Pour over chocolate; whisk until

smooth. Cool, stirring occasionally, to room temperature or until ganache reaches a spreading consistency, about 30 minutes.

6. Spread ganache over top and sides of cake; press the almonds onto sides. Cover and refrigerate for 30 minutes or until set.

Peach Blueberry Pie

What a flavor! That's what I hear most often after folks try this pie I invented one day when I was short of peaches to fill a full crust.

—**SUE THUMMA** SHEPHERD, MI

PREP: 15 MIN. • **BAKE:** 40 MIN. + COOLING
MAKES: 8 SERVINGS

- 1 **cup sugar**
- ⅓ **cup all-purpose flour**
- ½ **teaspoon ground cinnamon**
- ⅛ **teaspoon ground allspice**
- 3 **cups sliced peeled fresh peaches**
- 1 **cup fresh or frozen unsweetened blueberries**
  Pastry for double-crust pie (9 inches)
- 1 **tablespoon butter**
- 1 **tablespoon 2% milk**
  Cinnamon-sugar

1. In a large bowl, combine sugar, flour, cinnamon and allspice. Add peaches and blueberries; toss to coat.

2. Preheat oven to 400°. On a lightly floured surface, roll one half of dough to a ⅛-in.-thick circle; transfer to a 9-in. pie plate. Trim pastry to ½ in. beyond rim of plate. Add filling; dot with butter.

3. Roll remaining dough to a ⅛-in.-thick circle; cut into ½-in.-wide strips. Arrange over filling in a lattice pattern. Trim and seal strips to edge of bottom pastry; flute edge. Brush lattice strips with milk; sprinkle with cinnamon-sugar.

4. Bake 40-45 minutes or until crust is golden brown and filling is bubbly. Cool on a wire rack.

NOTE *Frozen fruit may be used if it is thawed and well drained.*

Lemon Cream Cake

Drizzling limoncello liqueur over the cake layers before frosting adds a tart punch to this refreshing confection.

—AMY FREDERICK ISLAND CITY, OR

PREP: 20 MIN. • **BAKE:** 25 MIN. + COOLING
MAKES: 12 SERVINGS

- 1 package yellow cake mix (regular size)
- 1¼ cups water
- 3 large eggs
- ⅓ cup canola oil
- 1 teaspoon lemon extract
- 1 carton (8 ounces) mascarpone cheese
- 1 cup heavy whipping cream
- ½ cup lemon curd
- ¼ cup limoncello, optional
  Fresh raspberries and lemon peel strips

1. In a large bowl, combine the cake mix, water, eggs, oil and extract; beat on low speed for 30 seconds. Beat on medium for 2 minutes. Pour into two greased and floured 9-in. round baking pans.

2. Bake at 350° for 22-26 minutes or until a toothpick inserted near the center comes out clean. Cool for 10 minutes before removing from pans to wire racks to cool completely.

3. In a small bowl, beat the cheese, cream and lemon curd until smooth. Place one cake layer on a serving plate. Drizzle with half the limoncello if desired; spread with half the cheese mixture. Repeat layers. Garnish with raspberries and lemon peel. Store in the refrigerator.

LEMON CURD

Lemon curd is a soft custard that's often used as a filling for baked desserts such as tarts and as a spread for scones and biscuits. The flavor and texture are similar to lemon meringue pie filling. Commercially prepared lemon curd is available in larger grocery stores alongside the jams and jellies or with the baking supplies.

Fluted Tiramisu Cake

Melted coffee ice cream adds a decadent depth of flavor to a white cake mix. A simple yet impressive dessert, this Bundt cake will rise above your highest expectations.

—CAROL GILLESPIE CHAMBERSBURG, PA

PREP: 20 MIN. • **BAKE:** 35 MIN. + COOLING
MAKES: 12 SERVINGS

- 1 package white cake mix (regular size)
- 2 cups coffee ice cream, melted
- 3 large eggs
- 1 tablespoon water
- 1 teaspoon instant coffee granules
- 1 can (12 ounces) whipped vanilla frosting
- ½ teaspoon ground cinnamon
- 1 tablespoon cinnamon-sugar

1. In a large bowl, beat the cake mix, ice cream and eggs at low speed for 30 seconds. Beat on medium for 2 minutes. Pour into a greased and floured 10-in. fluted tube pan.
2. Bake at 350° for 35-40 minutes or until a toothpick inserted near the center comes out clean. Cool cake for 10 minutes before removing from pan to a wire rack to cool completely.
3. Place water and coffee granules in a large bowl; stir until dissolved. Add frosting and cinnamon; beat until smooth. Frost cake. Sprinkle with cinnamon-sugar.

Citrus Cornmeal Cake

Cornmeal adds a rustic quality to this delicate dessert flavored with citrus and almond. It's sure to be a staple in your recipe collection and also makes a great hostess gift at parties.

—ROXANNE CHAN ALBANY, CA

PREP: 25 MIN. • **BAKE:** 25 MIN.
MAKES: 8 SERVINGS

- ½ cup lemon yogurt
- ⅓ cup honey
- ¼ cup olive oil
- 1 large egg
- 2 large egg whites
- ¼ teaspoon almond extract
- ¾ cup all-purpose flour
- ½ cup cornmeal
- 1 teaspoon baking powder
- ½ teaspoon grated orange peel
- 1 can (15 ounces) mandarin oranges, drained
- 3 tablespoons slivered almonds

1. Coat a 9-in. fluted tart pan with removable bottom with cooking spray. In a large bowl, beat the yogurt, honey, oil, egg, egg whites and extract until well blended. Combine the flour, cornmeal and baking powder; gradually beat into yogurt mixture until blended. Stir in orange peel.
2. Pour into prepared pan. Arrange oranges over batter; sprinkle with almonds. Bake at 350° for 25-30 minutes or until a toothpick inserted near the center comes out clean. Cool on a wire rack for 10 minutes before cutting. Serve warm or at room temperature.

Peachy Gingerbread Cake Roll

My father loved gingerbread, so I combined two or three recipes to create this one for him. This yummy version of a cake roll gets kudos every time I serve it.

—**DAWN DEPEW** BLACKLICK, OH

PREP: 25 MIN. • **BAKE:** 15 MIN. + COOLING
MAKES: 12 SERVINGS

- 4 **large eggs**
- ½ **cup sugar**
- ½ **cup packed dark brown sugar**
- ¼ **cup water**
- 3 **tablespoons butter, melted**
- 3 **tablespoons molasses**
- 1 **teaspoon vanilla extract**
- 1⅓ **cups all-purpose flour**
- 2 **teaspoons pumpkin pie spice**
- 1 **teaspoon ground cinnamon**
- ½ **teaspoon baking powder**
- ½ **teaspoon baking soda**
- ¼ **teaspoon salt**
  Confectioners' sugar

FILLING

- 2 **packages (8 ounces each) plus 3 ounces cream cheese, softened**
- 1¼ **cups peach preserves**
- 1¼ **teaspoons ground ginger**
- 1¼ **teaspoons ground cinnamon**
- ¼ **teaspoon ground nutmeg**
  Confectioners' sugar and sliced peaches, optional

1. Line a greased 15x10x1-in. baking pan with waxed paper; grease the paper and set aside.

2. In a large bowl, beat eggs for 3 minutes. Gradually add sugars, beating until mixture is thickened. Beat in the water, butter, molasses and vanilla. Combine the flour, pie spice, cinnamon, baking powder, baking soda and salt; fold into egg mixture. Spread batter into prepared pan.

3. Bake at 350° for 12-15 minutes or until cake springs back when lightly touched. Cool for 5 minutes. Invert onto a kitchen towel dusted with confectioners' sugar. Gently peel off waxed paper. Roll up cake in the towel jelly-roll style, starting with a short side. Cool completely on a wire rack.

4. For filling, in a small bowl, beat the cream cheese, peach preserves, ginger, cinnamon and nutmeg until smooth. Unroll cake; spread filling over cake to within ½ in. of edges. Roll up again. Place seam side down on a serving platter. Dust with confectioners' sugar and garnish with sliced peaches if desired.

Grandma's Chocolate Meringue Pie

My grandmother served chocolate meringue pie after Sunday dinner each week, usually with an apology that it was "too runny" or something else was wrong with it. Of course, it was never less than perfect!

—**DONNA VEST TILLEY** CHESTERFIELD, VA

PREP: 30 MIN. • **BAKE:** 15 MIN.
MAKES: 8 SERVINGS

- ¾ **cup sugar**
- 5 **tablespoons baking cocoa**
- 3 **tablespoons cornstarch**
- ¼ **teaspoon salt**
- 2 **cups milk**
- 3 **large egg yolks, beaten**
- 1 **teaspoon vanilla extract**
- 1 **pie shell (9 inches), baked**

MERINGUE

- 3 **large egg whites**
- ¼ **teaspoon cream of tartar**
- 6 **tablespoons sugar**

1. In a saucepan, mix sugar, cocoa, cornstarch and salt; gradually add milk. Cook and stir over medium-high heat until thickened and bubbly. Reduce heat; cook and stir 2 minutes more. Remove from heat. Stir about 1 cup of the hot filling into the egg yolks. Return to saucepan and bring to a gentle boil. Cook and stir 2 minutes. Remove from the heat and stir in vanilla. Pour hot filling into pie crust.

2. For meringue, immediately beat egg whites with cream of tartar until soft peaks form. Gradually add sugar and continue to beat until stiff and glossy. Spread evenly over hot filling, sealing meringue to pie crust. Bake at 350° for 12-15 minutes or until golden.

Coconut Banana Cream Pie

This pie features the perfect pairing of bananas and coconut, giving it a slightly tropical taste.

—TAMMY OLSON BRUCE, SD

PREP: 30 MIN. + CHILLING
MAKES: 6-8 SERVINGS

- 3 cups flaked coconut
- 7 tablespoons butter
- ¾ cup sugar
- ¼ cup all-purpose flour
- 3 tablespoons cornstarch
- ¼ teaspoons salt
- 3 cups half-and-half cream
- 4 large egg yolks, lightly beaten
- 2 teaspoons vanilla extract
- 2 large firm bananas, sliced
  Whipped cream and sliced bananas, optional

1. In a large skillet, saute the coconut in butter until golden. Reserve 2 tablespoons for garnish. Press the remaining toasted coconut onto the bottom and up the sides of a greased 9-in. pie plate. Bake at 350° for 7 minutes. Cool on a wire rack.
2. For filling, combine the sugar, flour, cornstarch and salt in a large saucepan. Stir in cream until smooth. Cook and stir over medium-high heat until thickened and bubbly. Reduce heat; cook and stir 2 minutes longer. Remove from the heat. Stir a small amount of hot filling into egg yolks; return all to pan, stirring constantly. Bring to a gentle boil; cook and stir 2 minutes longer. Remove from the heat. Gently stir in vanilla. Cool to room temperature without stirring.
3. Place bananas in the crust. Cover with cream mixture. Refrigerate until set, about 2 hours. Sprinkle with the reserved coconut. If desired, garnish with whipped cream and bananas. Refrigerate leftovers.

Susan's Favorite Mocha Cake

My family insists on my mocha cake for special occasions. They even call it "the best cake in the world." The flavors are simply wonderful.

—SUSAN BAZAN SEQUIM, WA

PREP: 30 MIN. • **BAKE:** 25 MIN. + CHILLING
MAKES: 16 SERVINGS

- 1 package chocolate cake mix (regular size)
- 1¾ cups sour cream
- 2 large eggs
- ½ cup coffee liqueur
- ¼ cup canola oil
- 2 cups (12 ounces) semisweet chocolate chips, divided
- 1 package (10 to 12 ounces) white baking chips
- ⅓ cup butter, cubed
- 1 tablespoon instant coffee granules
- 1 teaspoon rum extract
- 1 envelope unflavored gelatin
- 1½ cups heavy whipping cream, divided

WHIPPED CREAM
- 2 cups heavy whipping cream
- ½ cup sugar
- 1 teaspoon vanilla extract

1. In a large bowl, combine the cake mix, sour cream, eggs, liqueur and oil; beat on low speed for 30 seconds. Beat on medium for 2 minutes. Stir in 1 cup chocolate chips. Transfer batter to three greased and floured 9-in. round baking pans.
2. Bake at 350° for 24-28 minutes or until a toothpick inserted near the center comes out clean. Cool for 10 minutes before removing from pans to wire racks to cool completely.
3. In a microwave, melt the white baking chips, butter and remaining chocolate chips; stir until smooth. Stir in coffee granules and extract. Cool to room temperature.
4. In a small saucepan, sprinkle the gelatin over ¼ cup cream; let stand for 1 minute. Heat over low heat, stirring until gelatin is dissolved. Stir into chocolate mixture. In a large bowl, beat the remaining 1¼ cups cream until soft peaks form. Add to the cooled chocolate mixture; beat until stiff peaks form.
5. For the whipped cream, in a small bowl, beat cream until it begins to thicken. Add sugar and vanilla; beat until stiff peaks form.
6. Place bottom cake layer on a serving plate; top with half of the chocolate mixture. Repeat layers. Top with the remaining cake layer. Frost top and sides of cake with whipped cream. Refrigerate for at least 2 hours before serving.

Marvelous Cannoli Cake

A luscious cannoli-inspired filling separates the layers of this easy vanilla cake. Just like the fabulous Italian dessert, it's best served well chilled.

—ANTOINETTE OWENS RIDGEFIELD, CT

PREP: 30 MIN. + CHILLING • **BAKE:** 25 MIN. + COOLING
MAKES: 12 SERVINGS

- 1 **package French vanilla cake mix (regular size)**

FILLING:
- 1 **carton (16 ounces) ricotta cheese**
- ½ **cup confectioners' sugar**
- 2 **teaspoons ground cinnamon**
- 1 **teaspoon almond extract**
- 1 **teaspoon rum extract**
- 1 **teaspoon vanilla extract**
- 2 **ounces semisweet chocolate, finely chopped**

FROSTING:
- 2 **cartons (8 ounces each) mascarpone cheese**
- ¾ **cup confectioners' sugar, sifted**
- ¼ **cup whole milk**
- 2 **teaspoons almond extract**
- 1 **teaspoon vanilla extract**
- 1 **cup sliced almonds**
- 2 **tablespoons miniature semisweet chocolate chips**

1. Prepare and bake cake mix according to package directions, using two greased and floured 9-in. round baking pans. Cool for 10 minutes before removing from pans to wire racks to cool completely.

2. In a large bowl, combine ricotta cheese, confectioners' sugar, cinnamon and extracts; stir in chocolate. In another bowl, beat the mascarpone cheese, confectioners' sugar, milk and extracts on medium speed until creamy (do not overmix).

3. Place one cake layer on a serving plate; spread with 1 cup filling. Top with second cake layer. Spread remaining filling over top of cake to within 1 in. of edges. Frost sides and top edge of cake with 2 cups frosting.

4. Press almonds into sides of cake. Sprinkle chocolate chips over top. Refrigerate until serving.

Strawberry Ginger Tart

This tart heralds lazy summer days when strawberries are at their sweetest and juiciest. It's entirely customizable, too. You can substitute any refrigerated cookie dough for the crust.

—CHANTAL BOURBON MONTREAL, QC

PREP: 25 MIN. + CHILLING • **BAKE:** 20 MIN.
MAKES: 12 SERVINGS

- ¼ **cup butter, softened**
- ⅔ **cup sugar**
- 1 **large egg white**
- 1 **tablespoon minced fresh gingerroot**
- 1¼ **cups all-purpose flour**
- ¼ **teaspoon baking soda**
- ¼ **teaspoon salt**
- 1 **cup milk chocolate chips**

FILLING
- 1 **package (8 ounces) reduced-fat cream cheese**
- 3 **tablespoons confectioners' sugar**
- 2 **tablespoons 2% milk**
- 4 **cups halved fresh strawberries**

GLAZE
- ¼ **cup seedless strawberry jam**
- 1 **tablespoon crystallized ginger, finely chopped**

1. In a large bowl, cream butter and sugar until light and fluffy. Beat in egg white and ginger. Combine the flour, baking soda and salt; gradually add to creamed mixture and mix well. Press onto the bottom and up the sides of a greased 9-in. tart pan.

2. Bake at 350° for 12-15 minutes or until edges are lightly browned. Sprinkle with chips. Bake 4-5 minutes longer or until chocolate is melted; spread over crust. Cool on a wire rack.

3. In a small bowl, beat the cream cheese, confectioners' sugar and milk until smooth; spread over the chocolate. Top with strawberries. In a small microwave-safe bowl, microwave jam in 10-second intervals until melted; brush over strawberries. Sprinkle with ginger. Refrigerate for at least 2 hours before serving.

Neapolitan Cheesecake, page 222

223

217

227

Just Desserts

You'll always find room for dessert with this collection of sweet favorites. From **frosty specialties** perfect for topping off warm-weather meals to holiday classics that **make memories,** these tempting bites can't be beat. Turn here whenever you need a **simply impressive finale** to any meal!

Chocolate Banana Bundles

Banana and chocolate is such an irresistible combination that I make this quick dessert often. I sometimes sprinkle on a dash of sea salt. You can also top with any leftover butter and brown sugar mixture.

—**THOMAS FAGLON** SOMERSET, NJ

START TO FINISH: 30 MIN.
MAKES: 4 SERVINGS

- 2 tablespoons butter
- ¼ cup packed brown sugar
- 2 medium ripe bananas, halved lengthwise
- 1 sheet frozen puff pastry, thawed
- 4 ounces semisweet chocolate, melted
  Vanilla ice cream, optional

1. Preheat oven to 400°. In a large skillet, melt butter over medium heat. Stir in brown sugar until blended. Add bananas; stir to coat. Remove from heat; set aside.
2. Unfold puff pastry. Cut into four rectangles. Place a halved banana in center of each square. Overlap two opposite corners of pastry over banana; pinch tightly to seal. Place on parchment paper-lined baking sheets.
3. Bake 20-25 minutes or until golden brown. Drizzle with chocolate. Serve warm with ice cream if desired.
CARAMEL BANANA BUNDLES *Omit chocolate. Drizzle with caramel ice cream topping.*

I love making this treat for friends during the peak of apple-picking season. I plan a quick meal of soup and bread so we can get right to the scrumptious dessert!

—**LIBBY WALP** CHICAGO, IL

Apple Betty with Almond Cream

PREP: 15 MIN. • **COOK:** 3 HOURS
MAKES: 8 SERVINGS

- 3 pounds tart apples, peeled and sliced
- 10 slices cinnamon-raisin bread, cubed
- ¾ cup packed brown sugar
- ½ cup butter, melted
- 1 teaspoon almond extract
- ½ teaspoon ground cinnamon
- ¼ teaspoon ground cardamom
- ⅛ teaspoon salt

WHIPPED CREAM

- 1 cup heavy whipping cream
- 2 tablespoons sugar
- 1 teaspoon grated lemon peel
- ½ teaspoon almond extract

1. Place apples in an ungreased 4- or 5-qt. slow cooker. In a large bowl, combine the bread, brown sugar, butter, extract, cinnamon, cardamom and salt; spoon over apples. Cover and cook on low for 3-4 hours or until apples are tender.
2. In a small bowl, beat cream until it begins to thicken. Add the sugar, lemon peel and extract; beat until soft peaks form. Serve with apple mixture.

White Chocolate Cheesecake

This is my all-time favorite cheesecake recipe...and I have a lot of them! I've made this delicious cake so many times over the years—it's frequently requested as birthday cake.

—JANET GILL TANEYTOWN, MD

PREP: 40 MIN. • **BAKE:** 45 MIN. + CHILLING
MAKES: 12 SERVINGS

- 7 **whole cinnamon graham crackers, crushed**
- ¼ **cup sugar**
- ⅓ **cup butter, melted**

FILLING

- 4 **packages (8 ounces each) cream cheese, softened**
- ½ **cup plus 2 tablespoons sugar**
- 1 **tablespoon all-purpose flour**
- 1 **teaspoon vanilla extract**
- 4 **large eggs, lightly beaten**
- 2 **large egg yolks, lightly beaten**
- 8 **ounces white baking chocolate, melted and cooled**

STRAWBERRY SAUCE

- ½ **cup sugar**
- 2 **tablespoons cornstarch**
- ½ **cup water**
- 1½ **cups chopped fresh strawberries**
   Red food coloring, optional
   Melted white chocolate

1. In a small bowl, combine cracker crumbs and sugar; stir in butter. Press onto the bottom and 1 in. up the sides of a greased 10-in. springform pan.

2. In a large bowl, beat the cream cheese, sugar, flour and vanilla until well blended. Add eggs and yolks; beat on low speed just until combined. Stir in white chocolate. Pour over crust. Place pan on a baking sheet.

3. Bake at 350° for 45-50 minutes or until center is just set. Cool on a wire rack for 10 minutes. Carefully run a knife around edge of pan to loosen; cool 1 hour longer. Refrigerate overnight.

4. For sauce, in a large saucepan, combine the sugar, cornstarch and water until smooth. Add strawberries. Bring to a boil; cook and stir until thickened. Remove from the heat; stir in a few drops of food coloring if desired. Cool.

5. Spread strawberry sauce over top of cheesecake; drizzle with melted white chocolate. Refrigerate leftovers.

Very Berry Crisp

I love this recipe because it's easy, low-fat, versatile and delicious! The crispy topping is flavored with graham cracker crumbs, cinnamon and almonds and doesn't taste light at all. It's great with frozen yogurt or whipped topping.

—SCARLETT ELROD NEWNAN, GA

PREP: 20 MIN. • **BAKE:** 25 MIN.
MAKES: 8 SERVINGS

- 2 **cups fresh raspberries**
- 2 **cups sliced fresh strawberries**
- 2 **cups fresh blueberries**
- ⅓ **cup sugar**
- 2 **tablespoons plus ¼ cup all-purpose flour, divided**
- ⅓ **cup graham cracker crumbs**
- ⅓ **cup quick-cooking oats**
- ¼ **cup packed brown sugar**
- 2 **tablespoons sliced almonds**
- ½ **teaspoon ground cinnamon**
- 1 **tablespoon canola oil**
- 1 **tablespoon butter, melted**
- 1 **tablespoon water**

1. In a large bowl, combine the berries, sugar and 2 tablespoons flour; transfer to an 11x7-in. baking dish coated with cooking spray.

2. In a small bowl, combine the cracker crumbs, oats, brown sugar, almonds, cinnamon and remaining flour. Stir in the oil, butter and water until moistened. Sprinkle over berries.

3. Bake at 375° for 25-30 minutes or until filling is bubbly and topping is golden brown.

Mochaccino Pudding

I like to top this homey prize-winning pudding with chocolate-covered espresso beans and whipped cream. Pudding never tasted so elegant!

—MARIA REGAKIS SAUGUS, MA

PREP: 15 MIN. • **COOK:** 10 MIN. + CHILLING
MAKES: 6 SERVINGS

- 1 tablespoon boiling water
- 2 teaspoons instant espresso powder
- ¾ cup sugar
- ¼ cup baking cocoa
- 3 tablespoons cornstarch
- ½ teaspoon ground cinnamon
- ⅛ teaspoon salt
- 3 cups 2% milk
- 3 large egg yolks, lightly beaten
- 1 tablespoon brandy, optional
- 1 teaspoon vanilla extract
  Whipped cream and chocolate-covered coffee beans, optional

1. Combine boiling water and espresso powder; set aside. In a large heavy saucepan, combine the sugar, cocoa, cornstarch, cinnamon and salt. Stir in milk until smooth. Cook and stir over medium-high heat until thickened and bubbly. Reduce heat to low; cook and stir 2 minutes longer.
2. Remove from the heat. Stir a small amount of hot mixture into egg yolks; return all to the pan, stirring constantly. Bring to a gentle boil; cook and stir 2 minutes longer. Remove from the heat. Stir in brandy if desired, vanilla and espresso mixture. Cool for 15 minutes, stirring occasionally.
3. Transfer to dessert dishes. Cover and refrigerate for 1 hour. Garnish with whipped cream and coffee beans if desired.

Sunshine Cobbler

This scrumptious cobbler is a refreshing change of pace from everyday desserts. With a crispy homemade topping and a juicy filling, this recipe is a golden success!

—ANGELA LEINENBACH MECHANICSVLLE, VA

PREP: 25 MIN. • **BAKE:** 15 MIN.
MAKES: 6 SERVINGS

- 2 cans (8 ounces each) citrus salad, undrained
- ½ cup packed brown sugar
- 3 tablespoons all-purpose flour
- 1 can (11 ounces) mandarin oranges, undrained
- 3 tablespoons butter

TOPPING
- 1 cup all-purpose flour
- 3 tablespoons sugar, divided
- 1½ teaspoons baking powder
- ¼ teaspoon salt
- ¼ cup cold butter
- 1 large egg, lightly beaten
- ¼ cup 2% milk
- ⅛ teaspoon ground cinnamon
- 6 pecan halves
  Half-and-half cream, optional

1. Drain citrus salad, reserving ¼ cup juice. In a large bowl, combine the brown sugar, flour and reserved juice. Stir in citrus salad and oranges. Divide among six 6-oz. ramekins or custard cups; dot with butter.
2. In a small bowl, combine the flour, 2 tablespoons sugar, baking powder and salt; cut in butter until mixture resembles coarse crumbs. Stir in egg and milk. Drop by spoonfuls over fruit mixture. Combine cinnamon and remaining sugar; sprinkle over tops.
3. Bake at 425° for 15-18 minutes or until filling is bubbly and a toothpick inserted in topping comes out clean. Top each with a pecan half. Serve with cream if desired.

Nutty Caramel Ice Cream Cake

We made this frozen treat for a family birthday party, and we received endless comments on it. It's truly fantastic! Be sure to try the recipe with other ice cream flavors.
—**DAVID H STELZL JR** WAXHAW, NC

PREP: 30 MIN. + FREEZING
MAKES: 16 SERVINGS

- **4** cups crushed pecan shortbread cookies (about 52 cookies)
- **¼** cup butter, melted
- **6** cups butter pecan ice cream, softened
- **1** carton (8 ounces) frozen whipped topping, thawed
- **¾** cup slivered almonds, toasted
- **¾** cup milk chocolate English toffee bits
- **¼** cup caramel sundae syrup

1. In a large bowl, combine cookie crumbs and butter. Press 2 cups onto the bottom of a greased 9-in. springform pan. Spoon half of the ice cream into the prepared pan. Freeze for 20 minutes.

2. Repeat layers with remaining cookie crumbs and ice cream. Spread with whipped topping. Sprinkle with almonds and toffee bits. Cover and freeze overnight or until firm. May be frozen for up to 2 months.

TO USE FROZEN CAKE *Remove from the freezer 10 minutes before serving. Drizzle with syrup.*

Apple Roly-Poly

Apple Roly-Poly isn't very fancy, but it's genuine Down East fare. It came from my grandmother. With 13 children plus the men at Grandpa's sawmill, she had to do lots of cooking each day!

—MEGAN NEWCOMBE COOKSTOWN, ON

PREP: 25 MIN. • **BAKE:** 30 MIN.
MAKES: 12 SERVINGS

- 1¾ cups all-purpose flour
- ¼ cup sugar
- 4 teaspoons baking powder
- ½ teaspoon salt
- ¼ cup shortening
- ¼ cup cold butter
- ⅔ cup sour cream

FILLING

- ¼ cup butter, softened
- 1 cup packed brown sugar
- 2 teaspoons ground cinnamon
- 6 medium Granny Smith apples, peeled and coarsely shredded (about 5 cups)

TOPPING

- 2½ cups water
- 2 tablespoons brown sugar
- 1 teaspoon ground cinnamon
- ½ cup half-and-half cream

1. In a bowl, combine flour, sugar, baking powder and salt. Cut in the shortening and butter until crumbly. Add the sour cream and blend until a ball forms.

2. Roll out on a floured surface into a 15x10-in. rectangle. Spread with softened butter; sprinkle with remaining filling ingredients.

3. Roll up, jelly-roll style, starting with a long side. Cut into 12 slices. Place slices, cut side down, in a 13x9-in. baking pan.

4. For topping, combine water, brown sugar and cinnamon in a saucepan. Bring to a boil; remove from the heat. Stir in the cream.

5. Carefully pour hot topping over dumplings. Bake, uncovered, at 350° for 35 minutes or until bubbly. (Center will jiggle when dumplings are hot out of the oven but will set as dumplings stand for a few minutes.) Serve warm.

Best Maple-Cranberry Cheesecake

While this maple cheesecake may look like it is difficult to make, it's actually easy. If you have to make only one holiday dessert this season, it should be this one!

—TONYA BURKHARD DAVIS, IL

PREP: 30 MIN. • **BAKE:** 1¼ HOURS + CHILLING
MAKES: 16 SERVINGS (2 CUPS COMPOTE)

- 2 **cups graham cracker crumbs**
- ⅓ **cup butter, melted**
- 3 **tablespoons sugar**
- ½ **teaspoon ground cinnamon**

FILLING

- 1½ **cups maple syrup**
- 3 **packages (8 ounces each) cream cheese, softened**
- ½ **cup packed brown sugar**
- ⅔ **cup sour cream**
- 3 **tablespoons all-purpose flour**
- 2 **teaspoons vanilla extract**
- ¼ **teaspoon salt**
- 4 **large eggs, lightly beaten**

COMPOTE

- 2 **cups fresh or frozen cranberries, thawed**
- ⅔ **cup dried cranberries**
- 1 **cup maple syrup**
- ½ **cup packed brown sugar**

1. Place a greased 9-in. springform pan on a double thickness of heavy-duty foil (about 18 in. square). Securely wrap foil around pan.
2. Combine the cracker crumbs, butter, sugar and cinnamon; press onto the bottom and 1½ in. up the sides of prepared pan. Place the pan on a baking sheet. Bake at 375° for 8-10 minutes or until set. Cool on a wire rack. Reduce heat to 325°.
3. Meanwhile, place maple syrup in a small saucepan. Bring to a boil; cook until syrup is reduced to about 1 cup. Cool to room temperature; set aside.
4. In a large bowl, beat cream cheese and brown sugar until smooth. Beat in the sour cream, flour, vanilla, salt and cooled syrup. Add eggs; beat on low speed just until combined. Pour into crust. Place springform pan in a large baking pan; add 1 in. of hot water to larger pan.

5. Bake at 325° for 1¼-1½ hours or until center is just set and top appears dull. Remove springform pan from water bath. Cool on a wire rack for 10 minutes. Carefully run a knife around edge of pan to loosen; cool 1 hour longer. Refrigerate overnight. Remove sides of pan.
6. In a large saucepan, combine the cranberries, syrup and brown sugar. Cook over medium heat until the berries pop, about 10 minutes. Serve warm with cheesecake.

Pecan Kringle Sticks

My family loves this kringle's flakiness and that it's not too sweet—it just melts in your mouth. It also makes a beautiful presentation on a platter. The recipe makes four, so you can give a few as gifts.

—CONNIE VJESTICA BROOKFIELD, IL

PREP: 40 MIN. + CHILLING • **BAKE:** 20 MIN.
MAKES: 4 KRINGLES (6 SERVINGS EACH)

- 2 **cups all-purpose flour**
- 1 **cup cold butter, cubed**
- 1 **cup sour cream**

FILLING

- 1 **large egg white**
- 1 **teaspoon vanilla extract**
- ½ **cup sugar**
- 1 **cup chopped pecans**

ICING

- 1¼ **cups confectioners' sugar**
- 2 **tablespoons 2% milk**

1. Place flour in a large bowl; cut in the butter until crumbly. Stir in the sour cream. Wrap in plastic wrap. Refrigerate for 1-1½ hours or until easy to handle.
2. In a small bowl, beat the egg white and vanilla on medium speed until soft peaks form. Gradually beat in sugar on high until stiff peaks form. Fold in pecans.
3. Divide the dough into four portions. Roll one portion into a 12x6-in. rectangle; place on an ungreased baking sheet. Spread a fourth of the egg white mixture lengthwise down the center. Fold in sides of pastry to meet in the center; pinch seam to seal. Repeat.
4. Bake at 375° for 18-22 minutes or until lightly browned. Combine confectioners' sugar and milk; drizzle over warm pastries.

GRAND PRIZE
WINNER
★ ★ ★ ★

Chocolate-Covered Cherry Pudding Cake

Growing up, I remember my grandfather cherishing the chocolate-covered cherries we'd bring him for Christmas. He passed away this past year, and I came up with this rich recipe in his honor. It's delicious served with whipped topping.

—**MEREDITH COE** CHARLOTTESVILLE, VA

PREP: 20 MIN. • **COOK:** 2 HOURS + STANDING
MAKES: 8 SERVINGS

- ½ cup reduced-fat sour cream
- 2 tablespoons canola oil
- 1 tablespoon butter, melted
- 2 teaspoons vanilla extract
- 1 cup all-purpose flour
- ¼ cup sugar
- ¼ cup packed brown sugar
- 3 tablespoons baking cocoa
- 2 teaspoons baking powder
- ½ teaspoon ground cinnamon
- ⅛ teaspoon salt
- 1 cup fresh or frozen pitted dark sweet cherries, thawed
- 1 cup fresh or frozen pitted tart cherries, thawed
- ⅓ cup 60% cacao bittersweet chocolate baking chips

PUDDING
- ½ cup packed brown sugar
- 2 tablespoons baking cocoa
- 1¼ cups hot water

1. In a large bowl, beat the sour cream, oil, butter and vanilla until blended. Combine the flour, sugars, cocoa, baking powder, cinnamon and salt. Add to sour cream mixture just until combined. Stir in cherries and chips. Pour into a 3-qt. slow cooker coated with cooking spray.
2. In a small bowl, combine brown sugar and cocoa. Stir in hot water until blended. Pour over the batter (do not stir). Cover and cook on high for 2-2½ hours or until set. Let stand for 15 minutes. Serve warm.

Dulce de Leche Cheesecake

I'm originally from Paraguay, and dulce de leche reminds me of where I came from. If you can't find it at your grocery store, try caramel ice cream topping instead. It tastes different, but this decadent dessert will still be amazing.

—**SONIA LIPHAM** RANBURNE, AL

PREP: 40 MIN. • **BAKE:** 1 HOUR + CHILLING
MAKES: 16 SERVINGS

- 1¾ cups crushed gingersnap cookies (about 35 cookies)
- ¼ cup finely chopped walnuts
- 1 tablespoon sugar
- ½ teaspoon ground cinnamon
- 6 tablespoons butter, melted

FILLING
- 3 packages (8 ounces each) cream cheese, softened
- 1 cup plus 2 tablespoons sugar
- ¼ cup 2% milk
- 2 tablespoons all-purpose flour
- 1 teaspoon vanilla extract
- 3 large eggs, lightly beaten
- 1 can (13.4 ounces) dulce de leche

TOPPINGS
- 1 cup (6 ounces) semisweet chocolate chips
- 1½ teaspoons chili powder
- ½ cup dulce de leche
- 3 tablespoons hot water

1. Preheat oven to 350°. Place a greased 9-in. springform pan on a double thickness of heavy-duty foil (about 18 in. square). Securely wrap foil around pan. In a large bowl, combine the cookie crumbs, chopped walnuts, sugar, cinnamon and butter. Press onto bottom and 2 in. up sides of prepared pan.
2. In a large bowl, beat cream cheese and sugar until smooth. Beat in milk, flour and vanilla. Add eggs; beat on low speed just until combined. Pour into crust.
3. Pour dulce de leche into a microwave-safe bowl; microwave at 50% power until softened. Drop dulce de leche by tablespoonfuls over batter; cut through batter with a knife to swirl.
4. Place springform pan in a large baking pan; add 1 in. of hot water to larger pan. Bake 60-70 minutes or until center is just set and top appears dull.
5. Remove springform pan from water bath. Cool on a wire rack 10 minutes. Carefully run a knife around edge of pan to loosen; cool 1 hour.
6. In a microwave-safe bowl, melt chips; stir until smooth. Stir in chili powder. Spread over cheesecake. Refrigerate overnight. Remove sides of pan.
7. In a small bowl, whisk dulce de leche and hot water until smooth; drizzle over cheesecake.
NOTE *This recipe was tested with Nestle La Lechera dulce de leche; look for it in the international foods section. If using Eagle Brand dulce de leche, thicken according to package directions before using.*

1. Place a greased 9-in. springform pan on a double thickness of heavy-duty foil (about 18 in. square). Securely wrap foil around pan.

2. In a small bowl, combine the cookie crumbs, sugar and butter. Press onto the bottom of pan; set aside.

3. In a large bowl, beat cream cheese and sugar until smooth. Beat in the flour, cream and extracts. Add eggs; beat on low speed just until combined. Divide the batter into thirds.

4. In a microwave, melt chocolate chips; cool to room temperature. Stir melted chocolate into one portion of batter; pour over crust. In a food processor, puree strawberries. Add pureed strawberries and food coloring if desired to another portion; gently spread over chocolate layer. Place springform pan in a large baking pan; add 1 in. of hot water to larger pan.

5. Bake at 325° for 40 minutes or until center is just set and top appears dull. Gently spread remaining batter over top. Bake for 25-30 minutes or until top appears dull. Remove springform pan from water bath. Cool on a wire rack for 10 minutes. Carefully run a knife around edge of pan to loosen; cool 1 hour longer. Refrigerate overnight.

6. Remove sides of pan. Drizzle jam over cheesecake; garnish with strawberries and whipped cream.

Apple-Cranberry Crisp

Desserts are a special favorite of mine, and I clip out and save more dessert recipes than any other kind. This dessert can be assembled easily and cooked with a minimum of attention—you can prepare all the rest of your evening meal while it bakes.

—CANDIE TAKACS WEST CARROLLTON, OH

PREP: 20 MIN. • **BAKE:** 1 HOUR
MAKES: 8 SERVINGS

        3   cups chopped apples, unpeeled
        2   cups fresh cranberries
        ¾   to 1 cup sugar
TOPPING
        1½ cups old-fashioned or quick-cooking oats
        ½   cup packed brown sugar
        ⅓   cup all-purpose flour
        ⅓   cup chopped pecans
        ½   cup butter, melted

1. In a bowl, combine the apples, cranberries and sugar; transfer to an 8-in. square baking dish; set aside. Combine topping ingredients until crumbly; sprinkle over fruit.

2. Bake at 350° for 1 hour or until the fruit is tender. Serve warm with ice cream or whipped cream.

When I was a child, I loved Neapolitan ice cream. I thought it would be fun to create a cheesecake with the same flavors. This smooth, creamy layered beauty is the result. Each layer is rich with flavor.

—SUE GRONHOLZ BEAVER DAM, WI

Neapolitan Cheesecake

PREP: 45 MIN. • **BAKE:** 65 MIN. + CHILLING
MAKES: 12 SERVINGS

        1   cup cream-filled chocolate sandwich cookie crumbs
        3   tablespoons sugar
        3   tablespoons butter, melted
FILLING
        4   packages (8 ounces each) cream cheese, softened
        1⅓ cups sugar
        2   tablespoons all-purpose flour
        2   tablespoons heavy whipping cream
        1   teaspoon vanilla extract
        ½   teaspoon almond extract
        4   large eggs, lightly beaten
        ¾   cup semisweet chocolate chips
        1   cup fresh strawberries, hulled
        1   to 2 drops red food coloring, optional
        ¼   cup seedless strawberry jam, warmed
            Sliced fresh strawberries and sweetened whipped
            cream

Lemon Blackberry Parfaits

I love the freshness of lemon, so I paired it with seasonal blackberries to make this rich, creamy dessert that's so wonderful! Serve immediately if you like crisp graham crackers or within 4 hours for a moister crumb.
—**AMBER NEEDHAM** BELLBROOK, OH

PREP: 25 MIN. + CHILLING
MAKES: 6 SERVINGS

- 3 **large eggs**
- ½ **cup plus ¼ cup sugar, divided**
- ¾ **cup lemon juice**
- 1 **tablespoon grated lemon peel**
- 2 **tablespoons butter**
- 4 **ounces fat-free cream cheese**
- 1 **cup plus 6 tablespoons reduced-fat whipped topping, divided**
- 3 **cups fresh blackberries**
- 3 **whole graham crackers, crushed**

1. In a small heavy saucepan over medium heat, whisk the eggs, ½ cup sugar, lemon juice and peel until blended. Add butter; cook, whisking constantly, until mixture is thickened and coats the back of a spoon. Transfer to a small bowl; cool. Cover and refrigerate until chilled.
2. In a small bowl, beat cream cheese and remaining sugar until smooth. Fold in lemon mixture and 1 cup whipped topping. Spoon half of the cream cheese mixture into six parfait glasses. Top with half of the berries and half of the cracker crumbs. Repeat layers. Top with remaining whipped topping. Serve immediately.

Festive Napoleons with Thyme Cream

Considering the assembly required, we save these Napoleons for special occasions, but they're absolutely worth it. I like to experiment with unusual seasonings and thyme, which adds a surprising twist along with the honey and fruit.
—**BRIDGET KLUSMAN** OTSEGO, MI

PREP: 50 MIN. • **BAKE:** 10 MIN./BATCH + COOLING
MAKES: 10 SERVINGS

- 5 **large egg whites**
- 1 **cup turbinado (washed raw) sugar**
- 1¼ **teaspoons vanilla extract**
- ¼ **teaspoon salt**
- 1¼ **cups all-purpose flour**
- ⅔ **cup butter, softened**
- 2 **tablespoons plus 1½ teaspoons walnut or canola oil**
- 1⅔ **cups chopped walnuts, toasted**

CRANBERRY FILLING
- 4 **tangerines**
- 1 **package (12 ounces) fresh or frozen cranberries**
- ½ **cup turbinado (washed raw) sugar**

THYME CREAM
- 1 **carton (8 ounces) mascarpone cheese**
- 1 **cup (8 ounces) plain yogurt**
- ⅓ **cup honey**
- ½ **teaspoon minced fresh thyme**
    Additional chopped toasted walnuts

1. In a small bowl, beat the egg whites, sugar, vanilla and salt until foamy. Gradually beat in flour. Beat in butter and oil. Fold in walnuts.
2. With a pencil, draw five 3-in. circles on a sheet of parchment paper. Place paper, pencil mark down, on a baking sheet. Spread a heaping tablespoonful of batter over each circle. Bake at 400° for 8-10 minutes or until edges begin to brown. Remove to wire racks to cool completely. Repeat with remaining batter, making 30 cookies.
3. Using a vegetable peeler, remove peel from one tangerine; set aside. Peel and seed remaining tangerines and place in a food processor. Add the cranberries, sugar and reserved tangerine peel. Cover and process until chopped. Transfer to a large saucepan. Cook over medium heat until thickened, about 10 minutes. Cool.
4. For thyme cream, beat the cheese, yogurt, honey and thyme until thickened. Place one cookie on a small plate. Spread with 1 tablespoon cranberry filling and 1 tablespoon thyme cream. Repeat layers twice. Repeat with remaining cookies, cranberry filling and thyme cream. Sprinkle with additional walnuts.

Apple Tarragon Granita

Looking for a different twist on a classic Italian treat? Fresh tarragon complements the sweet, bright apple flavor of this icy grown-up dessert.

—DEBBY HARDEN LANSING, MI

PREP: 10 MIN. + FREEZING
MAKES: 6 SERVINGS

  3 **cups unsweetened apple juice**
  ½ **cup sugar**
  2 **tablespoons coarsely chopped fresh tarragon**
  4 **teaspoons lemon juice**

1. In an 8-in. square dish, combine all ingredients until sugar is dissolved. Freeze 1 hour; stir with a fork. Freeze 2-3 hours longer or until completely frozen, stirring every 30 minutes.
2. Stir granita with a fork just before serving; spoon into dessert dishes.

GIVE IT A TRY

Granitas, or ices, are simple to make and don't require an ice cream freezer. The mixture of water, sugar and a liquid flavoring needs to be scraped often as it freezes in order to give the dessert its characteristic crystalline texture.

Cranberry-Pear Crisp

Delicately spiced fruits are topped with scrumptious crunch—a clever use of oatmeal cookie mix.

—TONI PENDLEY SOMERSET, KY

PREP: 20 MIN. • **BAKE:** 30 MIN. + STANDING
MAKES: 9 SERVINGS

  3 **cans (15¼ ounces each) sliced pears, drained**
  1 **cup fresh or frozen cranberries, thawed**
  ¼ **cup sugar**
  3 **tablespoons all-purpose flour**
  ½ **teaspoon ground cinnamon**
  ¼ **teaspoon ground ginger**
  1 **package (17½ ounces) oatmeal cookie mix**
     Vanilla ice cream

1. In a large bowl, combine pears and cranberries. Combine the sugar, flour, cinnamon and ginger; sprinkle over pear mixture and toss to coat. Transfer to a greased 11x7-in. baking dish.
2. Prepare cookie mix batter according to package directions. Sprinkle over fruit mixture. Bake at 375° for 30-35 minutes or until fruit is bubbly and topping is golden brown. Serve warm with ice cream.

Baked Sweet Potato Pudding

I always have lots of leftover sweet potatoes, but when I make this, they're gone faster than you can say "Thanksgiving!" Any ice cream flavor will do, though vanilla bean seems to be an ideal companion for our tastes.

—JOYCE WELLING SWANTON, OH

PREP: 25 MIN. • **BAKE:** 50 MIN.
MAKES: 8 SERVINGS

- 4 **cups mashed sweet potatoes**
- ½ **cup heavy whipping cream**
- 3 **large eggs, separated**
- 2 **tablespoons lemon juice**
- 1 **teaspoon grated lemon peel**
- ½ **teaspoon ground cinnamon**
- ½ **teaspoon ground ginger**
- ¼ **teaspoon ground cloves**
- 1 **cup flaked coconut, divided**
- ⅓ **cup packed brown sugar**
- ⅓ **cup slivered almonds**
     Vanilla ice cream, optional

1. In a large bowl, beat the potatoes, cream, egg yolks, lemon juice, lemon peel and spices until smooth. Fold in ⅔ cup coconut.
2. In a large bowl with clean beaters, beat egg whites on medium speed until soft peaks form. Gradually beat in brown sugar, 1 tablespoon at a time, on high until stiff glossy peaks form and sugar is dissolved.
3. With a spatula, stir a fourth of the egg whites into sweet potato mixture until no white streaks remain. Fold in remaining egg whites until combined.
4. Transfer to a greased 11x7-in. baking dish. Sprinkle with almonds and remaining coconut. Bake at 325° for 50-55 minutes or until a knife inserted near the center comes out clean. Serve warm with ice cream if desired.

Date Nut Torte

I always get compliments on this sweet and nutty torte. It's wonderful after a meal or as a little snack with coffee. My husband, three children and five grandchildren all enjoy the dessert, too!

—JUNE HOVLAND ROCHESTER, MN

PREP: 15 MIN. • **BAKE:** 30 MIN. + COOLING
MAKES: 9 SERVINGS

- 2 **large eggs**
- ½ **cup sugar**
- ½ **cup packed brown sugar**
- ⅔ **cup all-purpose flour**
- 1 **teaspoon baking powder**
- ¼ **teaspoon salt**
- 1 **cup chopped walnuts**
- 1 **cup chopped dates**
     Whipped cream

1. In a bowl, beat eggs. Gradually add sugars and beat until well mixed. Combine the flour, baking powder and salt; add to egg mixture and stir until moistened. Stir in nuts and dates. Pour into a greased 8-in. square baking pan.
2. Bake at 350° for 30 minutes. Torte top will be crusty and the inside chewy. Cool. Cut into squares and serve with a dollop of whipped cream.

Homemade Fudge Sauce

Since I don't like store-bought sauces, I decided to create my own. I make it for family and company, and I'll often get asked for the recipe.

—TRUDY DEFELICE COLUMBIA, SC

PREP: 5 MIN. • **COOK:** 10 MIN. + COOLING
MAKES: 3 CUPS

- 1¼ **cups sugar**
- 1 **cup baking cocoa**
- ½ **teaspoon ground cinnamon**
- 1 **cup heavy whipping cream**
- ½ **cup milk**
- ½ **cup unsalted butter, cut into eight pieces**
- 2 **teaspoons vanilla extract**

1. In a heavy saucepan, stir together sugar, cocoa and cinnamon. Add cream and milk; mix well. Over medium heat, bring to a boil, stirring constantly. Cook for 2 minutes.
2. Remove from the heat; cool for 15 minutes. Add butter and stir until melted. Stir in the vanilla. Cool to room temperature. Cover and store in the refrigerator. Stir before serving.

Raisin Date Bread Pudding

I put all of my leftover bread and buns in the freezer, and when I've stashed away enough, I whip up a batch of this delicious pudding. It's truly the perfect dish for any occasion.

—**DAWN GREEN** HOPKINS, MI

PREP: 15 MIN. • **BAKE:** 55 MIN.
MAKES: 10-12 SERVINGS

- 4 **cups milk**
- 5 **cups cubed day-old bread**
- 1 **cup sugar**
- 8 **large eggs, beaten**
- ½ **cup butter, melted**
- ¼ **cup chopped dates**
- ¼ **cup raisins**
- 1 **teaspoon vanilla extract**
- ½ **teaspoon ground cinnamon**
- **Dash salt**
- **Dash ground nutmeg**
- **Additional sugar, cinnamon and nutmeg, optional**
- **Whipped cream, optional**

In a large bowl, pour milk over bread. Add sugar, eggs, butter, dates, raisins, vanilla, cinnamon, salt and nutmeg; stir to mix well. Pour into a greased 13x9-in. baking dish. If desired, sprinkle top with additional sugar, cinnamon and nutmeg. Bake at 350° for 55 minutes or until golden brown and a knife inserted near the center comes out clean. Serve warm with whipped cream if desired.

"DAY-OLD" TODAY

Can't wait until tomorrow to prepare Raisin Date Bread Pudding? You can dry the bread cubes in the oven!

For 5 cups of dry bread cubes, cut five to six slices of firm bread into ½ in. cubes. Spread in a single layer on a 15x10-in. baking pan. Bake at 300° for 10-12 minutes or until dry, stirring twice (bread cubes will continue to dry as they cool).

Caramel Pumpkin Tiramisu

I'm not fond of traditional tiramisu, so I used pumpkin and bourbon in place of coffee, and it's absolutely fabulous. I always make extra sauce and eat it over vanilla ice cream. I can't leave it alone!

—**MARY FILIPIAK** FORT WAYNE, IN

PREP: 35 MIN. + CHILLING
MAKES: 9 SERVINGS

- 18 **crisp ladyfinger cookies**
- ¼ **cup maple syrup**
- 2 **tablespoons bourbon**
- 1 **cup heavy whipping cream, divided**
- ¼ **cup sugar**
- ¾ **cup solid-pack pumpkin**
- 1 **teaspoon ground cinnamon**
- ½ **teaspoon ground ginger**
- ¼ **teaspoon salt**
- 4 **ounces cream cheese, softened**
- 3 **tablespoons confectioners' sugar**

SAUCE

- ¾ **cup caramel ice cream topping**
- 2 **teaspoons bourbon**

1. Using a serrated knife, cut six ladyfingers in half widthwise. In a shallow bowl, combine maple syrup and bourbon. Dip six whole ladyfingers and six halves into mixture; arrange in a single layer in an 8-in. square dish.

2. In a small bowl, beat ½ cup cream until it begins to thicken. Gradually add sugar; beat until soft peaks form. In a large bowl, combine the pumpkin, cinnamon, ginger and salt; fold in whipped cream. In another bowl, beat the cream cheese, confectioners' sugar and remaining cream until thickened.

3. Spread half of pumpkin mixture over ladyfingers in the dish. Dip remaining ladyfingers; arrange over the top. Top with remaining pumpkin mixture and the cream cheese mixture. Cover and refrigerate for 8 hours or overnight.

4. In a microwave, heat caramel sauce; stir in bourbon. Serve warm with tiramisu.

NOTE *This recipe was prepared with Alessi brand ladyfinger cookies.*

Corn Ice Cream

You have to give this novel ice cream a try. It's actually made with corn, sweetly flavored by vanilla extract and maple syrup. I plan to make this surprising treat every summer.

—**DIANA BURRINK** CRETE, IL

PREP: 40 MIN. + CHILLING
PROCESS: 15 MIN. + FREEZING
MAKES: 4 CUPS

- 2 **cups 2% milk**
- ¾ **cup sugar**
- ½ **cup maple syrup**
- 4 **large egg yolks, lightly beaten**
- 1 **can (14¾ ounces) cream-style corn**
- 1 **teaspoon vanilla extract**

1. In a large heavy saucepan, heat the milk, sugar and syrup until bubbles form around sides of pan. Whisk a small amount of hot mixture into egg yolks. Return all to the pan, whisking constantly.

2. Cook and stir over low heat until mixture reaches 160°. Quickly transfer to a bowl; place in ice water and stir for 2 minutes. Stir in corn and vanilla. Press waxed paper onto surface of custard. Refrigerate for several hours or overnight.

3. Strain custard, discarding corn. Fill cylinder of ice cream freezer two-thirds full; freeze according to the manufacturer's directions. When the ice cream is frozen, transfer to a freezer container; freeze for 2-4 hours before serving.

Butter Pecan Cheesecake

Fall always makes me yearn for this pecan cheesecake, but it's delicious any time of year. You'll want to put it on your list of favorite desserts.

—LAURA SYLVESTER MECHANICSVLLE, VA

PREP: 30 MIN. • **BAKE:** 70 MIN. + CHILLING
MAKES: 16 SERVINGS

- 1½ cups graham cracker crumbs
- ½ cup finely chopped pecans
- ⅓ cup sugar
- ⅓ cup butter, melted

FILLING
- 3 packages (8 ounces each) cream cheese, softened
- 1½ cups sugar
- 2 cups (16 ounces) sour cream
- 1 teaspoon vanilla extract
- ½ teaspoon butter flavoring
- 3 large eggs, lightly beaten
- 1 cup finely chopped pecans

1. In a large bowl, combine the cracker crumbs, pecans, sugar and butter; set aside ⅓ cup for topping. Press remaining crumb mixture onto the bottom and 1 in. up the sides of a greased 9-in. springform pan.

2. Place the springform pan on a double thickness of heavy-duty foil (about 18 in. square). Securely wrap foil around pan.

3. In a large bowl, beat cream cheese and sugar until smooth. Beat in the sour cream, vanilla and butter flavoring. Add eggs; beat on low speed just until combined. Fold in pecans. Pour into crust; sprinkle with reserved crumb mixture. Place springform pan in a large baking pan; add 1 in. of hot water to larger pan.

4. Bake at 325° for 70-80 minutes or until center is almost set. Remove springform pan from water bath. Cool on a wire rack for 10 minutes. Carefully run a knife around edge of pan to loosen; cool 1 hour longer. Refrigerate overnight. Remove sides of pan.

Sweet Corn Creme Brulee

The starch in corn acts as a natural thickener for this dessert and adds an extra sweetness. The caramelized sugar crust and fruit garnish make for a lovely presentation.

—MARYANNE JENSEN-GOWAN PELHAM, NH

PREP: 25 MIN. • **BAKE:** 45 MIN. + CHILLING
MAKES: 6 SERVINGS

- 1½ cups frozen corn, thawed
- 4½ teaspoons butter
- 3 cups heavy whipping cream
- 1 cup 2% milk
- 8 large egg yolks
- 1¼ cups plus 2 tablespoons sugar, divided
- 2 tablespoons vanilla extract
  Fresh raspberries and mint leaves

1. In a large saucepan, saute corn in butter until tender. Reduce heat. Add cream and milk; heat until bubbles form around sides of pan. Cool slightly. Transfer to a blender; cover and process until smooth. Strain and discard corn pulp. Return to pan.

2. In a small bowl, whisk egg yolks and 1¼ cups sugar. Stir a small amount of hot cream into egg mixture. Return all to the pan, stirring constantly. Stir in vanilla.

3. Transfer to six 6-oz. ramekins. Place in a baking pan; add 1 in. of boiling water to pan. Bake, uncovered, at 325° for 40-45 minutes or until centers are just set (mixture will jiggle). Remove ramekins from water bath; cool for 10 minutes. Cover and refrigerate for at least 4 hours.

4. If using a creme brulee torch, sprinkle custards with remaining sugar. Heat sugar with the torch until caramelized. Serve immediately.

5. If broiling the custards, place ramekins on a baking sheet; let stand at room temperature for 15 minutes. Sprinkle with the sugar. Broil 8 in. from the heat for 4-7 minutes or until sugar is caramelized. Refrigerate for 1-2 hours or until firm.

6. Garnish servings with raspberries and mint leaves.

General Recipe Index

This handy index lists every recipe by food category, major ingredient and/or cooking method, so you can easily locate recipes to suit your needs.

 RECIPES INCLUDE **NUTRITION FACTS** AND **DIABETIC EXCHANGES**

Alphabetical Recipe Index

This index lists every recipe in alphabetical order so you can easily locate your favorites.

⊘ RECIPES INCLUDE **NUTRITION FACTS** AND **DIABETIC EXCHANGES**